# Recapturing Freedom

# Sydney Institute of Criminology Series No 24

**Series Editors:** Chris Cunneen, Mark Findlay, Julie Stubbs
University of Sydney Law School

## Other titles in the series

The Institute of Criminology Monograph Series

# Recapturing Freedom

## Issues relating to the release of long-term prisoners into the community

DOT GOULDING

Foreword by
PROFESSOR DAVID BROWN

Hawkins Press
2007

Published in Sydney by:
  Hawkins Press
  An imprint of The Federation Press
  PO Box 45, Annandale, NSW, 2038
  71 John St, Leichhardt, NSW, 2040
  Ph (02) 9552 2200 Fax (02) 9552 1681
  E-mail: info@federationpress.com.au
  Website: http://www.federationpress.com.au

National Library of Australia
Cataloguing-in-Publication entry

  Goulding, Dot

  Recapturing freedom: issues relating to the release of long-term prisoners into the community

  Bibliography.
  Includes index.
  ISBN 978 1 87606 718 2 (pbk).

  1. Prisoners – Rehabilitation – Western Australia. 2. Ex-convicts – Rehabilitation – Western Australia. 3. Criminals – Rehabilitation – Western Australia. 4. Prisoners – Western Australia. 5. Prisons – Moral and ethical aspects – Western Australia. 6. Prisons – Western Australia – Psychological aspects. 7. Prisons – Social aspects – Western Australia. I. Title. (Series: Institute of Criminology monograph series).

364.609941

Text printed on
100% recycled paper

Typeset by The Federation Press, Leichhardt, NSW.
Printed by Ligare Pty Ltd, Riverwood, NSW.

# Foreword

When Dot Goulding set out on the research that lead to this book, she was no neophyte. She had been working in and around prisons in various ways for many years, as an activist and advocate, and a partner of a long-term prisoner. She was not naïve, understanding well the capacity of the prison system to reproduce criminality. Indeed her aim in the research was to identify the many difficulties and obstacles that beset prisoners in making a successful transition from prison to life outside the prison, to tease out the tears and ruptures in the processes of 'reintegration' or 'resettlement'. This aim was to be achieved by interviewing a number of long-term prisoners prior to their release and then progressively after their release.

But what Dot Goulding – even with her experience and understanding of prison life and the life of prisoners' families and friends – did not count on, was the depth, the weight and the force of the prison experience, propelling, even attracting, prisoners back from whence they had come, back behind the walls of the prison. So that within a relatively short period of time nine out of the 10 long-term prisoners who participated in the in-prison interviews were re-imprisoned for various reasons, sabotaging the program of post-prison interviews. The success of the prison, not in 'rehabilitating' but in consolidating criminal careers and identities, in reproducing criminals and prisoners, had been dramatically demonstrated in the lives of her participants, well beyond expectations based on current recidivism rates.

Her prison participants had not succeeded in 'recapturing freedom' but had been 'recaptured by the system'. The question is, why? In attempting to answer that question she realised that clues lay in the stories her participants told her, stories of their upbringing, their crimes, their experiences in prison, their ways of coping with life inside, their acculturation and desensitisation to violence, their senses of identity and constructions of gender, their forms of resistance to the prison regime, their anxiety about how they could cope with life outside prison, their fear of further failure. Key phrases participants used, such as 'I have identity in jail', a 'position here' indicated a sense of 'being someone' in prison, compared with being 'an alien', 'weird', 'like ET', 'I don't belong out there', in the outside world.

Prison then, is not only a place, a physical location, a 'total institution', but also a state of mind. Walking out its doors does not mean leaving it behind, when its rhythms and routines, its cultures and meanings, its 'mental, moral and social impacts' are still engaged, running in the minds of released prisoners attempting to 'recapture freedom', to become 'free citizens'. The great virtue of this book is that it gives the reader an insight into this mental world, the realm of Blake's 'mind forged manacles', the 'prisons in the mind' which bind and constrain unseen behind the prosaic term 'recidivism'.

Such insights can be gleaned from a range of sources including criminological, penological and sociological research studies, from prison literature, biography and film, from journalism and prison inquiries, from recidivism statistics. The author draws on all these sources to reveal the forces at work in the prison experience and the themes and concepts through which we can attempt to identify and understand them. But what marks this book out is the centrality accorded the voices of prisoners, the stories, narratives, musings, explanations, justifications, rationalisations, aspirations, anxieties and fears of those long-term prisoners who agreed to participate in the research study and who, along with the institution of the prison itself, were the central subjects of the research.

Such voices are not conjured easily, their expression relies on a substantial degree of trust between author and participants, a trust that the stories will not be used to further denigrate and stigmatise, nor woven into familiar skeins of good and evil, of recrimination and desert. A trust which is not automatically granted to all researchers but which must be won over time and continually renewed, a trust which in the context of lives lived in crime and punishment, has an intensely personal foundation.

The evident solidity of that foundation results in a book which makes a major contribution to understanding why the prison system reproduces criminality and turns out prisoners, and what we might do to change this. The author has completely vindicated the trust invested in her by her prisoner subjects; through her they achieve that which they are so often denied: a voice, they partake in an act of discursive citizenship.

It behoves us all, as individuals, as citizens, as communities, as a society, to listen to these voices, as much for our own good as for theirs, for in truth, the two are entwined.

Professor David Brown
Law Faculty
University of NSW, Sydney
September 2007

# Contents

# Acknowledgments

I would like to thank Emeritus Professor Trish Harris, past Director of the Centre for Social and Community Research, Murdoch University, for her assistance in the preparation of this monograph. Her guidance, moral support and patience throughout the duration of the research were particularly valuable. Thanks also go to my good friend, fellow justice activist and work colleague, Dr Brian Steels, for his continued encouragement and assistance throughout the research process.

I am indebted to Trisha Valliappan and Chris Holt of Federation Press, without their support there would be no book. Their advice and kindness are much appreciated. Thanks also go to Baroness Vivien Stern from the International Centre for Prison Studies, King's College, London; Professor Kerry Carrington from the School of Social Science, University of New England; and Professor David Brown of the Faculty of Law, University of New South Wales, for their constructive criticism, encouragement and kind remarks.

I owe a debt of gratitude to Dr Michael McCall, past Director General of the West Australian Department of Justice (now renamed Department of Corrective Services) who personally provided funds for the project. Without his most generous assistance the research for this book would not have been possible. I am grateful both for the financial assistance and the trust he invested in my ability to complete this project. Thanks also go to Professor Robert Harvey, past Executive Director of the West Australian Department of Justice, now Executive Dean at the Faculty of Business and Law at Edith Cowan University, for allowing me unrestricted access to the imprisoned men and women who participated in the research for this book.

I would also like to express thanks to my children, Samantha, Rory and Gareth and to my darling granddaughters, Rebecca, Katie and Claire for simply being there, keeping me grounded, and for never once telling me I was too old to do this.

Finally, and most importantly, I wish to thank those men and women prisoners and ex-prisoners who spoke so openly and honestly to me about their experiences of imprisonment. It is to the 'prisoner consultant' that I am most indebted. His generosity in sharing his extensive knowledge of the West Australian prison system and his particular contribution to the chapter on violence and brutality in prisons, have been central to the research.

Dot Goulding
September 2007

*... Behind high walls in prison cells*
*young men and women learn to dwell*
*year after year until it's time*
*to leave their punishment for crime;*
*and though they've waited long and hard*
*to walk out of that prison yard,*
*it's much more difficult they find,*
*to free the chains upon the mind.*

(Brenda Hodge: Greenough Regional Prison, 1994)

# Introduction

This book is about the effects of long term imprisonment on individuals and communities. I have defined "long term" imprisonment as a served prison sentence of three years or more. The research for the book was conducted within the West Australian prison system and, as such, specific issues related to the research topic will be analysed within a context of policies and practices of the West Australian Department of Corrective Services.[1] Initially the set task was to find more effective ways to successfully reintegrate long term prisoners into the community. Accordingly, the particular focus was the liminal space between prison and the wider community: that is, specifically, the transitional stage of imprisonment that occurs immediately before and after release. However, as a result of information gathered during in-depth interviews with several long term prisoners, the focus and intent of the research changed considerably and came to rest on the effects of imprisonment, *per se*. The change in focus will be discussed later in this introductory chapter.

## General background

The consequences of mass incarceration as a solution to social problems are serious. Society is being exposed to serious dangers to its security from creating an enormous alienated antisocial class hostile to society's values and bound together in crime. It will be a dangerous world when so many people have made their friendships in prisons, affirmed their values there and created business networks with their fellow prisoners. The large minority of young men who have learnt during their imprisonment to see society as their enemy could present a greater threat once they have been processed through the prison system than they did at the beginning of their criminal careers. (Stern cited in Bowen and Consedine 1999: 9)

---

1 The Department of Corrective Services (WA) has previously, during the time span of the research for this book, been known as the Department of Justice (WA) and before that the Ministry of Justice (WA). Following a recommendation in the Mahoney Report (November 2005) the Department of Justice (WA) was divided into two separate departments: The Attorney General's Department (WA) and the Department of Corrective Services (WA). Apart from direct quotations where the department is referred to in one of its historical titles, the Department of Corrective Services (WA) will be used throughout the text.

While imprisoning a person may prevent that individual from offending against the wider community whilst he or she is locked up, the vast majority of prisoners will be released from prison and returned to the community. Stern (1998: 11) suggests that:

> [T]heir stay in prison will probably leave them more prone to crime and will have damaged those elements that bond people to society, such as relationships with family and friends, the chance of a place to live and a job, the chance of being respected and esteemed by others.

Stern (1998: 22) goes on to say: "Basically prison is damaging, to the individual, the family and the community. It has few positive results and its costs are high". Also, according to Garland (1990: 166), prison fails to reduce crime but is retained, in the main, because of a "lack of any functional alternative". He further argues that one of the main reasons for the durability of the prison as an ongoing institution is its profound failure to rehabilitate prisoners and return them to the community as valued citizens (Garland 1990: 149).

There are many studies related to the counterproductive nature of imprisonment. These form the background to this book. In line with their arguments, my contention is that prisons do not rehabilitate inmates, do not act as a deterrent to crime and do not ensure ongoing public protection against those who commit criminal offences (Pratt 1997: 158-159, Stern 1998: 11). Although this text in many ways follows the arguments of Stern (1998), Garland (1990, 1997), Carlen (1994), Coyle (1994), and Pratt (1997), the main difference is in its focus on *how prisoners themselves experience imprisonment*. Ten long term prisoners and one ex-prisoner assisted in this task by sharing with me their experiences of imprisonment and subsequent release into the community. Their stories are central to the text, which is set within an exploration of the socio-political position of prisons within society in general. Also central to the analysis is the notion of prisons as "total institutions". My contention is that each of these factors – prisoner consciousness, the socio-political place of prisons and the nature of prisons as total institutions – is crucial to any complete analysis of the effects of imprisonment.

## Researcher's background

I have commenced the research for this book from the position of a prison reformer. In other words, I have some already held assumptions regarding the negative impact of imprisonment. These assumptions have not been simply pulled out of the air, but have developed during my many years working in and around prisons; as an advocate for prisoners, ex-prisoners and their families, as a justice activist, and prison reformer. Over the years, I have observed first hand the counter-productive nature of imprisonment and its ineffectiveness as an answer to the problem of crime. My contention that imprisonment fails the community in terms of its stated goals of crime deterrence and prisoner rehabilitation is based on a broad personal experience of the negative social and emotional impact of imprisonment.

This book draws also from my own close personal relationship with a prisoner. My ex-partner was incarcerated for six years. I supported him throughout his term of imprisonment and for some time after he was released. I have experienced, from a family's perspective, many of the problems associated with the transition from prisoner to free citizen. I have a real awareness that prison baggage is not shed at the prison gate, having lived through the anticipation, excitement and optimism of a loved one's imminent release from prison. However, I have also experienced the dark side of coping with the reality of someone who had lived for many years in a brutal and brutalising environment and whose social mores and values had become those of the subculture of the total institution. Goffman (1961: 56) describes this as the "fraternization process, through which socially distant persons find themselves developing mutual support and common counter-mores in opposition to a system that has forced them into intimacy". Here I refer to factors such as a dehumanised view of others, a hierarchical pecking order of emotional and physical intimidation, and a carefully gathered business and social network of acquaintances involved in various forms of criminal activity.

These experiences of living within my ex-partner's period of transition from imprisonment to freedom, together with my ongoing academic career stirred my sociological imagination and germinated into an idea for this book which builds upon prior research conducted with prisoners and their families (Goulding 1995, 1997). At the time of commencement of this study I was also heavily involved in prison reform and individual prisoner advocacy within the West Australian prison system.

From the commencement of my relationship with the prison system I felt a need to make things better. Consequently, this book began life as an idea that I might in some way contribute to a better community understanding of people who have served time in prison for criminal offences. This was to be my contribution to a more successful re-communalisation process that might assist some long term prisoners to more easily return to society as valued persons. I hoped my research would result in some innovative and proactive policy recommendations that would ease the transition from prisoner to free person. The consequence of which would be a safer community for all. A noble thought, a positive contribution to society. Assist marginalised prisoners, initiate strategies that may result in a safer and more equitable community and, along the way, publish a book. However, from its conception, throughout its tortuous development and after a long and painful birth process the resulting progeny this text – in many ways bears little resemblance to the original concept.

## Original research direction

Let me explain. Originally I had set about organising my research around issues related to the release of long term prisoners into the community. At that level it was to be an organised and practical process, an exploratory investigation into that stage of transition from imprisonment to freedom which had been impossible for both my ex-partner and me to negotiate. I felt quite strongly that my own experience in this area would be beneficial within the research process. In other words, I knew the right questions to ask and, over my years of involvement with prisoners and their families, I had developed a passion for the topic. At the early stage of the research process my intent was to interview a number of long term prisoners in the days leading up to their release and to repeat the interview process several weeks after their release. Specified open ended questions looking at issues such as anxieties, expectations and family and community supports were formulated, several logistical problems were overcome and off I went in search of answers.

Somewhat naively I had expected fairly straightforward answers to questions which were pragmatic in nature and which dealt with important issues concerning release. However, for several reasons related to the nature of total institutions (which will be explored later in the book), I was told stories, usually in a matter of fact manner, of the most heart rending experiences of childhoods bereft of affection and basic parental care, extreme violence experienced both within and without the prison, and of small children being forcibly removed from mothers.

For example one of the participants, Linda, who was serving three years, spoke about her first term of imprisonment when her baby daughter was taken from her in Bandyup Women's Prison a few days after her first birthday. She described the pain of enforced separation, how it was so intense that she wanted to die and how she coped by having a hit (heroin) to dull the pain. The three Aboriginal participants Judy, Simon and Beau all spoke of traumatic childhoods where they were forcibly removed from their parents and put into institutional care, subsequently suffering both physical and emotional abuse and becoming the second and third generations of their families who became part of the stolen generations. Also, Dick, institutionalised at four, addicted to heroin in his teens and serving his second lengthy prison term, described his struggle in prison to find out why he had become addicted to heroin:

> This time around I had some counselling to see why I used drugs. The prison psych hypnotised me and my head was full of this shit about my mother's death. I had a huge chip on my shoulders about that and I must have felt sorry for myself. Anyway I kept crying and saying 'my mother's dead' over and over and so she had to bring me out and we had to deal with this problem about why I kept remembering my mother getting shot. I was only four when it happened and it's because it's the last memory I have of her, you know. I've had to learn to deal with the fact that I don't really remember what it's like to feel a mother's love or what it is to really belong in a normal family situation. (interview: September 1999)

In sum, seven of the 11 participants had spent much of their childhood in institutional care, several being moved continuously between foster families and children's homes. Each of these participants claimed to have experienced ongoing physical and emotional abuse during their childhood. In addition to this, two of the remaining four participants spoke of witnessing their mothers being beaten and of being physically abused themselves by violent fathers.

I found that the interviews became almost unbearably intense emotional experiences and I often felt that I had made significant links with the participants. This was not a factor I had anticipated. I was totally unprepared for the emotions I experienced as I listened to these stories and it was at this point that the pains of change began in earnest.

## Evolution of research

In terms of the research direction, my first positive steps began to waiver and I began to tread cautiously along a different path. Although I had worked intensively with prisoners for several years, this particular interview process afforded me yet another way of seeing their lives. Most pertinent, and of particular concern to me, was the manner in which incidents of extreme and often life threatening violence were mentioned as though such events were a taken for granted aspect of everyday life. The interviews took on a life of their own as each res-- pondent told of his or her life and prison experiences. As each person's story emerged, I became increasingly concerned about the effects of imprisonment. Prisons appeared to be successful merely as an exercise in "populist punitiveness" (Bottoms cited in Pratt 1997: 252), a public outcry of what Durkheim describes as the "collective conscience at work" (Garland 1990: 23), where "vengeance is the primary motivation which underpins punitive actions" (Garland 1990: 32). In other words, I came to see that imprisonment as punishment is underpinned by a frac- turing of a collective moral order which, in turn, imparts a form of "legitimised vengefulness" (Feinberg cited in Duff and Garland 1994: 74). This, I believe achieves little, if anything, in terms of enhancing community safety and collectively healing the effects of crime.

The point here is that my initial hope of finding some practical solutions to the problems experienced by long term prisoners upon their release into the community became, instead, a daunting question. "What on earth do we do to people?". Alternatively, "what do we as a community, allow the state to do to people in our name?". As my inter- views progressed I repeatedly questioned the basic logic of imprison- ment. Why does the State, in the name of the community, send those who break laws to prison to become more socially deskilled, angrier, more brutalised and institutionalised and in the case of long term priso- ners, after several years release them back to a community which, in general terms, is unwelcoming of them, has few common social values with them, and then wonders why they re-offend?

As I listened to the participants' stories, particularly during the follow-up interviews, I became convinced that whilst the perception is that we *physically* lock people up in prisons, most importantly, what we do is *imprison their minds*. When the State, in the name of the com- munity, incarcerates people within the total institution of the prison, it sentences them to become enculturated into a distinct social subsystem that has few common values with the wider community. And when prisoners, particularly those who are long term, are released *physically* into the wider and mostly unforgiving community, *their minds are still generally securely imprisoned* within a subculture of brutality, iso- lation and deprivation. As Toch (1977: 122) argues:

> It is in this area that prison has its simplest and most obvious effect. For an environment designed to confine men physically, confines them psychologically as well. A prison creates a world that demands constricted acts, thoughts and feelings. It is a world

in which strong and tragic resentments are bound to fester and sometimes to explode.

The effects of this mental imprisonment became increasingly apparent as the interviews progressed and it was this factor that prompted me to change the focus of the book. The original objective had carried a clear intent to explore that area of transition between prisoner and free citizen in order to search for practical solutions to ease the change. Instead the research now centred on the mental, moral and social impacts that prisons have on inmates. This, in turn, led to further consideration of how prisons affect the wider community.

For the individuals concerned, there is no doubt that to be labelled "prisoner" or "ex-prisoner" is profoundly stigmatic as far as the straight community is concerned. When individuals are labelled in this way their behaviour patterns tend to adapt to and are interpreted within the framework of that label (Goffman 1963: 137). This factor is magnified when those labelled as bad, criminal and deviant are then placed within a closed, restricted physical and social environment exclusively with others labelled likewise. According to Goffman (1963: 32), this generally has the effect of initiating the formation of:

> a different value system ... evinced by the communality of behaviour which occurs when inmates interact among themselves ... They form and recognise symbols of prestige and disgrace; evaluate relevant situations in terms of their own norms and in their own idiom.

Duff and Garland (1994: preface to Morris 'A Paternalistic Theory of Punishment': 93) claim that imprisonment "often produces resentment, bitterness and alienation rather than moral reconciliation" and that "those who are punished may not share the values of the law abiding, or live in circumstances in which these values can be easily adhered to". These effects escalate when parents are imprisoned. This often ensures the enculturation of prisoners' children into a subculture of criminal activity as the threat of imprisonment for those children is diminished by its normalisation through familiarity. In other words, the threat of imprisonment as a deterrent to criminal activity is lost where it has become part and parcel of everyday life. For example, a study of four thousand prisoners in England and Wales demonstrated that "one third had a family member ... in prison already" (Stern 1998: 115) and a similar study of prisoners in the United States showed that "four out of ten in US prisons had a family member in prison". In Stern's (1998: 10) view, "[p]rison effectively creates tougher, more embittered individuals whose crimes upon release may well be more brutal and irresponsible".

In terms of communities, worldwide research (Bowen and Consedine 1999, Garland 1990, Pratt 1997, Stern 1998) repeatedly outlines the counterproductive and destructive nature of imprisonment. Yet, in Western Australia, over the past two decades, governments of differing political ideologies have condoned "law and order" and "war on crime" measures which have led to a substantial increase in incarceration rates. As Duff and Garland (1994: 31) argue, penal policy is determined, not so much by crime rates, but more by other prevailing social and political factors. Nonetheless, viewed in purely economic terms, expenditure on prisons reduces the amount spent on schools, hospitals, youth recreation centres and other positive and productive places. And, for each breadwinner imprisoned, there is the likelihood that his or her family will become dependent on welfare payments. There is also the actual cost of keeping just one person in prison. In Western Australia this is currently estimated at $239.10 per day or $87,500 per year (Department of Corrective Services WA Annual Report 2004-2005). Add to this the associated police, legal and court costs and the estimation blows out enormously.

The negative social and economic effects of imprisonment are, in general terms, well documented and indeed form the background to this book. However, there is a paucity of literature which focuses on the effects of imprisonment at the experiential or phenomenological level. This research hopes to contribute meaningful insight into the effects of imprisonment at that level. The text has four main thrusts. These are:

- To provide detailed insights into the impact of imprisonment on both individual prisoners and the community in general.

- To permit the silenced voices of prisoners to be heard.

- To provide an analysis of penal policy, discourse and practice with a specific focus on how policy, discourse and practice construct the notion of prisoner.

- To explore possible meaningful alternatives to imprisonment as it is presently constituted.

As already indicated, my understanding of the effects of imprisonment on individual prisoners is based on close observation of the West Australian prison system over a period of more than 10 years. Throughout these years, I have listened to many prisoners' interpretations of their own experiences. The extended research undertaken for this book involved in-depth interviews with nine long term prisoner participants plus a prisoner consultant and an ex-prisoner during initial and follow up discussions.

My analysis of penal policy and its discursive frame has been undertaken using secondary source data. The data was gathered through a review of contemporary sociological, criminological and penological literature, as well as papers from criminological and penological conferences, and scrutiny of Department of Corrective Services (WA) research reports, corporate strategy documents, mission statements, Director General's Rules and the *Prisons Act 1981* (WA). I also became familiar with penal policy in the West Australian prison system as a result of my involvement on a Department of Corrective Services task force reviewing prison visits in 1996. Further, I was a contributor to the department's reviews of prisoner grievance procedures, suicide management strategies and the current rewriting of the *Prisons Act* WA. I also appeared as a witness before the Standing Committee on Estimates and Financial Operations in Relation to the Financial Management of Prisons (Hon Mark Nevill MLC Chairman: 20 January 1999).

Finally, my analysis of penal practice also drew from my many years as an official prison visitor, prisoner advocate and prison reformer.

## Research format

As part of the research process, I interviewed nine long term prisoner participants in the days immediately prior to their release and planned to re-interview each participant three to six months after their release. I was, however, unable to locate the participant named "Simon" after his release from a regional prison. As a result of information gathered during these interviews, I elected to consult with one other long term prisoner (described as the prisoner consultant throughout the text) who subsequently provided much of the background information for the book. Also, at the writing up stage, I felt that more information was needed to fill in some gaps in terms of continuity of the study. At that stage I spoke again to the prisoner consultant and sought further assistance from an ex-prisoner who had recently been released from custody after serving a lengthy prison sentence. Finally, my work colleague, close friend and fellow prison reformer and justice activist, Brian Steels, who has also served time in prison, provided me with information of his own prison experience. This also became valuable background information for the study.

Tellingly, seven of the follow up interviews with the nine participants were conducted in prison as these participants had been returned to prison for either breach of parole conditions or had been arrested for further offences. The long term prisoner who was the consultant for background information, also returned to prison subsequent to his release after serving almost 15 years in prison. He experienced only two months of freedom in the community before being arrested for further crimes and is currently serving another long term prison sentence. Further, within the time span of the research one other participant returned to prison after two years out in the community and another returned to prison after three years of freedom. In summary, nine out of 10 long term prisoners who participated in this research experienced re-imprisonment for one reason or another. Also, the ex-prisoner involved in the research offended again, was convicted and served another prison term. This proportion of the group returning to prison is not completely consistent with the recidivism rate in Western Australia as a whole. (The recidivism rate for male Aboriginal prisoners is estimated to stand at 80 per cent, with the female Aboriginal rate being approximately 75 per cent. The overall recidivism rate for male prisoners is 48 per cent and for non-Aboriginal females is 29 per cent (Broadhurst 1988: 83)).

## Chapter outline

Chapter 1 outlines the context of the book. It briefly reviews the history of the prison in Western Australia, changing crime rates, current punishment trends, socio-economic, cultural and racial make-up of prison populations and which types of crime attract prison sentences. It also deals with changing rationalities of crime and punishment, investigates criminal justice policies in the era of welfarism, the changes of the past two decades, and the new penal order embodied in its characteristic formation. The prisoners' own words also begin to be heard within this chapter.

Chapters 2, 3, 4 and 5 all draw heavily on the prisoners' own accounts.

Chapter 2 combines the prisoners' narratives with Goffman's work to describe the nature of total institutions and their effect on inmates. In addition – and using a blend of interview material and academic research – this chapter explores the prison experience in terms of loss, describes the restricted physical and social environs of the prison, and addresses prisoner enculturation and institutional survival.

Chapter 3 turns to the ubiquity of surveillance in the prison environment and examines its use as a tool of control. It also explores the role of prison officers and the prisoners' perception of prison staff. The duality of prison culture is emphasised. The chapter ends by addressing prisoner resistance to institutionalisation.

Chapter 4 is centrally concerned with the questions of violence and brutalisation – issues which figured large in the interviews with all the male participants. As well as investigating how violence becomes rationalised within prison culture, the chapter deals with gender issues related to violence, the prevalence of sexual violence, and group logistics of violence within the prison environment.

Chapter 5 describes the participants' experience of "freedom" out in the community. On the basis of their own accounts, their expectations, anxieties and frustrations are detailed. Here, the participants describe the difficulties they faced on release, the positive and negative factors and, for most of the participants, their ultimate return to prison.

Chapter 6 concludes the text and reflects on the need for, and possible directions of, change. This discussion is set against the actual experiences of prisoners. During the research, participants offered suggestions for strategies to assist prisoners reintegrate more easily into the wider community. These are recounted together with recommendations supporting the proposed directions. The final part of the chapter turns to more fundamental reform of the prison system, and offers proposals for the introduction of a "restorative and transformative" element to West Australian prisons.

Appendix A describes the research design and introduces the reader to the micro-sociological component of the study, reflecting the research focus on the participants' own experiences of imprisonment. It provides a brief description of the symbolic interactionist, phenomenological and ethnomethodological perspectives influencing the study and comments on their usefulness and limitations in the context of this research. It outlines the methodology utilised within the research and provides an in-depth explanation of the reasons for using qualitative methods. It provides a description of the prisoner respondents and a brief explanation of the part played by the prisoner who became the background information consultant. The serious and complex ethical considerations associated with conducting research with extremely marginalised groups are discussed and my own role as researcher is reviewed.

# Chapter 1

# Context of the Book

## Prisons: the historical background in Western Australia

Western Australia was first established as a penal settlement in 1826 when "twenty three prisoners under the command of a Major Lockyer" (Thomas and Stewart 1978: 1) landed at what we now know as Albany. No prison was built at that time and "the idea of a penal settlement was abandoned by proclamation dated 7 March 1831, largely because it was intended to establish a settlement on the Swan River" (Thomas and Stewart 1978: 2). The new settlement on the Swan River established its first penal institution when, in 1829, and following the English trend of using the shells of old ships to house prisoners, a grounded cargo vessel, *The Marquis of Anglesea,* became Western Australia's first prison hulk. Subsequently, the Round House, Western Australia's first purpose-built prison, was constructed in Fremantle in 1831 to house both male and female prisoners.

The Round House prison was run according to the early English model. Thomas and Stewart (1978: 6) report that:

> [F]ollowing the English tradition, it was decided that the Quarter Sessions was to be the body which administered the prison ... that the superintendent was to report regularly to the Quarter Sessions, and that visiting magistrates were to inspect the prison at least once a month.

Thus the precedent was set for the administration of the West Australian prison system. In 1849 the first Act specific to prisons was introduced, declaring the penal institutions in Perth, Fremantle, Rottnest and Albany, to be "legal public gaols and prisons" and thus subject to regulatory controls (Thomas and Stewart 1978: 10). The institution which imprisoned Aboriginal Australians on Rottnest Island, however, was not included in these regulations.

Fremantle Prison, which became the main prison for the colony of Western Australia, was built between 1852 and 1859 using convict labour. Originally, Fremantle Prison had more than 500 cells plus four large dormitories and could hold 1000 prisoners. In 1888 women prisoners were moved to a separated section of the Fremantle Gaol from the old Perth Prison. Between 1904 and 1907 the New Division of Fremantle Gaol was built in order to introduce a new prison philosophy (Fremantle Prison: A Brief History, Department of Environment and Heritage 2005: 2) whereby prisoners were required to endure a regime of solitary confinement for their first three months of incarceration. "Although the theory of 'separation' was not applied in its full rigour for long" certain categories of prisoners were kept separate from the mainstream prison population (Thomas and Stewart 1978: 3). After almost 140 years as the State's main jail, Fremantle Prison was eventually decommissioned in 1991.

In 1856 transportation of convicts was abolished in Western Australia and there appeared to be few administrative problems associated with the growing penal system until the 1890s when full responsibility for prisons was transferred to the colonial government. At this time, Frederick Vosper, a journalist and editor of the *Coolgardie Times* who had himself served time in prison, expressed dissatisfaction with the local prison system. His complaints initiated the first Royal Commission into the Prison System in Western Australia of 1898-99. The Royal Commission was established in order to inquire into:

> the existing condition of the penal system of Western Australia, and to report on the method now in use for the punishment of criminals, their classification, the remission of sentences, and the sanitary conditions of Fremantle Gaol, as well as to enquire into all contracts for supplies of food and other materials for use in the said gaol. (Thomas and Stewart 1978: 52)

Prisoners were invited to give evidence to the Royal Commission and all evidence was published in the subsequent report. The Jameson Royal Commission of 1898 "condemned the structural inadequacies" of Fremantle Gaol (Megahey 2000: 17). Then, in 1911, a second Royal Commission recommended that the site of Fremantle Gaol "be sold and the revenue used to build a new prison" (Megahey 2000: 17). Megahey (2000: 18) questions why "a social institution which was clearly recognised as inherently defective continued to exist throughout most of the twentieth century". Historically, however, Royal Commissions in Western Australia have been less than effective in terms of the implementation of recommendations. This trend has continued into contemporary prison administrations as evidenced by the report of the Royal Commission into Aboriginal Deaths in Custody (RCIADIC) 1991 which laid out 339 recommendations. Significantly, and according to the spirit and intent of these recommendations, WA Deaths in

Custody Watch Committee claim that, more than 10 years on, less than 10 per cent of the RCIADIC recommendations related to custodial matters have been implemented in Western Australia (interview: Duffield, March 2001).

Until the early 20th century Aboriginal prisoners held in prisons around the State and on Rottnest Island were generally kept separate from non-Aboriginal prisoners. Chain gangs of Aboriginal prisoners were a common sight and the police often brought Aboriginal witnesses to towns in chains (Thomas and Stewart 1978: 122). Thomas and Stewart (1978: 121-122) suggest that penal policies affecting Aboriginal people were "demarcated by ... varying policies which, as always in penal administration, are a microcosm of what is happening in the wider society". They suggest that the early period of settlement was characterised by a liberal attitude towards Aboriginal peoples, which was in the main, encouraged by the British Government. Against this, others agree that during the early period of settlement, the white population of Western Australia demonstrated a deep seated dislike of Aboriginal Australians generated by fear as well as the desire for supremacy. Reynolds (1999: 135-139) challenges the notion of peaceful settlement of Australia and argues that:

> Despite the great disadvantages of their position the evidence from all over Australia establishes beyond doubt the considerable impact of resistance. This can be gauged by the reaction of Europeans ... and by the deep fear which Aborigines evoked among frontier settlers.

Reynolds (1999: 135-139) also claims that Aboriginal resistance was "scattered and sporadic" and that "the number of encroaching settlers and the effectiveness of their weapons" reduced the efficacy of Aboriginal resistance. The greatly diminished level of Aboriginal resistance towards the end of the 19th century ensured that the Aboriginal population was no longer considered to be "a considerable physical threat to the lives of white settlers", but had become instead "an irritant, especially because of their persistent killing of livestock" (Thomas and Stewart 1978: 122). Many Aboriginal people were sent to prison for extended periods of time, often on the basis of the "imposition of penalties for actions which were not an offence for non-Aborigines" (Aboriginal Affairs Planning Authority 1992). Thus began an incarceration trend that would have burgeoned out of all proportion by the mid-20th century and which has consistently remained alarmingly high into the 21st century.

By the beginning of the 20th century white Australia's widespread contempt for Aboriginal people was reflected in paternalistic legislation such as the *Aborigines Act* of 1905 and the *Native Administration Act 1936* (WA), which gave guardianship of all Aboriginal children to the Commissioner for Aborigines, allowed the removal of Aboriginal children from their families and permitted the implementation of a policy of absorption which threatened "the Aborigine's very existence as a distinct racial and ethnic community" (Haebich 1988: 349). As Choo (1989: 81) claims, the practice of removing generations of Aboriginal children from their "families, natural environments and social systems" produced a fundamental dislocation thus "creating a problem of massive proportions, the consequences of which we are still experiencing today". This is clearly illustrated in the disproportionate numbers of Aboriginal people currently held within West Australian prisons. According to the Aboriginal Justice Council Annual Report (1998: 43) Aboriginal people constituted 1924 out of 4574 or approximately 42 per cent of all receptions to West Australian prisons in 1997, while constituting only 2.5 per cent of the total State population. At the time of writing, Aboriginal people constitute 39.6 per cent of the total West Australian adult prison population, with Aboriginal women making up more than 50 per cent of all female prisoners within that system (Department of Corrective Services WA Monthly Graphical Report: January 2006).

There are now 13 prisons in Western Australia including the first private prison which opened its gates to receive its initial intake of 75 medium security male prisoners in May 2001 (Director General, Department of Corrective Services: 16 March 2001). The new prison has been built to house 750 prisoners but has the capacity to contain 1100. It is expected that up to 50 per cent of these prisoners will be Aboriginal Australians.

Between 1900 and 1960 prisons were built, populated and often decommissioned as communities established and sometimes moved on. Indeterminate sentences became a feature of punishment in Western Australia and open or minimum security prisons were introduced. Pardelup, near Albany, Wooroloo and Karnet Prison Farms are examples of "open" or minimum security prisons which are currently in use (Department of Corrective Services WA information pamphlets: An Introduction to Karnet, Pardelup and Wooroloo Prison Farms 1996). Until recently these prisons were not surrounded by high walls or razor wire perimeter fences and contained, in the main, minimum security prisoners nearing the end of their prison terms. However, because of several high profile escapes from Karnet Prison Farm in 2005, perimeter fences have now been erected around both Karnet and Wooroloo minimum security prisons at a cost of $11 million. These perimeter fences were put in place although, in his report of an *Inquiry into the Management of Offenders in Custody and in the Community* (2005: vii), Justice Mahoney argued that "it is essential to have open prisons. They are part of the process of re-socialisation of prisoners to reduce the risk of re-offending on release". Mahoney (2005: xvi) went on to recommend that:

> Government should avoid making decisions in relation to capital expenditure, such as the further fencing of minimum security prisons, until adequate needs based planning has been undertaken by the Department. (Recommendation 11)

> Government should not fence further minimum security prisons until a review of the operation of the fences at Karnet and Wooroloo Prison Farms is conducted, following two years operation of the new fences. (Recommendation 12)

In 1980 Canning Vale maximum security prison (now renamed Hakea and Western Australia's premier remand, receival and assessment facility) was commissioned adjacent to the CW Campbell Remand Centre at Canning Vale. This prison was supposed to break new ground by moving from an exclusive focus on the secure containment of prisoners to a combination of re-socialisation and prisoner security. In official terms, the aim was to provide the optimum balance between "the goals of security of imprisonment and retention of some level of human responsiveness in the inmates" (Emery et al 1973: v). Canning Vale Prison was originally designed to accommodate 325 prisoners who were to be held within the principles of 'unit management' (Department of Corrective Services WA information pamphlet: An Introduction to Canning Vale Prison 1996). The unit management regime was introduced to promote the use of "motivated staff members" to work in welfare oriented roles in order to "act as a very positive influence on inmates" (Emery et al 1973: 1). "Small domestically based groups of inmates housed in their own physically separate wings and blocks" together with "small shift-based groups of staff where the responsibility for decision making ... is that of a group of officers" (Emery et al 1973: 5) were to be established in Canning Vale Prison in an endeavour to maximise the resemblance between prison life and life in the wider community. More than 20 years later, it is questionable how successful these principles of unit management have been. Later in the book I will draw attention to the prevalence of a deep-seated "us and them" culture revealed by the accounts of the prisoners who participated in this study. This, I shall suggest, erodes the likelihood of prisoners and prison officers being able to engage in positive relationships based on mutual trust.

In September 1991 Casuarina maximum security prison was opened on the outskirts of Perth. This hi-tech prison was built to replace the, by then, defunct Fremantle Gaol. At the time of its opening, Casuarina Prison was said to be the most up to date, secure prison in the southern hemisphere (Ayris 1991: 1). The prison was built in an open campus style with six units plus a self care unit. The vast majority of cells in Casuarina were designed to contain only one inmate. However, by the time of the Christmas day riot of 1998, Casuarina had doubled up prisoners in many cells, was approximately 30 per cent over population capacity and had remained consistently overcrowded for more than four years (Smith 1999: 28).

## The women's estate

In 1969, Bandyup, the first West Australian prison built exclusively for women was commissioned. Bandyup maximum security prison was built to contain up to 80 women prisoners but has, in recent years, remained continuously overcrowded. Bandyup Prison houses minimum, medium and maximum security prisoners as well as remand (unconvicted) prisoners. There is no segregation of women prisoners based on security rating. Bandyup has a mother and child unit which can accommodate up to four mothers and their babies. However, official policy ensures that "[b]abies can only stay with their mothers until the babies are twelve months old. At that age, they must be sent to carers outside the prison" (Department of Corrective Services WA information pamphlet: An Introduction to Bandyup Women's Prison 1996).

Until the late 1990s Bandyup Women's Prison was the only prison specifically for women in the Perth metropolitan area. In December 1998, largely because of the ongoing overcrowding at Bandyup, Nyandi Pre-release Centre was opened to accommodate women of minimum security classification. The Nyandi facility, an annexe of Bandyup and previously used as a juvenile detention centre for girls, provided women prisoners with the opportunity to "serve part of their sentences in an appropriate minimum security pre-release facility and receive services to assist them to prepare for release" (Harding 2002b: 5). Nyandi Pre-release Centre was established as a temporary answer to the problems of overcrowding and lack of resources to facilitate women's resettlement needs in Bandyup prison. Nyandi was closed in May 2004 when the new low security Boronia Pre-release Centre for Women was opened.

Boronia Pre-release Centre for Women, opened in May 2004, represents a radical move forward in prison architecture and prisoner management philosophy within the West Australian system. The prison was conceptualised and developed over several years with genuine grass roots community consultation (Harding 2005: xxi). Boronia Prerelease Centre is designed to manage up to 70 minimum security women nearing release, within a community-style setting. That is, the women live in Ministry of Housing style houses rather than prison wings or units. There are 17 houses on site with up to five women living in a house where they are responsible for cooking, cleaning, budgeting and shopping for groceries from the Centre supermarket (Department of Corrective Services WA information leaflet 2006). Several houses have been set aside for women who are primary care givers for children and these women are permitted to keep their children with them until they are four years old.

## Prison inquiries

In the past two decades there have been several inquiries into the West Australian prison system. These include the *Report of the Inquiry into the Fire and Riot at Fremantle Prison on the 4th January 1988* (McGivern 1988), the *Report of the Inquiry into an Incident at Casuarina Prison on 25th December 1998* (Smith 1999), the *Report on an Inquiry into Deaths in Prisons in Western Australia* by the West Australian State Ombudsman (Ombudsman WA 2000) and, most recently, the *Inquiry into the Management of Offenders in Custody and in the Community* (Mahoney 2005) which was conducted in association with a directed inquiry by the Inspector of Custodial Services WA under the *Inspector of Custodial Services Act 2003* s 17; *Directed Review of the Management of Offenders in Custody in Western Australia*. Both inquiries reported to the West Australian Parliament in November 2005.

The McGivern Inquiry was established to investigate the cause of the Fremantle Prison riot of 4 and 5 January 1988. The main findings of the inquiry suggest that the poor physical conditions of the prison, the depressed human environment and an ineffective administration system were the major factors contributing to the general prisoner unrest which culminated in the riot. McGivern (1988: 14) described the physical conditions in Fremantle Gaol as substandard. He reported that the prison was seriously overcrowded, the cells were small, unsewered and vermin infested, and that prisoners were "compelled to eat, sleep and defecate" in their cells. McGivern (1988: 16) also claimed that the most common complaints among prisoners were the "selective and punitive attitudes of a few prison officers". This factor was also highlighted by the prisoner consultant who was involved in the riot. He described the build up to the Fremantle riot in this way:

> *There was a concerted effort over a period of around six months of frustration of having grievances about appalling conditions ignored and laughed at. These things built up over a period of time, plus there were some real arseholes of officers giving us a hard time for no real reason. There were three main things that brought the tension to a head and finally triggered the riot, basically the straws that broke the camel's back. First, prisoners' mail was getting passed around by officers who were reading it and laughing at it and taking the piss out of the letters in front of other prisoners and officers. Second, an 80-year-old grandmother visiting her grandson got strip-searched in her wheel chair. She was one of about 30 or 40 family members who'd been strip-searched that week so the tension was building up to flashpoint by the time this old grandmother was strip-searched. Then, the final nail in the coffin was on the morning of the riot, a young prisoner who hadn't made his bed, or something equally trivial, got handcuffed and belted around by officers. That was the last straw and the riot erupted.* (interview: September 1998)

McGivern himself had more than 30 years experience in the West Australian prison system, having served as a prison officer and superintendent, and had retired from the prison service only two years before the riot (Megahey 2000: 27). His report concluded that "consideration of prisoners' evidence led to a clear recognition that ill-treatment of prisoners by officers, albeit relatively few in number, was a fact of prison life and a justifiable source of grievance". He recommended that there should be "commitment on behalf of the Department and the administration of the prison, together with the prison officers, to develop an atmosphere in which prisoners believe they are being treated reasonably and fairly" (McGivern 1988: 65).

The report into the Casuarina riot (Smith 1999: 95) claims that there were three main causes of the riot: "systemic neglect", a "tinderbox" situation and a final "spark". The characteristics of systemic neglect were presented as failure to provide for an expanding prison population and failure to provide support and direction to achieve primary goals of corrections (Smith 1999: 96). The "tinderbox" situation was described as "an overcrowded prison system manifesting various symptoms of staff and prisoner stress and decreased services to prisoners and failure to address the growing drug problem" (Smith 1999: 98-100). Finally, the "spark" was said to arise from the minimal control capability combined with maximised condition for disruption and drug intoxication, confrontation and collective violence (Smith

1999: 102-103). The associated factors in terms of prison management were "rapid change of positions at Director General and Executive Director levels, some system failure at highest level and failure to provide for an expanding prison population" (Smith 1999: 97). The main conclusion of the Smith Report was that overcrowding of the prison for an extended period of time together with decreased services to prisoners, increased prisoner grievances, increased demand for drugs and very little effective staff training were the "sparks that combusted within the tinderbox" (Smith 1999: 102). Until the opening of Acacia Prison (West Australia's first privately run prison), more than two years after the riot, Casuarina prison remained both overcrowded and under-resourced.

The *Report on an Inquiry into Deaths in Prisons in Western Australia* by the West Australian Ombudsman (December 2000) took more than two years to complete. This report highlighted the shortcomings already identified 18 months previously in the Smith Report. The Ombudsman (2000: 6) also noted that:

> One of the strongest themes to have emerged from my inquiry is that the Ministry [Department of Corrective Services] has always been able (sometimes with the help of recommendations made externally) to identify what has been needed to be done to improve our prison system. Where the Ministry has failed, in my opinion, is in its apparent inability over the years to move beyond the awareness and planning stages to the implementation and achievement stages.

The major recommendation from this report was that:

> [The responsibility] for the control of the prison health service should not lie with the Ministry – but, rather, should be placed in the hands of a new entity which is quite separate from the Ministry ... which should be funded in its own right ... to provide a health service within prisons that is equivalent ... to health services in the community. (Ombudsman WA 2000: 7)

However, this recommendation was rejected by the then Minister for Justice, Peter Foss, and to date, prisoner health services are still run by the Department of Corrective Services. However, various prisoner welfare and reform groups (in particular, the Prison Reform Group of WA, Deaths in Custody Watch Committee WA) have continuously lobbied for the transfer of prisoner health services from the Department of Corrective Services to the Health Department. Then, in April 2004, the Office of the Inspector of Custodial Services embarked on a thematic review of prisoner health services (Harding 2006: 1). According to Harding (2006: 4):

Deficiencies in prisoner health services became apparent to the Office of the Inspector of Custodial Services from the time its operations first commenced in June 2000. These deficiencies were manifest in areas such as dental services, mental healthcare, management of chronic illnesses, the control of blood-borne viruses and the availability of culturally appropriate health services for Aboriginal prisoners ... In a context where the social determinants of health and the health status of offender populations, is markedly worse than that of the general population, resources and funding were clearly insufficient. To compound matters, such services as were available were sometimes undermined by attitudinal values; the prisoner remained first and foremost a prisoner rather than a patient.

In July 2005 the Office of the Inspector of Custodial Services produced a draft report which was circulated to the Department of Corrective Services, The Health Department and a range of stakeholders including non-government organisations, government agencies and prison reform groups. In September 2006, Report No 35 of the Office of the Inspector of Custodial Services, the *Thematic Review of Offender Health Services* was presented to Parliament. The main recommendation was: "That responsibility for the provision of health services for prisoners and juvenile detainees should be transferred from the Department of Corrective Services to the Department of Health". Surprisingly, the Department of Corrective Services who had consistently, over a period of more than 10 years, remained opposed to relinquishing responsibility for prisoner health services "made a remarkable turnaround ... by an acceptance of the proposition that this is the right way to go ... it now recognises that limitations on the present capacity to deliver health services constitute a risk, both legal and political" (Harding 2006: 2). Consequently, the future of prisoner health care in Western Australia seems set to improve provided the transition to the Health Department goes ahead.

In April 2005 the Premier of Western Australia directed that an inquiry be held into the management of offenders. The reason for initiating the inquiry was a series of serious incidents leading to widespread public concern regarding the management of offenders within the West Australian criminal justice system. These incidents included the following; in 2003 an offender committed murder whilst on parole, early in April 2005 two long term prisoners escaped custody, and a prison employee was held hostage and seriously assaulted by a prisoner (Mahoney 2005: 15). These incidents were selected for investigation from a succession of many other disturbing events that took place within the same time frame. Some of the other serious incidents that occurred within that time span included the escape of nine high security prisoners from a holding cell at the Supreme Court and a prisoner gaining repeated access to the Department of Corrective Services confidential computer database.

The terms of reference for the Mahoney Inquiry required the:

> examination of the whole of the corrections system of Western Australia and a number of related matters; the assessment of the organisational structure, role and performance of the Department of Justice in its relevant aspects; and the development of a plan of 'implementable strategies' for the future. (Mahoney 2005: 5)

At the Inquiry's conclusion, Justice Mahoney handed down 148 recommendations. Arguably, the most notable of these were Recommendations 8, 19 and 73-76. Recommendations 73-76 involve the abolition of the then Department of Justice, which was to be divided into two new departments, namely the Department of the Attorney General and the Department of Corrective Services. The Department of the Attorney General was to oversee courts, the Public Advocate, the Public Trustee and provide support for the secretariat of the Parole Board. The newly formed Department of Corrective Services was to retain responsibility for the administration of offenders (adult and juvenile) in custody and the community (Mahoney 2005: xxvii).

Both the Mahoney Report and the Directed Review of the Management of Offenders in Custody recommended a total review of the prisoner classification system (Mahoney 2005, Recommendation 8: xvii) with the Inspector of Custodial Services adding that the current classification system "does not differentiate between males and females" even though the body of literature "argues that a male-based or normed classification system will negatively impact upon women" (Harding 2005: 22). Both reports also recommend that any future infrastructure planning for prisons should be based on a "Regional Prison" model in order to better serve the needs of Indigenous offenders and keep them within proximity of their homelands (Harding 2005: 94, 133, 160, Mahoney 2005, Recommendation 19: xvi).

At the time of writing, the then Department of Justice has been divided into the two recommended departments; Attorney General's Department and Department of Corrective Services. However, substantial confusion remains regarding the separation of roles and to date there has been no implementation of the recommendation to the prisoner classification system. In addition, the regionalisation of the prison system has not yet eventuated.

The content of these reports serves to illustrate the more general point that extensive inquiries, however carefully conducted, remain unable to instigate positive legislative or policy change within the prison system unless they have political backing. In this context it is pertinent to note that, to date, Australian governments from both sides of politics have not yet taken account of the requirements of the United Nations Human Rights instruments such as the *Standard Minimum Rules for the Treatment of Prisoners* or the *Basic Principles for the Treatment of Prisoners* when legislating on prison conditions and prisoners' treatment. International human rights instruments such as these are not legally enforceable. Importantly, the *Australian Standard Correctional Guidelines* which were first issued in 1989 by all State Justice or Corrective Services Ministers are not legally binding in any Australian State (Heilpern 1998: 135).

To take a case in point, while section 5.31 of the *Australian Standard Correctional Guidelines* states that "collective punishment must not be used", for almost a year after the 1998 Casuarina riot, prisoners, most of whom did not participate in the riot and many of whom were not held in Casuarina at the time of the riot, were collectively punished by being held in constant lockdown in their cells at Casuarina prison for a minimum of 22 hours per day. Albert, who was taken to Casuarina Prison as a remand prisoner two months after the riot, described the lockdown situation as he experienced it:

> Here I am on remand because I couldn't make bail for something I had nothing to do with anyway. I've been here for five weeks, convicted of nothing and I've been doubled up in a cell that's meant for one person. The place is still overcrowded, the screws are paranoid, there's no privileges, no case conferences, it's impossible to call your lawyer and no one could care less. I'm locked up in my slot (cell) for twenty three hours a day with someone I don't particularly like. I don't see the sun at all and it's real hard going – even for me and I've done a fair bit of time. I'm being punished for a riot that happened when I wasn't even in jail. (interview: September 1999)

[Albert was released two weeks after this interview. As he claimed, his arrest had been a case of mistaken identity.]

## Current trends

### Imprisonment rates

Over the past 25 years Australia's prison population has almost tripled. In 1980 the average daily prisoner count was 9746. In the March quarter of 2006 the average daily number of prisoners was 24,425

(Australian Bureau of Statistics, March 2006). The national average imprisonment rate for Australia during March 2006 was 156 prisoners per 100,000 of the adult population (ABS, March 2006). Of the average daily number of prisoners in Australia during the March quarter 2006, approximately 93 per cent were male. Also in the March quarter 2006, there were 5842 Aboriginal Australians in custody. This figure means that approximately 19 per cent of the Australian prison population is of Aboriginal or Torres Strait Islander descent. In other words, the national imprisonment rate for Indigenous Australians is 15 times the non-Indigenous rate.

The incarceration rate in Western Australia is the highest of any Australian State. According to Australian Bureau of Statistics figures the West Australian incarceration rate is now 227 per 100,000 of the adult population (ABS, March 2006). At the time of writing there are 3510 people in custody in West Australian prisons (Department of Corrective Services, weekly statistics, 20 July 2006). This figure represents a prison population increase of more than 50 per cent in the past five years.

Most alarmingly, the West Australian Aboriginal incarceration rates are even higher than the national average, with the Aboriginal rate of imprisonment currently standing at 3268 per 100,000; more than 20 times that of the non-Indigenous imprisonment rate (ABS, March 2006). According to the Department of Corrective Services WA weekly statistics (20 July 2006) there are currently 1391 Aboriginal Australians in custody, constituting almost 40 per cent of the total West Australian prison population. In addition to this, women are being sent to prison in Western Australia at a rate of 35.8 per 100,000. This figure represents the highest imprisonment rate for women of any Australian State or Territory, including the Northern Territory and is almost twice the national rate of 20.4 per 100,000 and almost three times the Victorian rate of 13.4 per 100,000. In particular, the rate of imprisonment of Aboriginal women is increasing alarmingly (ATSIC Social Justice Report 2004: 3). Within the West Australian context, Aboriginal women, who make up approximately 3 per cent of the general female population, constitute more than 50 per cent of the female West Australian prison population (Department of Corrective Services WA Monthly Graphical Report, January 2006).

The statistics surrounding imprisonment suggest that incarceration has become the tool of first resort in Western Australia as far as combating crime is concerned. This trend is repeated in many other western societies. As Coyle (1994: 3) argues, "we talk without thinking about alternatives to imprisonment. It is as if imprisonment were the first option of the sentencer and other forms of judicial penalty only to be used when imprisonment is not appropriate". Yet high incarceration rates and punitive prison regimes do not necessarily help to reduce crime rates. For example, the Victorian incarceration rate is the lowest of any Australian State at 91 per 100,000 (ABS, March 2006) and the *Victorian Political News* claims that the Victorian crime rate is almost 20 per cent below the national average. "Victoria had 5349.34 victims of crime per 100,000 population compared to the Australian average of 6683.07" (VPN September 2000: 1).

The relationship between incarceration rates and crime rates is complex and unstable. As Coyle (2001: 6) argues:

> One should be very cautious of any suggestion that an increased use of imprisonment is an efficient form of crime control. There is little evidence from anywhere in the world that there is any relationship between high rates of imprisonment and low rates of crime. Indeed the contrary is often the case. High rates of imprisonment are frequently an indicator of the break down of society's sense of community values.

One of the reasons why it is so difficult to say whether higher incarceration rates either increase or decrease criminal behaviour relates to the influence of demographic factors. There is, for example, a clear correlation between both age and gender and levels of criminal activity, with younger people, and young men in particular, the most likely to offend. So, when there is a heightened proportion of young men within the population it is reasonable to expect an increase in crime rates. Stern (1998: 285-286) points out that in the United States "between 1960 and 1980 the number of young men in the US nearly doubled (a rise from 11.9 million to 21.4 million). Crime rates also increased. Since 1980 the population of young men has slightly decreased, as have crime rates". Unless this is taken into account, the reduced crime rates over the past two decades could misleadingly be used as evidence to support the more punitive policies introduced over this period.

It could also be suggested that there is a simpler relationship at work. On this count, increased incarceration rates simply reflect an increase in criminal activity – they are a response to it. However, according to Zimring and Hawkins (1997: 30), "[t]here is no general tendency for penal systems to expand in proportion to general growth in crime". Further, as Carlen (1994: 313) points out, "in times of economic crisis societies become less tolerant and punish offenders more harshly". Alongside this, it is my contention the growth in prison populations reflects a growth in the *fear* of crime rather than a real growth in serious offending.

This fear of crime combines with the more punitive criminal justice policies which are largely based on the political expediency of notions of a "war on crime". So-called "tough on crime" policies currently appear to be the preferred option of many western governments. Such policies include, but are not limited to, mandatory sentencing and truth in sentencing legislation, reduction in parole opportunities, increases in both duration and numbers of prison sentences and reduction in bail opportunities.

Moreover, in the context of the *fear* of crime, electronic and print media within the genre of current affairs and news programs have greatly heightened public anxieties regarding levels of crime in the community. On this, the Glasgow Media Group expresses real concern regarding the "agenda-setting role of the media ... especially in its alleged use of slanted stereotypes and its tendency to affirmation of the status quo" (Jary and Jary 1991: 259). David, who had recently been released from prison and was experiencing a brief period of freedom in the community, reflected on his perception of society's views of crime in this way:

> *Attitudes seem to have changed in this area. Society's view on a crim is a lot stronger and harder. I walked through the city and saw a little rally happening – citizens against crime, I think. I never saw that before. I saw all the placards about lock em up for longer, flog em, hang em, and I felt like stoning the fuckwits because it pissed me off. They don't have an iota of an idea what it's like in prison or what prison does to people. Prison just made me more violent.* (interview: November 1998)

There is no doubt that crime is news. However, images of the elderly as the most likely victims of violent crime are misleading. Young men between the ages of 16 and 25 years are most likely to be both the victims and perpetrators of violent crime in Western Australia and women and children are more likely to be assaulted in their homes by family members or friends than they are by strangers on the street or home invaders. In short, media induced panic together with politically expedient law and order campaigns have effectively initiated some sectors of the community to call for more punitive approaches to crime. This, it can be suggested, is at least one of the factors behind the growth in prison populations.

## Who goes to prison?

In general terms criminal activity occurs right across the socio-economic spectrum. The crimes that attract most public attention and notoriety – at any event in terms of the volume of criminal charges laid – are characteristically those attributed to individuals from low socio-economic backgrounds. These typically constitute street crimes and property offences such as car theft or burglary. Such crimes often attract the "serious deep-ended punishments such as imprisonment" (Duff and Garland 1994: 306). Indeed, each of the long term prisoners who participated in the research for this book was serving a term of imprisonment attributed to property crimes and/or crimes of violence: robbery, burglary, robbery with violence, armed robbery and various types of assault. In comparison, the less publicised crimes of the powerful – fraud and corporate crime, for example – are generally more leniently treated, although they may, as Garland (Duff and Garland 1994: 306) suggests, "produce significantly greater social harm in terms both of monetary loss and of physical injury and death".

Prison populations are often indicative of prevailing worldwide patterns of social injustice and discrimination. According to Stern (1998: 117): "Prisons contain higher proportions than would be expected of people from groups that suffer from racism and discrimination". In support of Stern's argument, Simon, an Aboriginal prisoner serving a five year sentence, commented on the disproportionate numbers of Aboriginal Australians held in West Australian prisons:

> We make up maybe 2 per cent of the population but in this parti-
> cular prison it's about 30 per cent Aboriginal. Some prisons like
> Roebourne, Broome and Eastern Goldfields it's almost 100 per
> cent Aboriginal prisoners. It's pure and simple systemic racism
> and it starts with the police on the streets picking us up for things
> that whitefellas typically get away with. They'll pick us up for
> trivial things like drunk and disorderly, street drinking, public nui-
> sance things and that's generally how the typical Aboriginal kid
> gets started into the system and then it's all downhill from there.
> (interview: August 1998)

This trend is reflected worldwide with minority ethnic groups being disproportionately represented within prison populations. According to Mauer (2003: 4) in the United States, for example:

> Overall rates of incarceration, based on total populations, obscure
> the broad variation by which imprisonment impacts various demo-
> graphic groups. In this regard, African American males are clearly
> the most heavily affected by current policies, with one of every
> eight black males in the age group 25-29 currently in prison or jail.

Data from the Department of Justice demonstrate that a black male born today has a 29 per cent chance of spending time in state or federal prison in his lifetime.

This trend is mirrored in England and Wales, New Zealand, Canada and many other western societies. In socio-economic terms, "[p]risons are mainly occupied by the casualties of social policies: those, and the children of those, who have not managed to get for themselves a position with income, employment, family security and social acceptance" (Stern 1998: 121). And, as Carlen (1994: 309) argues:

> Whatever else prisons may be for, they have always housed large numbers of the poor, the unemployed, the unemployable, the homeless, the physically ill and the mentally disturbed. From time to time ... these staples of the prison population have been augmented by large contingents of other 'problem' populations such as ethnic minority groups, political protesters, and ... unemployed *youth* ... as commentary on the blatant inequities of the criminal justice system.

Carlen's argument is well supported by the gross over-representation of Aboriginal people in the West Australian prison system, the number of people imprisoned because of an inability to pay fines and the high percentage of the prison population who have either psychological or psychiatric disorders and/or intellectual disabilities.

## Worldwide punishment trends

The world average incarceration rate is approximately 140 per 100,000 of the total population but "within that average there are wide variations" (Coyle 2001a: 2). Currently, there are more than 2 million people incarcerated in the United States of America. The State of California now boasts the "biggest prison system in the western industrialised world ... the state now holds more inmates in its jails and prisons than do France, Britain, Germany, Japan, Singapore and the Netherlands combined" (Schlosser 1998: 52). In the State of Texas, the incarceration rate is "a staggering 1014 per one hundred thousand – that means that one per cent of the whole population of the state is in prison" (Coyle 2001a: 2). Overall, the USA currently incarcerates its people at the rate of 714 per 100,000 of the national population (Walmsley 2005: 1). This represents a tripling of the prison population in just over 10 years yet, according to Stern (1998: 285):

> Serious violent crime is at about the same level it was ten years ago, in spite of the massive growth in incarceration. The level of violence in America's inner cities, after this massive investment ...

is still higher than in any comparable country. Not a great achievement for the expense and social disruption that has been caused.

In many instances longer terms of imprisonment have accompanied higher incarceration ratios. Coyle (2001a: 5) writes, "for an increasing number of men and women the period of exclusion is becoming longer and longer. In the United States in particular a significant proportion of prisoners will spend the rest of their lives in prison". The significance of this phenomenon is that prison systems will have to adapt in order to accommodate large numbers of very old prisoners who are likely to suffer all of the emotional, psychiatric and physical ailments of senility.

The Russian incarceration rate is only slightly less than that of the United States. According to Stern (1998: 64), "this may not cause much surprise. In many ways Russia and its history seem interwoven with exile, imprisonment, forced labour and suffering". Currently there are approximately 1 million people incarcerated in Russian prisons. This equates to an incarceration rate of 685 per 100,000. Moreover, appalling conditions, poor nutrition, and gross overcrowding in Russian prisons have contributed to epidemic proportions of prisoners diagnosed with tuberculosis. Stern (1999: 39) records that "[f]ilth, squalor, overcrowded conditions, malnutrition, and lack of drugs all contribute to a horrifying statistic: an estimated 50 per cent of Russia's one million prison inmates are infected with the TB bacillus, and close to 10 per cent are sick with active TB". In short, approximately 100,000 Russian prisoners have active tuberculosis.

In contrast, some Northern European countries have relatively low incarceration rates and prison regimes which are more closely related to general community norms. The Danish, Swedish and Dutch incarceration rates are each 70, 75 and 123 per 100,000 of the national population respectively (Walmsley 2005: 5), around one tenth of the incarceration rate in the United States and Russia (Stern 1998: 32). In these countries the negative stereotyping of prisoners that flourishes in countries with relatively high incarceration rates seems less prominent. For instance, when Dutch prisons are filled to capacity, the authorities utilise strategies to avoid overcrowding. Thus, for example, prisoners who are nearing the end of their sentences can be considered for early release. In addition, and more significantly, newly sentenced offenders who are not deemed a danger to the community can be sent home from court until a prison cell is available. When a cell becomes free, they are requested to present themselves and, if they comply, are rewarded by remission of time served. Offenders who do not comply are eventually arrested and serve their full sentence as handed down by the court (Nieuhaus: 2000).

In the Netherlands, prisoners who feel that they have been treated unjustly by the prison authorities may complain to "a committee made up of ordinary citizens" who, "if they find the complaint justified ... can overturn the prison authorities' decision" (Stern 1998: 23, Nieuhaus 2000). Prisoners in open prisons in the Netherlands can generally go home at weekends. In Germany, too, unless they present a risk to the community, prisoners are entitled to 21 days home leave per year. The German incarceration rate is 96 per 100,000 (Walmsley 2005: 5) and the German prison population has reduced by approximately 30 per cent in the past decade (Stern 1998: 31).

India, the largest democracy in the world, incarcerates its citizens at the rate of 29 per 100,000 (Walmsley 2005: 4). The Japanese incarceration rate is 58 per 100,000 of the national population. Indeed, the Japanese prison population has more than halved in the past 50 years and has "resisted all the trends of the developed world" (Stern 1998: 33). It should be noted that when Japan's incarceration rate was at its highest in 1950 immediately after World War Two, the country was, in effect, under the control of the United States and its allies. However, culturally, Japan has a tradition of shaming, apology, reparation and forgiveness and this may, in part, account for the limited use of imprisonment as a strategy to control and limit criminal activity.

In concluding, it is worth noting that many countries, including Australia, had no concept of imprisonment until they were colonised by western democracies such as Britain. Coyle (2001c: 4) suggests that:

> In these countries the idea of taking large numbers of able-bodied young men, who should be contributing to the economic and social well-being of society, and locking them behind the high walls of a prison, where they are a burden on the community, makes little sense in terms of local cultural norms ... In many of these countries the problems facing their prison systems remain immense since some of the worst prison conditions are to be found in countries which were formerly ruled by imperial powers.

## The new penal order

### A New Right Alliance

I have argued that in the past decade the use of imprisonment as a strategy to combat crime has increasingly become the tool of first resort in a number of western countries, including Australia, Great Britain, and the United States of America. What sort of political ideology does this reflect? In answering this question I explore whether these high rates of imprisonment and more stringent prison regimes sit more comfortably within a neo-conservative or neo-liberal framework or, alternatively, whether they belong within an alliance of both ideologies which, together, make up the new penal order. To this end I consider neoliberalism in terms of the "ascendancy of consumer discourses" (O'Malley and Palmer 1996: 142), relating this to factors such as home security, private policing and prisons for profit within the context of risk management and individual responsibility. This is linked with small government and the associated "erosion or decentring of state services" and the productive or entrepreneurial individual (O'Malley and Palmer 1996: 142). I also investigate the parallel ascendancy of neoconservatism in terms of mandatory sentencing, longer custodial terms and more punitive prison regimes. As O'Malley and Garland argue (1996: 142), the combination of these trends suggests that the new penal order embodies an unstable alliance between neo-liberalism and an increasingly influential neo-conservatism. I examine these possibilities with specific reference to practices within West Australian prisons.

## Neo-liberalism

Over the past two decades there has been increasing displacement of welfarist policies within many western democratic criminal justice systems. Pratt (1997: 133) claims that: "A sense of dissatisfaction with welfarism" produced, from the late 1970s on, support for a "sweeping move away from welfarism, and towards neo-liberalism ... towards a much more fundamental reorganisation of economic and social life". There are two dominant themes within neo-liberalism. These are an ideological commitment to the free market and the reduction of the power of the State. Neo-liberal ideals are anti-State as a matter of political principle in terms of individual liberty as well as in terms of economic efficiency (Heywood 1992: 81). Neo-liberal rationalities encourage individuals to be both self reliant and entrepreneurial and, by the same token, prefer that private enterprise rather than the State should provide services such as public transport, energy supply and telecommunications. In short, the notion of small government and the implementation of privatisation policies are central within a neo-liberal framework.

With regard to the criminal justice system, nco-liberalism's concern is the provision of "a secure framework within which individuals can pursue their own lives and their own choices of the good" (Duff and Garland 1994: 3). In this case, the prime justification of the State's right to punish is the right of individuals to conduct their lives free from the risk of crime. This implies that "the state's power must also be strictly limited to ensure that it enhances rather than improperly constrains individual freedom. The liberal principles which permit the state to punish, thus also set definite constraints on its power" (Duff and Garland 1994: 3). Further, the state's attention needs to focus on the individual agency of those who are guilty of breaking the law as well as the rights of law-abiding citizens. Within a neo-liberal criminal justice system, offenders are assumed to be "responsible moral agents" (Duff and Garland 1994: 15) capable of choosing whether or not to offend. This contrasts with the welfarist emphasis on the socio-economic determinants of crime.

O'Malley (1999: 14) argues that neo-liberalism cannot be called upon to explain all of the current developments within the criminal justice system. On the one hand, it accounts for the privatisation of state services, the reduction in state responsibility, an increase in free market involvement and the call for increased community responsibility for crime management. On the other hand, it is less able to explain trends such as mandatory sentencing legislation, truth in sentencing and other variations of "three strike laws". All these bear the stamp of attempts to build up the authority of the state that fit within a neo-conservative framework.

## Neo-conservatism

The essence of neo-conservatism is the restoration of authority and control within the state (Heywood 1992: 88). O'Malley (1999: 15) argues that "for neo-conservatives, discipline is essential for the social good". He suggests, further, that the neo-conservative concept of the "social" has "very specific organic overtones that do not sit well with neo-liberals' radical individualism ... consequently the freedom and enhanced autonomy that is central to neo-liberalism cannot occupy a central place in conservative thinking" (O'Malley 1999: 15). For neo-conservatives the state is central to the preservation of law and order within society and both the free market and the individual are subordinate to state authority. Another notion characterising certain elements of neo-conservatism is the belief that "the mass of people, because of their inherent qualities, including ignorance and selfishness, are unlikely to create a satisfactory social order through their own efforts" (Jary and Jary 1991: 115).

Accordingly, issues of law and order are fundamental within a framework of neo-conservatism. O'Malley (1999: 15) points out that under a neo-conservative order:

The state, particularly in its role as the preserver of order and the governor of the nation is the privileged symbol of political rule, and allegiance to the state has nothing to do with a neo-liberal partnership. This strong assertion of state sovereignty in turn privileges both law and order as crucial, more important than the market and the individual.

A parallel argument is proposed by Garland (1990: 25) who, drawing on Durkheim's concept of social solidarity invested in a collective moral order, suggests that penal policy formulated in the name of an outraged "collective conscience" is, in the main, underpinned by notions of legitimised vengeance. In this way, neo-conservative penal policies often exhibit the punitive and reactionary characteristics of a positive retributivist model of punishment (Duff and Garland 1994: 13). Under this model, punishment is seen to be "not merely permissible, but required by justice, since law-abiding citizens suffer injustice if offenders are allowed to get away with their unfair advantage" (Duff and Garland 1994: 13). Positive retributivist methods indicate that "the guilty must always be punished to the full extent of their desert" (Duff and Garland 1994: 7). In short, a positive retributivist mode of punishment promotes the principle of "just deserts", calculating the severity of the sentence to fit the severity of the offence. This effectively diminishes judicial discretion in support of greater State control with the introduction of variations of "three strike" laws or mandatory sentencing legislation.

## Neo-liberalism, neo-conservatism and the formulation of criminal justice policies

The logical outcome of neo-liberalism as far as crime is concerned is that individuals are increasingly exhorted to take more responsibility in ensuring their own safety against the associated risks of criminal activity. Inherent within neo-liberalism is the argument that crime is a negative inevitability of everyday life which "requires the active involvement of the citizenry in tandem with the police" (O'Malley 1999: 12). To this end, innovations such as Crime Stoppers, Neighbourhood Watch and Safe Houses have been established nation-wide as the State attempts to abrogate primary responsibility for control of criminal activity within communities.

Running parallel with these initiatives is the promotion of an entrepreneurial culture. Entrepreneurialism promotes free market involvement in areas of home security. The items bought become, in effect, a practical demonstration of individual responsibility related to crime prevention. No longer is a barking dog seen to be a sufficient precaution against home burglary. Increasingly the insurance industry either obligates or encourages individuals wishing home risk cover to obtain marketable items such as window locks, security screens and burglar alarms in order to secure such risk cover. Furthermore, commercial organisations and businesses such as banks and pharmacies now employ private security guards as a visible deterrent to potential criminals.

Another possible consequence of entrepreneurialism is the privatisation of a number of criminal justice operations. Recent legislation in Western Australia enables specific court and prison functions such as court security, prisoner movement, health care and education to be serviced, at least in part, by the private sector (Western Australia Court Security and Custodial Services Bill 1998). Even more crucially, the first private for profit prison in Western Australia has been commissioned with the capacity to house up to 1100 prisoners. The irony of the private for profit prison is that it needs to be full of prisoners in order to maximise profit.

A real concern here is that when a privately run prison relies on the concept of a "full house" for its profit base then the motivation for prisoner rehabilitation, sentence remission and other incentives for earliest possible release may be diminished. This has been evidenced in certain other jurisdictions where the private prison industry is entrenched. For example, in the United States where private prisons contain almost 90,000 of the country's prison population (Schlosser 1998: 64), prisoners are often incarcerated for longer "than is necessary for justice to be served" in order to maximise profit (Schlosser 1998: 64).

Corrections Corporation of America is the parent company of Australian Integrated Management Systems (AIMS) which was initially contracted to run the West Australian private prison. It has been claimed that this company now builds prisons in the United States "entirely on spec – that is, without any contract to fill them. 'If you build it in the right place' a CCA executive said, 'the prisoners will come'" (Schlosser 1998: 64). Furthermore, Corrections Corporation of America recently acknowledged that Australia is the targeted area for projected market growth of the company (SBS Documentary *Business Behind Bars: Pt 1*, October 2000). Already Australia has the dubious reputation of housing 20 per cent of its prisoners, the highest percentage of any country, in private for profit prisons (SBS Documentary *Business Behind Bars: Pt 1*, October 2000).

O'Malley (1999: 13) argues that, over and above private prisons, we have seen the creation of "enterprising prisoners". In prison regimes where this applies prisoners are said to "enlist as agents in their own rehabilitation, and as entrepreneurs of their own personal development" whilst taking part "in the government of their own confinement" (O'Malley 1999: 14). The idea underpinning "enterprising prisoners" relates, at least theoretically, to responsible citizenry amongst prison inmates. However, as Pratt (1997: 187) argues, "[f]or such regimes of self help and responsibility to come into effect, prisons themselves must change ... warehousing ... is actually counterproductive: it denies the model of the rational, responsible subject". Yet warehousing of prisoners becomes inevitable when incarceration rates increase, resources decrease in real terms and the cost of effective prisoner rehabilitation becomes an unaffordable commodity within prison systems which are already stretched beyond their limits.

The neo-liberal "new vision" for prison systems in western societies characteristically displays a corporate discourse built around "mission statements", "strategic plans", "world's best practice" and "client satisfaction". Arguably, this is at odds with the pragmatic day to day running of overcrowded institutions and masks the real problems of prisoners being permitted to aspire, even in small part, to governing their own confinement. In the case of Western Australia, the concept of self governance stands in stark contrast to the policy of zero tolerance imposed by many prison officers and superintendents following the 1998 Christmas Day Riot at Casuarina maximum security prison (prisoner interviews, February-September 1999).

Accordingly, as argued earlier, the neo-liberal emphasis on personal responsibility sits side by side with a number of neo-conservative and – in this case – retributive measures. Other examples of retribution in the West Australian prison system include prisoners in Casuarina being subjected to ongoing lockdown in their cells for a minimum of 22 hours per day for a period of more than 10 months subsequent to the riot. Several years after the riot, the regime in Casuarina is substantially more retributive than it was before the incident (personal observation, personal conversation: prison chaplain, prisoner interviews 1999-2002). In line with this, the original open campus style layout of Casuarina prison has been changed substantially. Each of the six units is now surrounded by high security fences topped with razor wire and with gates securely locked. Prisoners, who previously could move relatively freely around the prison, cannot now move from their unit even to the restricted outside yard without a prison officer unlocking the door for them. In addition to this, Unit One now has an additional punishment area (outside the unit but still within the unit's perimeter fence), which is built in the manner of sheep or cattle pens. Prisoners

37

may be held in these pens at the discretion of senior prison personnel (personal observation: June 2000).

Prisoner support groups such as Deaths in Custody Watch Committee and the Prisoners' Advisory Support Services WA (Inc) have exposed other examples of neo-conservative positive retributivist measures. Deaths in Custody Watch Committee Executive Officer, Kath Mallott (*The Australian* newspaper: September 1999) protested to senior management of the Department of Corrective Services about the use of a "five point restraint bed with a mask, commonly known amongst prisoners and staff as the 'Hannibal Lector' bed". Although the original five-point restraint bed was removed from Casuarina prison subsequent to Ms Mallott's complaint, it has since been replaced by another and is now known as "the blue bed". According to the Inspector of Custodial Services, Professor Richard Harding (2001: 23), one prisoner claimed to have been strapped to the "blue bed" for more than 24 hours and was "obliged to urinate into his pants". Harding acknowledged that "generally, the extent and similarity of anecdotal evidence arguably amounted to some sort of evidence that these practices do occur".

In sum, the small government and free market ideals inherent in neo-liberalism form an uncomfortable but powerful alliance with the neo-conservative push toward increased State control through harsher sentencing trends and more punitive prison regimes. Taken together these mean that the more empowering aspects of neo-liberalism – in particular the idea of prisoners who could take part in their own rehabilitation – are effectively negated. As Duff and Garland (1994: 27) argue:

> It makes little sense to insist on a framework of sentencing which treats offenders as moral agents, responsible for their actions, but then to subject them to infantilising, disciplinary regimes in which all opportunities for responsible and moral choice are removed.

# Chapter 2

# The Prison Experience

### Prisanalasys

*How do I feel,*
*When my cell is invaded*
*By two screws*
*And a dog?*
*How do I feel,*
*When I am stripped*
*Naked*
*And asked to display*
*My scrotum*
*And anus?*
*How do I feel,*
*When my letters are read*
*By cold eyes*
*Behind closed doors?*
*How do I feel,*
*Writing to my children*
*So one day*
*They will know I loved them?*
*How do I feel, anger within,*
*Insight disoriented,*
*Encaged, enraged ... ... Disengaged.*
*How do I feel,*
*Out of control*
*(out of sight*
*out of mind)*
*how would you?*

Craig White: Casuarina Prison, 1997

In this chapter the participants' stories of their experiences of imprisonment are positioned within the frame of "total institutions" as described by Goffman. It is here that the prison experience is explored through more extensive use of the participants' own stories. This chapter deals with issues such as the officially sanctioned stripping of the individual's prior social identity upon entry to prison and the institutional strategies used to build up the individual's new self image as prisoner. As Goffman reminds us, this "stripping" of one identity and "building up" of another in individuals is most clearly illustrated in total institutions such as prisons. Imprisonment is also looked at in terms of confinement of prisoners' physical and social space and restrictions of choice and meaningful work options. In addition, imprisonment in terms of loss; loss of family, loss of rights to sexual relations and loss of civil rights is explored.

Because I rely heavily on the prisoners' own words in this and the following chapters, I make use of different fonts to signify the diversity of voices. The prisoners' and ex-prisoner's voices are represented by *italics*. My own questions, prompts and journal notes are also in *italics*, but bracketed. The general analysis, theoretical discussion and quotes from the academic texts are all in Times New Roman.

## Self, imprisonment, institutionalisation and mortification

> The self, then, can be seen as something that resides in the arrangements prevailing in a social system for its members. The self in this sense is not a property of the person to whom it is attributed, but dwells rather in the pattern of social control that is exerted in connection with the person by himself and those around him. This special kind of institutional arrangement does not so much support the self as constitute it. (Goffman 1961: 168)

### *Prior social identity and the construction of self as prisoner*

Identity is about how we see ourselves. It is also about how we are perceived by others, signifies a sense of belonging or connectedness, and, as Gilligan (1988: 5) points out, is always relational. That is, our sense of self must always be in relation to "other": people, places, things. We identify ourselves through our family and other social relationships, cultural connections, shared values and our personal place in the world. When the framework within which individuals make meaning of their lives is forcibly removed and replaced with another, a sense of dislocation and loss of identity occurs (Taylor 1990: 27-28). A dislocation and loss of identity of this kind occurs when individuals are forcibly removed from their normal social environment and placed in total institutions such as prisons. Put simply, transitional stress is caused when an individual is placed in an alien environment such as prison where his or her prior life experience is largely irrelevant and unhelpful. Berger and Luckmann (1967: 35) suggest that this kind of forced transition is experienced "as a kind of a shock. This shock is to be understood as caused by the shift in attentiveness that the transition entails. Waking up from a dream illustrates the transition most simply".

Goffman (1961: 14) argues that an individual enters prison with a preconceived sense of identity which is relational to "certain stable social arrangements in his home world". These social arrangements provide individuals with the framework within which their lives have meaning. As Taylor (1990: 27) states:

> To know who I am is a species of knowing where I stand. My identity is defined by the commitments and identifications which provide the frame or horizon within which I can try to determine ... what is good, or valuable, or what ought to be done, or what I endorse or oppose ... it is the horizon within which I am capable of taking a stand.

Upon entry to prison previous supportive social arrangements are immediately and deliberately removed. Through the implementation of various admittance procedures, which strip the prisoner of "self" and are reinforced throughout the sentence, the social identity held by individuals before incarceration is taken away and systematically replaced by an institutional self. Further, the social framework within which the individual made meaning of his or her life is replaced by the narrow and restricted physical and social confines of the prison. Accordingly, when individuals enter prison they endure an enforced shedding of their previously established social identity (Goffman 1961: 14).

Before entering prison, individuals can claim certain rights and rely on established relationships. Immediately upon entry to the prison these rights and relationships are removed. Prisons are experienced as places of "low trust, high vigilance, uncertainty and discomfort" (Toch 1977: 42) where the prevalence of the "perceived threat" demands constant personal caution against physical danger. In his interview, Brad spoke extensively about his first days in prison:

> The first time I went to prison I didn't know what to expect. I guess I was scared. I was told to strip naked in front of some other prisoners and I had to shower with them. I remember being embar-

*rassed because I was heavy at the time and also worried in case anyone would try to fuck me up the arse, but the screw (prison officer) was there watching us shower ... Then I was made to squat, run my hands through my hair, let a screw look in my mouth, all this while I was standing there naked. My belongings – the clothes I had worn from court, and my wallet and all that – were taken away and I was given a set of prison greens. A green tracksuit and some prison sneakers. I remember feeling embarrassed because the tracksuit was too tight, so were the jocks and singlet. I also remember thinking I'd at least be able to keep my wallet with me as it had no money and no credit cards in, just a card with my tax file number and some photos. My photo was taken at reception and I was given an ID card with a prison number.* (interview: April 2001)

As a general rule, upon admittance to a prison, prisoners are photographed and a brief record of personal history is taken. Prisoners are then instructed to remove all of their clothing and other personal possessions such as jewellery. This occurs in the presence of prison staff and usually in the presence of other prisoners, all of who may be unknown to each other. Prisoners are then told to shower and may also be required to use a de-lousing substance. The prison, now having stripped the prisoners of their clothes and possessions, must then replace these with institutional things. Goffman (1961: 18) describes this as "a leaving off and a taking on, with the midpoint marked by physical nakedness".

Prisoners are issued with institutional clothing, or "prison greens". Prison clothes are uniform in character and generally standard issue. They are anonymous and uniform, simultaneously identifying the wearer as prisoner and, as always, a compulsory member of the institution. Within the prison environs the prisoner's capacity to appear before others in the manner in which he or she would wish is thus minimal. The identity kit with which the individual has previously faced the world has been removed and replaced with that of the institution. The "stripping off" of the individual's community identity gains momentum and the construction of self as prisoner begins.

Prisoners' civilian possessions are taken away, listed, packed and stored in an area which is inaccessible to them. For the duration of their custodial period prisoners cannot access their personal possessions except via approval of prison staff. The dispossession of personal property signifies a momentous loss of the self which is invested in such personal possessions. However, the most significant loss may be less related to tangible things as the prisoner's right to be called by his or her full name. Goffman (1961: 18) contends that "loss of one's name can be a great curtailment of the self". Added to this, is the degradation whereby the prisoner is given an institutional number which he or she is required to remember. John illustrated this when he said: *"I'm Carter (fictional surname) and I'm 1972916 (fictional ID number) … In a prison once you've come in and gone through all the processes like getting rid of your own clothes and changing into prison clothes and once you do some time, the world outside of these walls doesn't exist"* (interview: September 1998).

## *Institutionalisation*

Toch (1977: 120) suggests that "[i]nstitutions that insist on uniformity undermine self respect and foster apathy and dependence. They encourage pliability, but they do so by making the sick sicker and the helpless more helpless". Brad described the transition from a relatively autonomous social being to prison inmate when he spoke of his admittance to prison for the first time:

> *Well, I suppose first of all I was scared because all this was the unknown. I didn't feel safe or secure and I was worried because I'd heard that young blokes like me got raped and that sort of thing was common. So I was worried about my personal safety first off. Then after a few days I stopped worrying so much and started to adjust to the routine. I watched the other blokes who'd done time and learnt the ropes I suppose. I sussed out who to avoid, what times certain things were done, to look out for dangerous situations, that sort of thing. I quickly learnt to call screws 'boss' or 'sir' and that while I was inside I would have very little choice and that most screws would say no to any request no matter how small. I was basically told when to eat, sleep, shower and shit. So, in one sense, I lost the ability to make even trivial decisions about my life. I didn't realise that, of course, until I tried to cope with normal life the first time I got out. I just felt a lot of anger in the first few months in jail. I had too much time to think and I never had a positive thought. I would get really pissed off with my girlfriend if she was out when I phoned her or if she was late for a visit. The screws would taunt me if they could see I was wound up. They'd say she was out screwing someone else and that would play on my mind and I'd be a bastard to her when she visited so I took all my anger out on her. Some things you adjusted to quickly, other things took longer, like coping with me being on the inside and her being on the outside. At some stage I got smart and learned to conform just to do my time easier.* (interview: April 2001)

Goffman (1961: 133) suggests that "[t] moral aspects of this career, then, typically begin with the experience of abandonment, disloyalty and embitterment". The individual must adjust to the desegregated life of the prisoner, living the rigidly organised round of social, work and leisure activities within the physical bounds of the prison in the company of others of similar institutional status.

> The barrier that total institutions place between the inmate and the wider world marks the first curtailment of self. In civil life, the sequential scheduling of the individual's roles ... ensures that no one role he plays will block his performances and ties in another. In total institutions ... membership automatically disrupts role scheduling, since the inmate's separation from the wider world lasts around the clock and may continue for many years. (Goffman 1961: 14)

Goffman (1961: 62-63) suggests that prisoners, once "colonised" in this way, tend to develop a degree of satisfaction with life in the prison. However, my observations and conversations with prisoners over the years suggest that prisoners adapt in order to make the best of an adverse situation rather than because they become satisfied with prison life. In Brad's words, *"[y]ou learn to conform to the degree you have to just to avoid confrontation with other crims or the screws. You do this in order to do your time easier"* (interview: April 2001). Further, any adaptation that does take place may be influenced by the lessening of shame over the years. Individuals incarcerated for the first time feel varying degrees of shame at their circumstances. As Mark remembered, *"I withdrew into myself at first. I think I was in shock or something. I didn't want anyone to know what I was in for but I was put into unit six (protection unit) so it wasn't hard to guess. I didn't talk to anyone. It was weeks before I spoke to other prisoners"* (interview: August 1998). Accordingly, first time inmates may begin their social and moral career as prisoners by avoiding contact with others so incarcerated. Usually, though, these prisoners gradually accept their situation. Brad illustrated this by saying, *"I can remember my feelings of fear and shame as if they were yesterday. That was the first time I went inside. The next time I went to prison I felt nothing except being pissed off at the bloody inconvenience of it all"* (interview: April 2001).

## Processes of mortification

I asked Beau about degradation ceremonies and processes of mortification used within the prison. In particular, I wanted information about strip-searches and urine tests. Beau described his heightened anger during cell searches and explained that *"[y]ou expect to be strip-*

*searched and it's usually no sweat but when a mongrel screw (prison officer) ramps your slot (searches your cell) and throws around your personal possessions, maybe letters from your missus, photos of your kids and such ... that's when you're most likely to go right off"* (interview: December 1998). According to each of the participants, such indignities and degradation ceremonies abound in prisons. Cell searches in particular appeared to cause the greatest degree of humiliation for most of the participants. Brad, too, spoke of this:

> *Well, I was strip-searched regularly throughout both sentences. In one prison I was strip-searched before and after every visit but that was the practice there. At first it was embarrassing but you just become used to that sort of thing. It becomes a routine thing, something you do almost every day. Me, I found getting my slot ramped (cell searched) more degrading because I had family photos there, personal things. It made me ashamed and angry when I saw my photo album emptied onto the floor and dirty footprints on photos of my mother and my girlfriend. Sometimes I'd have to stand by my door and watch when that happened and you'd see these bastards throwing your personal stuff around and you knew you just had to stand there and take it or else cop a beating or be sent down the back (punishment area). Compared to that even urine tests were a piece of piss – pardon the pun. As a known drug user I was piss tested regularly but it would sometimes be embarrassing if I couldn't piss on demand and had to stand there, usually naked, in front of screws waiting for me to pee for them.* (interview: April 2001)

At any time, prisoners may be subjected to strip-searches, urine tests, being obligated to provide particular responses to prison staff or told to stand by their cell doors. Body orifice searches may be authorised by senior prison staff, to be carried out in the presence of prison medical staff. Aungles (1994: 166) points out that "[t]he institutionalised power of prison officers is manifested in their right to strip prisoners, even to the right to invade the body of prisoners for ingenious hiding places". Dick spoke about being strip-searched in this way:

> *Here in Casuarina we're strip-searched on the way through to our visits ... we have to change from (prison) greens to visits gear then we're strip-searched on the way out again, a bit more thoroughly ... and we might have to squat and lift our balls for the screws. That might be embarrassing only if you have a hard on.* (interview: September 1998)

Within the West Australian prison system the procedure for prison staff to obtain a urine sample permits prison staff to remove the selected prisoner from his or her cell, place of work or other location within the prison, take the prisoner to an allocated place, order him/her to strip naked and remain with the prisoner until he or she can produce a urine sample. Peter spoke of the difficulty involved in trying to produce a urine sample on demand: *"Imagine trying to piss in a jar in front of two screws. You're usually buck naked and feeling very fucking disadvantaged ... even if you need to piss you can find it hard to squeeze it out with screws maybe making comments about the size of your wedding tackle"* (interview: May 1998). Failure to produce a urine sample results in prison charges and the imposition of negative sanctions such as loss of privileges or loss of remission for prisoners. And so the motivation for prisoners to comply with such processes is high.

> An important part of the theory of human nature in many total institutions is the belief that if the new inmate can be made to show extreme deference to staff immediately upon arrival, he will thereafter be manageable – that in submitting to these initial demands, his 'resistance' or 'spirit' is somehow broken. (Goffman 1961: 89)

In short, processes of mortification are effective tools of institutionalisation and are generally reinforced throughout any given prison term. Goffman (1961: 50) argues that the efficacy of these strategies is further enhanced when they are used in conjunction with the implementation of the prison privilege system, which is discussed in the next chapter.

## Imprisonment as confinement

### Restrictions of physical and social space

Prisoners can no longer move between the social worlds of family, work and recreation. They must remain locked within the narrow physical and social confines of the prison. In short, all of the prisoner's social roles are played within an extremely limited physical and social space. Linda described the boredom and restrictions of her life in Bandyup women's prison:

> *I've spent so much time in punishment and that's awful. In chogy (punishment) you spend 23 hours in a bare cell with only the floor to sit on. No one to talk to. You don't see anyone. It fucks with your mind, especially if you're sick like I was. You spend a lot of time depressed and crying. Even in mainstream it's boring. Two hours work a day pulling weeds or in the kitchen. I worked in the kitchen*

*before I went down the back (punishment cell). You might spend
time chatting with your mates, read a book or watch some TV after
lockdown.* (interview: December 1998)

Within prison walls a prisoner's choice of companions is also severely
restricted. Dick explained, *"You can't really avoid anyone properly in
jail. There's nowhere to go. Basically you try to avoid dickheads but if
you get put in a slot with a dickhead then how are you going to avoid
him? It's just not really possible"* (interview: September 1998). Judy
also described this phenomenon: *"Unless you lock yourself in a toilet
you can't spend time alone in here. It's so overcrowded. Almost all
slots are doubled up and there are more than six girls sleeping on mat-
tresses in the gym. It's hard to avoid people you don't want to see"*
(interview: January 1999).

Prisoners' activities are generally pre-arranged, tightly scheduled
and not subject to choice. Judy told of her tightly scheduled and physically restricted regime within the overcrowded women's prison:

> *It's pretty much the same thing every day unless there's an
> extended lockdown for some reason, which is even worse ... I
> usually waken up early but it gets hot in the slot and there are two
> of us in there ... one on a mattress on the floor, so you have no
> choice but to stay in bed until unlock at 7.30 am ... there's no floor
> space with the extra mattress ... so at unlock there's a rush for the
> shower block and muster (prisoner count) is at 8 am. I sleep in the
> bed, not on the floor. That was my slot first and I have seniority
> here. I've done more time.*
>
> *(What would you normally do for the rest of the day?)*
>
> *The same thing ... breakfast is in the canteen ... then I go to work
> for two or three hours ... lunch is in the canteen ... I hang around
> in the compound (yard) till tea, which is also in the canteen. Then
> it's lockdown at 6.45 pm and I either read or watch TV from my
> bed because there's no room in the slot to move around with the
> extra mattress on the floor ... A couple of weeks ago we had a
> pregnant girl sleeping on a mattress on the floor in this block and
> she woke up screaming with a rat running over her feet.* (inter-
> view: January 1999)

Day to day life within prisons involves restriction in one form or
another. Daily routines are confined to the physical areas of individual
cells, units and other strictly controlled areas within the prison. The
prisoner consultant briefly described his general experience of imprisonment:

*I live in a room this big (about 6' x 8'). I'm locked in it for between 13 and 17 hours a day ... they could put Cindy Crawford in one corner and Elle McPherson in the other and a gold plated toilet seat but you are still locked in that small space for at least 13 hours a day. Day in, day out, year in, year out. You can't walk out there and say hello to your mum or get a drink from the shop or even from the fridge ... I'd rather be out there in the gutter with absolutely nothing ... and the bottom line is, it doesn't matter which jail you're in, it's all jail. Every prison is the same. It's just a prison.* (interview: August 1999)

John lives in the protection area of a maximum security prison. Protected prisoners are those who are thought to be under threat from the general prison population and, as such, are kept within a secure area of the prison physically separate from mainstream prisoners. (It is worth noting here that Toch (1977: 44) suggests that there is a certain additional stigma attached to prisoners who are held in protection units. This may exacerbate physical danger if these protected prisoners come into contact with prisoners from the general prison population.) Living under protection further restricts the physical movements and social choices of protected prisoners. John described his life in this way:

*I've got a TV and I've got a cassette player in my cell. By the same token if you play up officers have the power to take those from you. The inside of the cells are pretty bland. The same bleak colours are all around. Over the years some things have changed ... but they (prison officers) still have the power to confine you to your cell so you learn to shut off from it all. Not only do I have physical brick walls around me, but, in my mind, I've created an actual emotional brick wall.* (interview: September 1998)

[I note here that John's mention of the "emotional brick wall" supports one of the main claims of this study; that is the ability of the prison as total institution to securely imprison the mind as well as to confine the body.]

The physical and social restriction that prisoners experience is greatly magnified within punishment areas of prisons. David's time spent in the Special Handling Unit of a prison illustrates this most clearly:

*The officers come around at 7.40 am with my breakfast. The small yard adjoining my cell is opened but I don't go out there because it's the size of a shoebox. An hour later the screws come around with a mop and bucket and tell me to clean out my slot. I eat all meals in my cell. If I'm lucky an officer will let me into the main exercise yard after the other prisoners have finished. I have tea in*

*my cell at 4.30 pm and I'm lucky if I get 20 minutes to half an hour
in the main yard. The rest of my day is spent in the cell. At least 23
hours a day in my cell.* (interview: September 1998)

Indeed, two days before his release into the community David was
held in the special *segregated* area of the Special Handling Unit. That
is, he was not permitted *any* form of contact with other prisoners and
was, in real terms, serving the final part of his eight year custodial term
in solitary confinement. This is how he described his situation:

> *The special handling unit where I live is a segregated punishment
> area. I'm not allowed to work. I have a self contained cell. It's
> designed so the prisoner doesn't leave the cell. Everything you
> need is in the cell so you don't need to come out.*
>
> *(Are you really in this cell for 24 hours each day?)*
>
> *Yes almost, but sometimes I get 20 minutes in the exercise yard on
> my own ... I have a television and I read, but I'm not allowed
> access to the library. I get to choose books from the discarded
> book box. I can speak (to other prisoners) through the walls. You
> know, yell over the top but you certainly can't come into face to
> face contact. You can see other prisoners who are passing if you
> peep through the grille on the door. Well, you see legs walk past. I
> don't really have much choice about what I do.* (interview: Sep-
> tember 1998)

When interviewed, David was only two days away from release into
the community. For several months before his release he had no face to
face contact with anyone other than prison officers with whom he
refused to communicate.

Linda also spent much of her last few months in prison in conditions of severe punishment. She described her experience in this
way:

> *For the last seven months I've done five months under close
> supervision and eight weeks chogy (punishment) in the punishment
> block. I did chogy in a segregation cell which is not natural
> for anyone. There's no mattress during the day, nothing to sit on,
> nothing to lie on. There's a toilet and a basin and the toilet hasn't
> got a seat on it. You have to sit or lie on the floor and you're
> in that cell for 23 hours a day. You're allowed a lead pencil, three
> sheets of writing paper and three books ... Mostly you go through
> a real misery and downer. Your mind becomes your own worst
> enemy when you're put in isolation. It's hard to explain to people.
> I'm trying to explain to you how bad it feels ... It's barbaric. You
> wouldn't do that to your dog.* (interview: December 1998)

Punishment areas of prisons are, by their very nature, less visible than general accommodation units. Civilian staff, visiting program facilitators and official visitors rarely if ever, visit punishment areas. Because of this, conditions in these most austere parts of prisons can, and often do, deteriorate badly without public notice.

## Restrictions of choice: prison food

Prison food was a contentious issue amongst most of those I interviewed. This was particularly so in the male maximum security prisons where the "regothermic" method of food preparation was used. There, prison prepared food was described as bland and overcooked. In these cases, participants often chose to purchase snack foods such as noodles, biscuits and/or tins of beans or sardines from the prison canteen. Because they were only permitted to earn between $10 and $40 per week, the participants' capacity to spend on food was limited and the choice in the prison canteen was, in any event, restricted. Peter outlined his meals regime:

> *If you eat prison food you eat in the dining area but I rarely eat prison food so I eat on my own in my cell. Apart from that I usually try and stay out of my cell as much as possible but you're locked down here for at least 13 hours a day and sometimes more.*

> *(Why don't you eat prison food?)*

> *Well, basically, it's crap. It's cooked days before you get it. It's frozen and reheated, everything is cooked together and everything tastes the same ... you only eat it if you run out of snacks in your cell.* (interview: May 1998)

Dick also avoided eating prison prepared meals:

> *The food in the blocks is no go. Noodles, sardines, tuna – things like that you can buy from the canteen. You usually buy that. The prison food is regothermic. That means it's cooked at Canning Vale prison. Pre-cooked, frozen, defrosted, sent to us and heated up in regothermic trays ... I mean the food's cooked a week beforehand ... it all tastes like shit.* (interview: September 1998)

David summed up the general participant opinion of regothermically prepared prison food by saying, *"[p]rison food is bland, regothermic. A sausage tastes the same as a potato which tastes the same as cardboard"* (interview: November 1998).

## Restriction of work options

Employment opportunities within the prison are extremely limited and often require low levels of skill. In his study, Goffman (1961: 10) observed that "sometimes so little work is required that inmates, often untrained in leisurely pursuits, suffer extremes of boredom". John acknowledged a high degree of boredom as he described his work routine:

> Well I work in the unit. I'm an auxiliary. I clean the unit and all that means is that I work for a couple of hours a day. Dust here and there and wipe the bench tops down ... it's only three days a week ... the rest of the day is mundane, routine ... I'll spend up to 16-17 hours a day in the cell. About the only time I'll come out my cell is to get some hot water to make coffee or fill my thermos or get my meals. (interview: September 1998)

Albert also spoke of the mundane nature of prison work and said that he starts work *"at 7.30 am in the laundry"*:

> I'm usually finished work by 10 am and that's my day as far as work is concerned ... then, if I'm not helping people with their research, I'll just hang around and have a coffee and a chat for an hour or so to kill time until lunchtime. Sometimes after lunch I'll have a sleep or play tennis. (interview: June 1999)

Employment opportunities are particularly restricted within the women's prison where they are generally gender specific. The choice of work within Bandyup women's prison is limited to cooking, cleaning, washing and ironing, gardening and sewing. Linda said, *"I usually work in the garden but there's only gardening, kitchen, laundry or textiles anyway"* (interview: December 1998). Judy further highlighted the humdrum nature of work within the women's prison: *"I usually work in the garden, pulling weeds or planting seedlings. That's for two to three hours a day ... then you just hang around. There's nothing much to do, not a lot of space and I can't go anywhere"* (interview: January 1999).

Other features of prison based employment were suggested in personal conversations I had with prisoners and industrial officers in Casuarina prison. The original intention of prison industry was to provide job training and skills to prisoners so that they might be meaningfully occupied whilst in prison and acquire employment experience which could be useful in the wider community. This potential, however, is lost when prisoners are transferred to another prison where that particular trade training is not available. This is also problematic for industrial prison officers who must try to run workshops profitably and is frustrating for prisoners when their skills training is incomplete (personal conversations with prisoners and industrial officers: Casuarina prison, December 2001).

Coyle (2001a: 11) contends that:

> One is drawn to conclude that the idea that the majority of prisoners, do, or indeed can ever, spend significant parts of each day in useful work is rather like the fable of the Emperor's New Clothes. It does not happen, everyone knows that it does not happen, yet there is a conspiracy of silence about it.

Another dimension of prison employment concerns the payment of prisoners. Inmates are paid only a fraction of prevailing community rates of pay, and face considerable restrictions on how they spend that meagre amount of money. Goffman (1961: 10) draws attention to the contrast between this and accepted community arrangements when he observes that:

> In the ordinary arrangements of living in our society, the authority of the work place stops with the worker's receipt of a money payment; the spending of this ... is the worker's private affair and constitutes a mechanism through which the authority of the work place is kept within strict bounds.

Within West Australian prisons a canteen system is utilised as one of the main areas in which prisoners spend their money. Prison staff organise the purchase of canteen stock and are largely in control of the limited range of goods available for purchase by prisoners. Prison officers maintain a physical presence within the canteen during hours of business and are privy to the knowledge of individual prisoner purchases. Further, and since the riot in Casuarina Prison on Christmas day 1998, prisoners in Casuarina are no longer permitted to go to the canteen and, at the time of writing, can only make their purchases from a canteen list. This further restricts movement and choice within that prison. Albert claimed that *"[t]his is just another way of frustrating us ... not only can they see what we're spending our money on, but they've also got a record of it ... The main thing, though, is that our lives are so restricted anyway and a visit to the canteen was something to look forward to"* (interview: November 1999).

All of these factors mean that work in prisons has a different role – psychologically and economically – than it does in the community. In addition, because it is the institution's responsibility to cater for prisoners' basic needs, the incentive for work may have much less significance for prisoners than it has for those in the wider community who must buy food, pay rent and pay for other associated living expenses. The prisoner consultant explained the general attitude towards prison work:

> *Most prisoners will work just to fill in time, to make the time go quicker. They're certainly not in it for the high wages. Top wage here is around $40.00 per week. Some blokes work to pay for their smokes and that sort of thing and some will work to buy their kids a can of coke and a packet of chips in visits but, let's face it, we get fed and the rent's paid. I work or study depending on what's available in whatever prison I'm in but I do it to make the day go quicker.* (interview: August 1999)

Taking all these elements together, Goffman (1961: 11) suggests there is a fundamental incompatibility between the prison as total institution and "the basic work-payment structure of western society".

It should also be noted that some prisoners see themselves as victims of systemic oppression and refuse to labour for the institution, which they view as the oppressor. Beau has always chosen to study during his prison terms and clearly felt that it would be wrong of him to work for the prison system. He explained:

> *I don't feel that I would be doing the right thing by myself if I was to do manual labour for the Ministry of Justice. Well the way I see it is why should they benefit from my labour, my hard work and sweat when I can use my time to enhance my own personal development. They got so many of us bros (brothers) in here for slave labour. I guess it's out of protest, a political thing.* (interview: December 1998)

## Imprisonment as loss

The prison experience involves considerable loss. Such losses include, but are not necessarily restricted to: loss of family; loss of rights to private sexual relations; and loss of certain civil rights.

### Loss of family

For many prisoners, loss of unrestricted family contact is particularly difficult. Such loss may become permanent as the quality of relationships diminishes during long terms of enforced separation. Upon release from prison some prisoners may be able to re-establish previously held social and familial roles but the accounts of those I interviewed suggested that there is inevitably some sense of loss. This was particularly painful for the two women prisoners who, in the wider community, had been the primary care givers for their children. Linda spoke of her pain when her baby was taken from her in prison:

> *I have a small daughter. She's a jail baby so to speak.*
>
> *(Was she born in prison?)*
>
> *No, she was a couple of months old when I came in and she stayed with me in the nursery until she was 12 months old and then she was taken from me and put into care. She was 12 months old and she was forcibly taken from me, her mother. It was the most awful thing I can remember. It was unbearable pain. When they took her from me I wanted to die ... I just went and saw a friend and had a hit (heroin) to try and dull the pain.* (interview: December 1998)

In her book, *Don't Let Her See Me Cry*, Helen Barnacle talks about her experience of being parted from her child whilst in prison. Here, she describes the painful anticipation of their approaching separation:

> I loved my little girl so much, yet I had to let go of her. Sometimes I found myself watching her in a daze, daydreaming, the thoughts moving in a circular fashion around the inside of my skull, a seemingly empty cavity being filled with unanswerable questions: What's it going to be like handing her over at the gate? How am I going to do that? Am I going to cry? Is it going to feel like a razor slicing through my heart? ... What's it going to be like in here for four years without her? What's it going to be like for her out there without me? Then came the inevitable emotional shutdown ... I could feel it all moving in too close and there was only one thing I knew of that would fix it. (2000: 233)

Like Linda, Helen Barnacle retreated into the oblivion provided by heroin. After she had handed her child over to her brother at the prison gates she recalled:

> I turned around and walked back to ... my unit ... I mixed the powdery substance with water in a spoon, lit a match underneath ... and then sucked it up into the syringe ... The substance moved quickly through my veins to my heart, easing the pain as reality blurred. (Barnacle 2000: 237)

Judy was also separated from her children. She told me how she knew she was *"going inside and had to make arrangements for my girls so they wouldn't go into care. My mum said she'd have them and that was good"*. The deepest trauma for Judy was in her mother's home the night before she was sentenced. *"I just cried and cried ... I kept going to look at their little faces asleep in their beds"* (interview: January 1999).

54

Prison inmates cannot contribute to family life socially, economically or culturally on a regular day to day basis. They are also reliant on others for maintaining what contact they have with their children. For example, Linda's small daughter lives with a foster family:

> [W]elfare bring her in twice a week ... I am so grateful ... I guess if it wasn't for the lady who brings her in, I wouldn't get to see my daughter. Some of the women in here have small children and don't get to see them ... some girls only get to see their kids once a month and they get really upset. (interview: December 1998)

Judy relies on her mother who brings the children regularly for visits, *"my mum brings in my kids to see me every week. She looks after them while I'm in here. She's been great. Sometimes my cousins come in too. They help my mum with the kids"* (interview: January 1999).

None of the male participants had ever been primary carers for their children. Only Beau had lived in a family situation with his children and their mother. He had what he termed a good relationship with both his son and daughter although, throughout most of his current prison term, he had not seen his children. He illustrated his sense of loss as a parent in this way:

> I'd like to spend time with my kids. I miss them ... when I'm on the outside my son and I are very close ... we go off together and do men's business ... my ex-missus put most of the work in with the kids but I love them too ... I've spent so much time in here and he's almost a teenager now ... I haven't seen my kids for months now and it's killing me. (interview: December 1998)

None of the male participants had regular visits from their children. On this, Aungles (1994: 86) suggests "the prisoners' fatherhood is virtually never a civil status that is at issue. The masculinity of the prison is a denial of the man's parenthood". She also points out that:

> Parenthood is the major issue in the political technology of the penal discourses when the social science gaze falls upon women prisoners ... the official discourses too reflect this bias. There are no official records in Australia detailing the numbers of children of male prisoners. The series of articles about bonding and absence of prisoner parents ... are almost exclusively about women prisoners. (1994: 87)

Goffman (1961: 138) suggests that family contact through social visits has limited significance in connecting prisoners to the outside world because of the short duration of visits and conditions of overt control and surveillance. The controlled nature of family contact generally curtails the spontaneity of normal social relationships, highlights the prisoner's degrading circumstances and inhibits the prisoner's prior social role relationship to his or her family. Goffman (1961: 139) also suggests that at the end of the visit "the visitor nonchalantly goes back into a world that the inmate has learned is incredibly thick with freedom and privileges". Brad recounted how he would *"get so pissed off and angry at my girlfriend and even my mother. They would just get up at the end of a visit and go wherever they wanted. I was angry and frustrated because I felt they had no idea what it was like for me to have no control over my life"* (interview: April 2001).

Against Goffman's arguments about the limited value of prison visits, accounts of the participants in this study suggested that the brief allocated visit time did permit a window of opportunity for some temporary escape from prison pressures when they could partially reclaim previously held social roles. For example, Brad said, *"I always felt good when my mum visited me. There was no pressure to be macho when she was there. She had no agenda. There was no hassle. She was just my mother and I was just her son but I still hated it when she left. I felt a bit abandoned by her then"* (interview: April 2001).

## Loss of right to private sexual relationships

Hearn and Parkin (1987: 74) write that "most imprisonment can be seen as primarily a restriction of contact and communication, and particularly sexual contact, from lovers, partners, spouses and other sexual intimates". Many of those I interviewed spoke about the loss of sexual intimacy. David, who described himself as bi-sexual, explained that although sexual contact was readily available for him in prison his capacity to engage in sexual intercourse was severely restricted. He put it this way, *"If, say, I was caught fucking my cell mate, even if it was consensual sex, we'd both be charged and put down the back (in punishment). Look, even if a screw looks in your slot and you're having a wank you could be charged. I've known blokes get charged for wanking"* (interview: September 1998).

Dick's account centred on how the loss of a sexual relationship affected his capacity to communicate effectively:

> *Obviously, I haven't had a woman for a long time ... the last time I got out I found myself wimping out. I couldn't communicate with women ... long term prisoners should be allowed to have private visits so that you can learn to communicate again, you know, talk, lay down together, relax, get that feeling of knowing each other again.* (interview: September 1998)

In many cases, too, the enforced separation led to a loss of intimacy, the breakdown of relationships and difficulty forming new ones. Beau told me that *"because I've spent so much time inside I lost that sense of tenderness and intimacy with my wife. That definitely contributed to our marriage break up ... when I got out before I was basically desperate to root and that's what I did, I treated her like a root"* (interview: December 1998).

## Loss of civil rights

Imprisonment also incurs the loss of certain civil rights. The right to organise and congregate, and the right to vote in particular jurisdictions, are lost for sentenced prisoners serving specific terms of imprisonment. On the other hand, remand prisoners have not yet been convicted and therefore generally retain the right to vote in all elections and referendums. However, Western Australian prisoners have since late 2006 lost their right to vote in State elections where previously those serving less than 12 months retained the vote (*Electoral Act 1907* s 18(1)) and convicted prisoners serving custodial terms of more than three years lose the right to vote in federal elections (*Roach v Electoral Commissioner* [2007] HCA 43). Because of the nature of the Australian political system, in particular the discrepancy between rights to vote at federal and State elections (as well as some confusion regarding the status of parolees), there is often uncertainty at the level of individual institutions regarding voting rights, with many prisoners and prison staff unsure of who must and must not vote. For instance, during the time span of the research for this book, several remand prisoners at Bandyup Prison were told they had no voting rights in a Commonwealth referendum. Some were not registered to vote at the relevant prison address, while in fact they had a legal obligation to do so. This dilemma was brought to the attention of executive personnel of the Department of Corrective Services and last minute arrangements were made to allow the women to vote (personal involvement).

Goffman (1961: 16) describes the loss of such rights as a form of "civil death". In tune with this notion of "civil death" the prisoners' narratives also speak of loss on a host of issues such as separation and bereavement. Beau expressed a deep-seated fear about this:

> *Apart from not being able to see my kids, there are other family issues which really worry me ... My mum's a pensioner now ... I mean I owe my mother my life so I'm obligated to take care of her in her old age ... I worry about what might happen to her while I'm in here ... so when I get out I won't be going too far from my mum because she's all I have left.* (interview: December 1998)

# Chapter 3

# Patterns of Surveillance and Control

*Body Search*

*Each time we are forced*
*To endure their searching hands*
*I stand in line waiting for my turn*
*Hold my breath waiting for it to pass*
*They laugh and say 'oh, look!*
*The birds are spreading their wings out to dry!'*
*We force a smile, and with arms outstretched*
*Submit .... Waiting for it to pass ...*

Brenda Hodge: Bandyup Women's Prison, 1987

## Surveillance

Prisons are responsible for the organisation and compulsory containment of large numbers of people. Accordingly, surveillance is central and constant, operating to "induce in the inmate a state of conscious and permanent visibility that assures the automatic functioning of power" (Foucault 1977: 201). In essence, effective surveillance allows control of the many by the few through promoting mass conformity to prison rules and regulations.

David, who spent much of his sentence in punishment cells, told of his experience of surveillance in the Special Handling Unit at Casuarina prison in the days leading up to his release. He described his situation in this way: *"I'm being managed under observation. In the cell there's cameras. Everything I do is monitored. I can't even use the bathroom without being exposed to everyone who's watching ... My life at the moment consists of a cell six feet by eight feet and what I do in that cell is seen by all"* (interview: September 1998).

The prisoner consultant's description of surveillance in the punishment area in Fremantle prison where he served much of his sentence, was similar. He said, *"[a]t that stage there was no camera sur-*

*veillance in the SHU (Special Handling Unit) but there was nowhere you could go without being seen. There was a glass control box with tinted glass so you couldn't see in but they could see out. Also they could see you anywhere in the yard"* (interview: September 1999).

To ensure surveillance is as effective as possible, prisons typically utilise a central place of observation. Bentham's panopticon provided the archetype whereby a central guard could see each and every prisoner, but they, in their turn, were unable to know whether or not they were under direct observation at any given time. It was this, which, according to Foucault (1977: 201), invoked self regulation with prisoners assuming "a state of conscious and permanent visibility that assured the automatic functioning of power". Within modern prisons hi-tech cameras and central viewing platforms now perform the functions of the panopticon. Foucault suggests that:

> It must be possible to hold the prisoner under permanent observation; every report that can be made about him must be recorded and computed. The theme of the panopticon – at once surveillance and observation, security and knowledge, individualisation and totalisation, isolation and transparency – found in the prison its locus of realisation. (cited in Rabinow 1984: 217)

## Overt surveillance

In the modern prison system it is useful to distinguish between overt and covert surveillance. Overt surveillance entails the actual presence of prison staff. It is obvious and occurs within almost all areas of the prison. David described the level of surveillance in this way, *"there's nowhere you can go and nothing you can do without someone being able to see you. Even if I sit on the toilet for a crap, a screw can look into my slot ... you just have to learn to live with that"* (interview: September 1998).

Overt surveillance can also involve invasive physical procedures such as the strip-search process, body orifice searches and urine testing described in the previous chapter. Linda explained how these physical procedures were linked to particular observation strategies:

> *If, say during visits a screw thought you'd got some drugs passed in a water balloon, either mouth to mouth or if they thought you'd hidden it in your vagina they wouldn't do an orifice search unless they called the doctor in. Screws can't do that. What they would most likely do is to put you in a dry 'obs' cell.*
>
> *(Could you explain what a dry 'obs' cell is?)*

59

*Okay, it's an observation cell which has no sink or flushing toilet. A dry cell. They would leave you in there for, I think, up to 48 hours where they can keep you under observation. You would have to pee and shit in a bucket and they'd keep you there long enough for you to pass anything you might have ingested. Then, if any drugs were found, you'd be charged. You'd also be urine tested.* (interview: December 1998)

In some prisons, prisoners are strip-searched as a matter of routine both before and after prison social visits. For example, in Casuarina prison inmates are strip-searched both prior and subsequent to visits and must change from normal prison greens into special grey visit attire. The prisoner consultant told me that:

*The idea of special visits attire and strip-searching prisoners before and after visits at Casuarina was supposed to be so that visitors wouldn't be searched, but they still strip-search visitors there. They say it's random, and sometimes it probably is, but they can and do use it as a method of control over prisoner behaviour.* (interview: August 1999)

Although it was common practice to randomly target prisoners' visitors for strip-searches during the time span of the interview process for this study, this has now been stopped and visitors suspected of carrying contraband are required to have non-contact visits. The use of "sniffer dogs" to detect drugs is another form of physical surveillance that has increased over recent years. It is used in prisoner units, visit areas and at the front gates of prisons when social visitors are entering the prison. On this, Dick noted that *"the drug dogs are never used in areas used exclusively by prison staff ... the prison authorities are afraid of what they might find. A dog can't tell the difference between a brown uniform and prison greens"* (interview: November 2000).

## Covert surveillance

Under covert surveillance the presence of the observer is not so readily apparent. It involves a one-way flow of information from the observed to the observer, magnifying the power differential between the two, with the observer able to gain knowledge and power over the observed (McHoul and Grace 1993: 7). The significance of covert surveillance is "that even if there is no guardian present, the power apparatus still operates effectively. The inmate cannot see whether or not the guardian is in the tower, so he must behave as if surveillance were perpetual and total" (Foucault cited in Rabinow 1984: 19).

Covert surveillance operates through two main channels. The first involves the mundane process of record keeping. Like other bureaucratic institutions, prisons like to gather information on each and every inmate. This information is kept on record in a prisoner's file, including a brief personal history, family background and detailed information regarding prison behaviour, prison movements and medical history. In Goffman's (1961: 75) words:

> Just as an article being processed through an industrial plant must be followed by a paper shadow showing what has been done by whom, what is to be done, and who last had responsibility for it, so a human object, moving, say, through a prison system, must be followed by a chain of informative receipts detailing what has been done to and by the inmate and who had most recent responsibility for him.

This type of record keeping produces a one-way flow of information from the person whose details are being recorded to the recorder and subsequently to the institution. While the prison has the power to record details about the prisoners – and, in this sense, to render him or her "visible" – no complementary capacity is vested in the prisoner. In addition, only *selected* information regarding prisoners, as deemed fit by the institutional authority, is recorded. Thus while prisoner behaviour, medical history and prison charges are recorded as a matter of routine, details about the physical punishment of prisoners or incidents of self harm, especially in punishment areas of prisons, may be comparatively sparse. The inadequacy of current records is recognised in Recommendation 12 of the *Report of an Unannounced Inspection of the Induction and Orientation Unit and the Special handling Unit at Casuarina Prison,* which states "that record keeping in relation to major events – particularly the use of the 'blue bed' (five point restraint bed), chemical agents, abnormal restraints, cell extractions and self harm incidents – be radically improved" (Harding 2001: 31).

The second main channel through which covert surveillance operates depends on high tech equipment such as surveillance cameras, listening devices, walk-through metal detectors and, in some prisons, the use of biometric identification technology.

## The impact of surveillance

The prevalence of surveillance devices – overt and covert, traditional and high-tech – means that prisoners must assume that they are being observed at all times (Foucault 1977: 202). Simon outlined this:

> *There are few places in the prison that you can't be seen by prison*
> *officers. There are surveillance cameras in every area of the prison*
> *and the screens are watched all the time. Even though there are no*
> *cameras in your cell, at any time, day or night, officers can look*
> *through the hatch or unlock and enter your cell so you more or less*
> *have to assume you're being watched all the time.* (interview:
> August 1998)

Surveillance also affects the personal and emotional lives of prisoners.
In this study, most of the participants were very wary of revealing
information about themselves to both the prison authorities and other
prisoners. Linda put it this way, *"You tend to keep personal infor-*
*mation pretty close to the chest in here ... you're never sure who might*
*dog (inform) on you or what petty piece of information might be exag-*
*gerated out of all proportion and result in you getting in the shit"*
(interview: December 1998).

Most tellingly, surveillance affected the quality of family visits.
Visiting areas and visiting groups are subject to the whole panoply of
surveillance strategies: high tech surveillance cameras, strategically
situated mirrors, the constant physical presence of prison staff and
sniffer dogs to detect drugs. Dick said that because of this *"you lose*
*that intimate contact because you're sitting on one side of the table*
*and she's sitting on the other. You know you're being watched. You've*
*got a camera above you so you don't want to be nice and gentle to*
*your lady. Just a quick kiss g'day and you don't see her for another*
*week. What's that?"* (interview: September 1998).

## "Us and Them": prisoners and prison staff

### The dual culture

Unsurprisingly, prisons are marked by a distinct, and often adversarial,
split between prisoners and staff, an "us and them" distinction, reflecting the disparity between the observers and the observed, the guards
and the guarded. This surfaced and re-surfaced in the interview
accounts, with the prisoner consultant reflecting on how the hierarchical nature of the rift affected how staff spoke to prisoners. In his
words:

> *In this system it's a general occurrence that most screws will speak*
> *to most crims in any way they want. For example, today when I*
> *was called over to this interview the screw that had to unlock the*
> *door for me told me to 'get a fucking move on'. He called me 'an*
> *awkward cunt' because he had to get up out of his chair. He was*

*only unlocking and then locking a door to let me through. The point I'm trying to make is screws can treat crims however they like. On the other hand, I have seen, on many occasions, prisoners who might be having a bad hair day, say to an officer, 'fuck off' or 'get fucked you dog' and the officer will react so angrily, drag the prisoner off kicking and screaming and lock him in an observation cell and treat him like shit ... They (prison officers) are very sensitive when someone's called them a cunt.* (interview: September 1999)

John also dwelt on the power differential between staff and inmates, exacerbated by the "total" nature of the prison:

*In prison you're like a community and it's not like living in the suburbs. If something goes wrong you can't go out and walk around the block to get away from it. If it's a problem with a prison officer then he can make your life unbearable. He can have you put in punishment for however long or he can put you in with another prisoner who's say, a predator, and might assault you ... so you learn to live with it and you call him 'mister', 'sir' or 'boss'. You get into that routine where you're told when to get up, when to eat, when to go to bed and when to shower. You might spend 10 or 12 years living like that.* (interview: September 1998)

In general terms, prisoners live their lives, for a state sanctioned period of time, entirely within the prison walls, whereas prison staff work within these walls only for the duration of their shift and then they return to the world outside. The fact that prisoners have extremely limited contact with the wider community while staff "are socially integrated into the outside world" (Goffman 1961: 7) intensifies the profound distinction between prison staff and prisoners and promotes the development of two diverse cultures within the institution. The prisoner consultant spoke of the difference in this way:

*Prisoners live their entire sentences, which might be a decade or more, behind these walls and razor wire. We might have the odd trip out to hospital or court, but we come and go cuffed and chained in the meat wagon (prisoner transport) and don't experience anything of the outside world except as prisoners. Our world, if you like, consists of confinement and restriction of every kind. Most of these limits that are put on us are enforced by officers who see us and treat us as arseholes or low-lives. We all get lumped in together as crims – so we find it convenient for our own reasons to see them, by and large, as dogs and cunts. Two separate groups, each with a need to openly dislike the other in order to maintain integrity within their own group.* (interview: September 1998)

John reinforced this perception of "us and them" when he talked about *"blokes that have been in the system for a while and have gone through the old days where you couldn't even approach the officers never mind talk to them, they can still see the imaginary line"* (interview: September 1998).

These two cultures, Goffman (1961: 111) suggests, have a fundamentally moral character:

> [They] stage a difference between two constructed categories of persons – a difference in social quality and moral character, a difference in perceptions of self and other. Thus every social arrangement ... seems to point to the profound difference ... in a prison, between an official and a convict.

This difference between two constructed categories of person is underpinned by specific patterns of deference. Although these patterns pertain in all institutional hierarchies, within total institutions, and most particularly prisons, they are most clearly formalised and sharply demarcated. All prisoners are required by institutional practice and tradition to defer to all prison staff and, consequently, all prison staff expect to be the recipients of such deference (Goffman 1961: 115). Most obviously, and as John commented, inmates are required to refer to prison officers as *"sir"*, *"mister"*, *"miss"* or *"boss"* whilst themselves being referred to by their surname only (interview: September 1998). Several of the participants involved in this study received varying degrees of punishment for refusing to defer to prison staff. For example, David said that he often found it difficult *"to call some screws 'boss', especially some of these bastards in the SHU (Special Handling Unit). I call them nothing, they wind me up, and I end up getting more prison charges – usually loss of remission which means I serve more time"* (interview: September 1998). These punishments ranged from loss of privileges such as removal of stereos and televisions to loss of remission, the imposition of solitary confinement and time spent in observation or punishment cells.

The prisoners I interviewed spoke about their resentment of such extreme forms of control. The prisoner consultant said that prison staff *"use a form of mental brutalisation with their privilege system ... it's a form of control ... people in here can't handle that, having their TV, or their contact visits or their phone calls taken away ... the thought of that drives them mad"* (interview: September 1999).

According to him, the most feared tool of control was the imposition of loss of contact visits, usually for drug use. He outlined a likely scenario:

64

*If I get caught smoking pot they stop my contact visits for six months. I've got to have visits in a glass box where the speaker cuts out every second word and you've got to shout and everyone can hear every word you say. What does this do to a bloke that's got a family? That's part of the ongoing punishment for smoking pot – non-contact visits. The bottom line is that they're trying to say that we've stopped your contact visits because we believe that your visitor brought in the drugs ... Anyway, for smoking pot you cop that punishment, but this prisoner might have four little children and a missus and three years to do. There's a family that's pulled apart for three years and trying to do everything to maintain their relationship; write letters, make phone calls, have visits with the wife and kids and, remember, visits are the only times he can hold his kids. Then they say tough shit, you're not holding your kids for six months. That family is starting to fall apart. The bloke in jail is starting to get frustrated and angry. If he gets angry at the wrong time and says something to a screw he might get non-contact for another six months.* (interview: September 1999)

Toch (1977: 102) points out that "orders given by others can be painful because they are clearly efforts by someone to impose his will on yours, ways of emphasising that you are lower in status, and a means of insuring that you have less say over your affairs". He also suggests that "reciprocity of communication builds links between men who are governed and those who are governing them. It makes it possible to negotiate, to question and to build relationships that ameliorate the impact of power" (Toch 1977: 118). Such reciprocity of communication rarely occurs between prison staff and prisoners and, as Coyle (2001b: 3) points out:

> There is one important distinction to be made between the prison and all other public institutions. All men and women who are in prison are held there against their will ... The prison is, therefore, first and foremost a coercive institution. Its essence consists of one group of human beings depriving another group of human beings of their liberty.

## The role of prison officers

Goffman (1961: 74) suggests that prisons present themselves to the community as "rational organisations designed consciously ... as effective machines for producing a few officially avowed and officially approved ends". These aims include crime deterrence, incapacitation, retribution and the rehabilitation and re-communalisation of prisoners. Notwithstanding the emphases on rehabilitation and re-communalisation, prisons continue – and in a sense, *must* continue within the logic of the current system – to act as warehouses for the secure containment of prisoners. It may be reasonable to claim, then, that prison is a particular type of total institution which has been structured for public protection against intentional threat and, as such, does not have as its primary concern "the welfare of the persons thus sequestered" (Goffman 1961: 83). These insights were reflected by Dick, who commented that *"prison officers aren't welfare workers ... how could an officer be a welfare worker when the next minute he could turn the key on you or put you in shackles ... it's a conflict of interest ... but as far as prison officers being prison officers, as it is, they are the enemy. That's it"* (interview: September 1998).

Goffman (1961: 114) suggests that lower ranking prison officers are more likely to be the long term employees within the prison and consequently it is this group that becomes the "tradition carriers" of the institution. Furthermore, it is generally the lower ranking officers who must "personally present the demands of the institution to the inmates" (Goffman 1961: 114). That is, it is this group who are most likely to administer negative sanctions on a day to day basis within the prison. Accordingly, it is this group of staff which usually attracts most resentment and hostility from prisoners. Dick described this, *"you might cop a charge for any old thing, sometimes you front the VJ (Visiting Justice), sometimes you might just get confined to your slot – whatever – it's the unit officer that locks you up or takes your TV. It's him that gets that pleasure"* (interview: September 1999). Similarly, the element of hostility and distrust noted by Goffman was voiced by David who said, *"I try and minimise my contact with prison officers as much as I can. I don't like them and they don't like me ... I haven't eaten a proper meal since I've been down here (Special Handling Unit) because their (prison officer's) hand dishes it up ... I don't trust them"* (interview: September 1998).

[Here I would like to note that, on the basis of personal observation and conversations with prisoners and industrial officers in Casuarina Prison (December 2001), a different relationship appears to prevail between industrial prison officers and the prisoners who work with them – at least in that particular prison. There the atmosphere seemed to be closer to mutual respect between prisoners and officers.]

## Welfare responsibilities

Within the West Australian prison system all civilian welfare officers have been replaced by prison officers under the prevailing unit management regime. Under unit management prison officers are assigned to a "unit" with the aim of fostering professional relationships with prisoners in these units. (A unit is a wing of the prison where prisoners live. Units usually consist of prisoners' cells, shower blocks and casual recreation areas.) As part of the unit management regime, it is expected that prison officers should carry out basic welfare roles (Department of Corrective Services presentation to stakeholders: March 2000). In Aungles' (1994: 186) view this type of policy shift has "paradoxically reinforced rather than undermined the relationship between prisoners and prison officers as that of soldiers and enemies". Her view was echoed by a number of the participants in this study. Thus, for example, when asked if he might approach a prison officer for help with a personal problem, Beau responded in this way:

> I've never taken my problems to any representative of the powers that be. The way I see it, and it's part of the survival thing as well, if you go and tell your problems to the powers that be they tend to use that vulnerability against you in a form of emotional blackmail. I learnt that at an early stage so then I just closed off to them and I wouldn't tell them shit.

> (Are there any circumstances where you would approach an officer for help with a problem of a personal nature?)

> No I wouldn't, due to the lack of confidentiality. (interview: December 1998)

Judy also talked about her lack of trust of officers, emphasising, conversely, the importance of her friends:

> (Whom would you turn to for support with a personal problem?)

> My friends. They're real staunch.

> (What about prison officers?)

> Are you joking? Not likely. You tell them your problems and the whole jail would know all about it within a minute. Some of them are okay but you wouldn't trust any of them. (interview: January 1999)

Peter similarly said that he'd turn to his friends for assistance if he was anxious, adding: *"I wouldn't talk to a screw about things like that"* (interview: May 1998).

John's response centred on the internalised barriers between prisoners and staff:

> Being in the position of a prisoner there's still the mental barrier of them and us and there's an invisible line ... there's an apprehension of actually approaching an officer and asking them for

*something because you get so used to prison officers just running your life for you that you don't see the person, you only see the uniform, just a shape with a shirt and a pair of boots on.* (interview: September 1998)

Simon was the only participant who said that he would ask for any sort of help from a prison officer, and even his response was qualified: *"If I had a problem with an officer I might turn to another officer for help or I might write to the Super. Anything trivial or personal I'd take to a friend and ask him. I wouldn't go to an officer with a personal problem. No way"* (interview: August 1998).

## Strategies of control

In controlling the behaviours of those held in custody, prison authorities rely on a host of different strategies. The participants in this study were keenly aware of two in particular. First, control over information vital to them; second, control over their family visits and other links with the outside world. As described by the participants, these strategies were not mutually exclusive but had the effect of highlighting and entrenching the binary characteristics of prison culture and the asymmetrical power relationship between prisoners and prison officers.

### Control over vital information

The participants' accounts suggested an almost routine exclusion from information often vital to their daily lives within the institution. Albert, who was on an indeterminate sentence at the Governor's Pleasure, found this particularly frustrating as he waited for his release date to be ascertained. He told me that he was *"waiting for a decision from the Attorney General. He's the main man. I could be out next week, but, on the other hand, it could be weeks, even months. I have no way of knowing"* (interview: June 1999).

Another important factor is that prisoner case conferences were said to be routinely conducted without the prisoner's presence. For example, Judy claimed, *"I've never been to any of my case conferences. I don't know of anyone who has been to their case conferences"* (interview: January 1999). Case conferences deal with, amongst other things, issues that can affect prisoner security rating, possible transfer of prisoners to another institution or even parole related information. While some prison staff may relate such information to prisoners prior to case conference rulings being activated, others may simply transfer to another unit or institution without notice or explanation. Goffman (1961: 9) suggests that exclusion from information which directly affects prisoners' lives "gives staff a special basis of distance from and control over inmates".

Linda was moved on more than one occasion, without notice, to regional prisons many hundreds of kilometres from her home base. She said, *"they've treated me like shit, you know. I've been shanghaied to other prisons throughout my sentences. I've been sent to Greenough and Roebourne jails and no one could visit me there because it was just too far away"* (interview: December 1998).

David spoke in similar terms. A few weeks before his release, he was sent to a remote northwest regional prison with, he said, no explanation for the transfer provided: *"They hi-jacked me to Roebourne prison ... I was there a week and then they flew me back. That must have cost them thousands of dollars in air fares for me and the Senior Officer who was cuffed to me. Two single fares for me and two return fares for him"* (interview: September 1998).

Albert said he was moved without notice from a minimum to a maximum security prison farm after being charged with returning a "dirty" urine sample. Although it was later found that the sample had been labelled incorrectly, and although the prison authorities at some point acknowledged their mistake, Albert, who, as previously stated, was on an indeterminate sentence told me that he *"spent an extra 18 months inside, most of it in maximum, most of it not knowing when I'd get out and most of it feeling pretty pissed off with the injustice of it all"* (interview: June 1999). As part of the interview, I asked Albert how the uncertainty of his indeterminate prison sentence (of which he had already served 10 years) was affecting him. He responded that he had to put up with it and *"just try not to think about it too much but it does get to me sometimes. It's really hard when you can't access any information that affects your future in such a big way"* (interview: June 1999).

## Control over family visits

For most of the prisoners interviewed, visits were of tremendous importance. Their comments indicated how visits temporarily disrupted their identity as prison inmate and, at least for the duration of the visit, allowed them to become dad, mum, brother, sister, husband and so on. Beau, whose family had not visited for several months, put it this way: *"I used to look forward to seeing my kids ... my kids make me laugh, make me happy ... when he used to visit, I'd ask my son if he'd been a good boy for his mum ... I've got a really close connection with my son. I love my kids as much as they love me"* (interview: December 1998).

Two types of prison visits are permitted within the West Australian prison system; non-contact visits and contact visits. Non-contact visits take place in cubicles where prisoners and their visitors are separated by solid transparent barriers, and telephone handpieces are normally used to permit verbal communication. Contact visits occur in a communal visit area and prisoners and their visitors are allowed a limited degree of physical contact. The controls exercised over family visits through surveillance and strip-searches have, as we have seen, a profound affect. Brad remembered:

> *Some visits ... (were) ruined when my girlfriend was strip-searched before a visit. If that happened she was usually crying and upset and that got me pissed off major league ... then if a screw told us off for sitting too close or kissing during a visit she'd get embarrassed and I'd get angry. Once I saw another crim's missus getting told off by a screw for sitting too close and she reacted by shouting 'I don't have to put up with this crap' and then she just stormed out of the visit. Whacko, end of relationship and, really, who could blame her? What had she done to deserve that?* (interview: April 2001)

In many cases, these control procedures are tolerated by those who wish to retain family contact with prisoners through social visits. Brad said that his girlfriend *"put up with regular strip-searches just to be able to have contact visits. She got upset every time she was strip-searched but the thought of having non-contacts or not visiting at all was even more stressful for her"* (interview: April 2001). In other instances, prisoners may discourage family or friends from visiting as the stress and potential humiliation is too great to bear. Simon told me that *"I really don't like visits in here (Bunbury prison) because of the conditions in visits. It causes me grief, well an amount of stress, especially if they get strip-searched. I've had to learn to cope with stress and cut it down to a manageable level. Visits heighten it"* (interview: August 1998).

David similarly chose not to have visits because *"they were giving my visitors a lot of grief coming through the gates. Strip-searches all the time and so forth. So I spoke to my visitors and told them not to come any more"* (interview: September 1998). The prisoner consultant spoke generally about the effects strip-searching families has on both visitors and inmates:

> *Look I know a number of prisoners whose visitors just stopped coming when they were strip-searched. Not just friends but wives,*

*children, mothers ... they don't want to be strip-searched ... Priso-*
*ners get uptight about their families being strip-searched. They go*
*right off. Not many people know, but that's what started the Fre-*
*mantle prison riots. An 80-year-old woman, a prisoner's*
*grandmother, in a wheelchair, was one of about 30 or 40 people*
*who'd been strip-searched that week ... These prisoners whose*
*families were searched had no past history with drugs.* (interview:
August 1999)

Because contact visits are classified as a privilege, visits can be used as
one of the tools whereby prison staff modify prisoners' behaviour. In
relation to this Goffman (1961: 50) points out that privilege systems are
used as a strategy whereby prisoners are offered rewards in exchange
for compliance and deference. Such privileges are "held up to the
inmate as possibilities, these few recapturings seem to have a reinte-
grating effect ... assuaging withdrawal symptoms from ... one's lost
self" (Goffman 1961: 49). The loss of these privileges or "rewards" has
the opposite effect. Dick described his experience of losing contact
visits in this way: *"[I]'ve had my phone calls stopped when I played up,*
*and once, when I had a dirty piss test, I lost my contacts (visits) for six*
*months. When you lose phone calls and contact visits you really hurt.*
*You hurt, and your family is hurt too"* (interview: November 2000).

The prisoner consultant said that the prison staff justified *"just*
*about anything they do"* by *"linking visitors with some sort of security*
*problem in the prison"* (interview: August 1999). He went on to speak
about the importance of *"little things"* that could be so easily taken
away:

> *It's little things like prisoners on non-contact visits – they're not*
> *allowed to bring food down for their visitors now. You know a can*
> *of drink, a packet of chips or chocolate for the kids. He (named*
> *superintendent) stopped all that. I know it doesn't sound like much*
> *but it's a lot when you get so little. It's good for a dad to be able to*
> *bring his kids something. For me this is a really important issue*
> *because if you maintain the family unit while you're in prison then*
> *you've got the best form of rehabilitation ... Yet the prison system*
> *as it is does everything to stop family visits being successful.* (inter-
> view: August 1999)

The knowledge that contact visits were a privilege signified to
each prisoner that there was always a possibility of that privilege being
removed. This operated as an effective management tool for prison
authorities, and was deployed in relation to the behaviour of prison
visitors as well as prisoners themselves. Beau illustrated this when he
said, *"my missus used to bring the kids in to visit. She'd be stressed out*

*in case they ran amuck ... she'd spend a lot of the visit just keeping them quiet and in their seats. That'd piss me right off and spoil the visits"* (interview: December 1998).

Aungles (1994: 173) supports Beau's observation in this way:

> The work of maintaining contact with imprisoned men then becomes an exercise in anticipating and avoiding prohibited behaviours ... Women then become involved in controlling their own behaviour and the behaviour of their children and of the prisoners themselves, not only over specific incidents but through the more diffuse policy of 'keeping your head down' and not causing trouble.

Aungles claims that prison officers deploy a number of strategies to remind visitors of their subordinate position within the confines of the prison. Thus, for example, she cites undue delays in social visitors being permitted to enter prisons for visits. "The delays can also be interpreted as a general demonstration of the arbitrary power of prison officers over the prisoners ... when undermining the visit becomes a punishment deliberately meted out" (Aungles 1994: 122).

An overall view of the impact of the privilege/punishment system was provided by the prisoner consultant who reflected that:

> *To me prisoners have been bought. TV, visits, phone calls ... all these privileges are used by the authorities as a tool and they use the threat of taking these luxuries away if you misbehave ... All this privilege system does is reinforce how quickly privileges can be taken away and keeps prisoners as selfish, self absorbed individuals who won't support each other. That's why the privilege system's such a great management tool. If prisoners organised together for their mutual benefit the authorities would lose control.*
> (interview: September 1999)

## Imprisonment and resistance

### Day to day resistance

Although most of the participants in this study complied with the great body of institutional rules and regulations throughout their sentences, several offered what can be described as ongoing, day to day resistance. These forms of resistance rarely threatened the good order and security of the prison as such. Rather, they presented as relatively minor misdemeanours which often attracted some sort of punishment. For example, several of the participants were heroin addicts and, when the opportunity presented itself, they thwarted prison rules and continued to use heroin during their terms of imprisonment. Linda described her drug use, during her current sentence, as sporadic and went on to say:

> This time I've not been too bad. I know it sounds like a lot, but this sentence I've only had six or seven dirty urines in three years. When I was younger and doing jail I was in trouble all the time.
>
> (How much time have you spent in punishment this sentence?)
>
> This last lot was for just over five months. I got done for a dirty urine test. I was out of punishment three days in the middle of that lot. (interview: December 1998)

Beau's resistance took the form of refusing to participate in any work activities. He also said that he acted as a spokesperson and adviser for his people, telling me that *"the powers that be have allowed me a bit of leeway because I've been around ... and they know that I can be a troublemaker so if, for example, I have to go in a two out cell I get the choice to pick who I'll go two out with"* (interview: December 1998). Albert's resistance was restricted to refusing to work for more than two or three hours per day. He said, *"for $25 per week I think they're not doing too bad. So, I finish work about 10 o'clock and then I relax"* (interview: June 1999).

Realistically, these forms of resistance pose no threat to the smooth running of the prison. However, they may be viewed as important to the prisoner's sense of self, for as Goffman (1961: 320) suggests "our sense of being a person can come from being drawn into a wider social unit; our sense of selfhood can arise through the little ways in which we resist the pull".

## Uncompromising resistance

David challenged the authority of prison staff so often that he served:

> [T]hree or four stints in the Special Handling Unit, sometimes for eight to 10 months at a time ... and every time I've ended up assaulting a prison officer ... I was only sentenced for 21 months originally and I've done eight years.
>
> (Was the extra time for offences in prison?)
>
> Yes, for offences in prison. For violence against prison officers. (interview: September 1998)

Equally, the prisoner consultant was involved in what can only be described as an extreme and sustained form of resistance to the prison regime and became involved in the organisation of the Fremantle Prison Riots of 1988. As a result, he attracted an additional custodial term and spent more than four years of his sentence under a punishment regime in Special Handling Units. He said, *"I got a lot of extra time for that one. I went into the SHU immediately after the Fremantle riots ... from memory I spent three years in the SHU at Fremantle and the rest in Casuarina SHU. Four and a half years all up in the SHU"* (interview: August 1999).

Both of these prisoners followed Goffman's (1961: 62) notion of the "intransigent line" – whereby prisoners blatantly refuse to cooperate with authority – and, as a result, attracted further criminal charges within the institution and spent more time in custody under the most austere and punitive conditions. When prisoners display this type of resistance it is likely that the institution will show "as much special devotion to the rebel as he has shown to it" (Goffman 1961: 62).

Within the context of rebellious or uncompromising resistance, Toch (1977: 110) suggests that:

> [S]uch views cement perceptions of personal consistency and build a favourable self image. Where others are duped by handouts and surface gestures, the rebel, who can 'see through' authoritarian benevolence, stands as a tower of insight, sophistication and principle.

The prisoner consultant echoed something of this in his remarks when he described his ongoing resistance as his way of exercising his principles and beliefs. He claimed that *"in prison you have to develop some principles. You have to stand up and be counted and you have to learn to support each other in certain circumstances"* (interview: September 1999).

In contrast to David and the prisoner consultant, most of the participants tended to eventually adjust to prison life to the degree necessary to keep out of trouble and feel relatively comfortable within the cultural reality of the prison environs. This response is in line with Goffman's (1961: 65) suggestion that most "intransigent" resistance to the norms and values of the institution is "typically a temporary and initial phase of reaction, with the inmate shifting to situational withdrawal or some other line of adaptation". The relative lack of sustained, overt resistance therefore needs to be read as a sign of the power of the institution and a decision, on the part of its inmates, to manage "the tension between the home world and the institutional world" (Goffman 1961: 65).

# Chapter 4

# Violence and Brutality in Prison

### Solitary Confinement

*Have you ever been ordered to strip*
*Before half a dozen barking eyes*
*Forcing you against a wall –*
*Ordering you to part your legs and bend over?*
*Have you ever had a door slammed*
*Locking you out of the world,*
*Propelling you into timeless space –*
*To the emptiness of silence?*
*... have you ever begged for blankets*
*from an eye staring through a hole in the door*
*rubbing at the cold air digging into your flesh –*
*biting down on your bottom lip, while mouthing*
*'please, sir'?*
*have you ever heard screams in the middle of the night,*
*or the sobbings of a stir-crazy prisoner,*
*echo over and over again in the darkness –*
*threatening to draw you into madness?*
*Have you ever rolled up into a human ball*
*And prayed for sleep to come?*
*Have you ever laid awake for hours*
*Waiting for morning to mark yet another day of being alone?*
*If you've never experienced even one of these,*
*Then bow your head and thank god,*
*For it's a strange thing indeed –*
*This rehabilitation system!*

Robert Walker: Aged 25, died Tuesday 28 August 1984,
Fremantle Prison (Prison the Last Resort: 1988 p 15)

Violence and brutality abound in prisons. During the research for this book I came to believe that among prisoners there is an almost universal acceptance of violence as a normal everyday occurrence within the prison system. Although I did not directly ask about violence during the interviews, the male participants consistently spoke about it. The prisoner consultant told me that *"[p]risons are violent places. You live with tension every minute in here, no matter who you are. The hardest, most violent, most infamous and most vicious prisoners live with constant tension. Fights, violence can break out just like that. That's just how prisoners live. Violence is an everyday reality"* (interview: August 1999).

As the interviews progressed it became apparent that physical violence, in one form or another, is a very common occurrence in prisons. Prisoners and, to a lesser extent, prison staff live with violence on a day to day basis. Moreover, the interviews with the male prisoner participants and the prisoner consultant indicated a collective, apparently nonchalant, attitude to even the most extreme acts of physical violence. It was as if each of the male participants, at least, had become thoroughly desensitised to violence in all its forms. It was this factor which initially prompted me to enlist the assistance of the prisoner consultant, hence the reliance on his interview material within this chapter. He told me that:

> In terms of violence, the desensitising process within prisons is very quick. It's a survival thing. It's not just a physical thing it's a mental survival too. You've got to be violent in your mind as well as sometimes physically violent, and it's such a common occurrence in prison – violence at lower levels, fights and that sort of thing, occasionally knives and occasional serious bashings. It's so common that you have to become blasé about it ... if you let it affect you it'll affect your whole prison life. Desensitisation is nearly automatic. (interview September 1999)

The perceptual frames promoting violence are marked by a positive attitude towards the use of violence, a lack of general social connectedness or sense of belonging (except to the group), and a perception of provocation from others. Within prisons, this can create a 'subculture' of violence. Genders and Morrison (1996: 36) describe subcultural explanations in this way:

> This standpoint purports that individuals become criminally violent through a process of socialisation whereby they learn that the use of violence is an acceptable and normal way of dealing with particular problems or situations. Within this context it is possible to

conceive of a subculture as providing a framework of references and values within which certain individuals make decisions.

David is known throughout the prison system as a violent prisoner. Nevertheless, he claimed that he was not a particularly violent person before his term of incarceration. He first came to prison as a 20-year-old heroin addict on a two year prison sentence. During his period of incarceration David became a problem prisoner with a record of serious violence towards other prisoners and prison staff. This led to further criminal charges within the prison system and the extension of his sentence from two to nine years. David also has a prison history of self mutilation. I asked him what he thought had made him act so violently given that he had claimed to be relatively non-violent before he went to prison. He told me:

> *Most of my adult life has been spent in prison and I started off by being violent whilst under the influence of drugs in prison. Prison makes people more angry and violent. It doesn't stop them offending. I have suffered most violence in prison and have become an extremely violent person in prison myself. The prison officers could antagonise me by being sarcastic, trying to upset me and winding me up, pulling my chain basically. I'd react violently and that's what I am now, a pretty violent person. Before, I'd have to struggle to act violently. Now, I have to struggle not to.* (interview: November 1998)

David's claim that prison officers were at least, in part, responsible for his violent tendencies is a relatively common assertion amongst prisoners. As Toch (1977: 40) argues, "[a] prison inmate can begin to see his keepers as potential sources of violence. This view is harrowing because it removes the most prominent source of institutional stability and control and makes for an environment that has a person totally at its mercy". Such perceived threats to personal safety increase the degree of tension within the prison environment and hence the likelihood of outbreaks of violence. When I asked the prisoner consultant whether prison staff attempted to stop violence when it occurred, he responded in this way:

> *It depends on who is involved and what the issue is about. If it's somebody who's well known and is likely to turn violent on them (prison officers) they tend to turn a blind eye unless it gets out of hand ... In the past prison officers and administration have promoted violence for their own reasons ... It's a good tactic, turn prisoner against prisoner, a model of control.* (interview: September 1999)

Foucault (1977: 10) suggests that "those who carry out the penalty tend to become an autonomous sector: justice is relieved of responsibility for it by a bureaucratic concealment of the penalty itself". This, he comments, is because "it is ugly to be punishable, but there is no glory in punishing. Hence that double system of protection that justice has set up between itself and the punishment it imposes". Seen another way, public apathy together with the general lack of accountability and transparency of prison systems may have the effect of encouraging the formation of a subculture wherein both prisoners and their keepers develop their own code of ethics.

## Theories of violence

There are two main theoretical approaches to criminal violence. These are the "individual's rational choice" and the "social approaches" (Indermaur 1996: 3). While Genders and Morrison (1996: 29) argue that "[s]ocial explanations of crime and criminal violence stand in sharp contrast to explanations which locate the causes of crime within the individual", I prefer a dialectical approach which incorporates both approaches. That is, I position violence as a rational choice of individuals within a context of their prior and continuing social and cultural conditioning. I also underline the point that violence stands to be heightened when individuals, many with a social and cultural conditioning that accepts violence as a rational act, are incarcerated together within the limited physical and social space of the prison.

Genders and Morrison (1996: 30) observe that the interconnectedness of factors such as past experiences, personal values, motivation, the use of drugs and alcohol, and situational opportunity must be taken into account when exploring the causes of violent behaviour. In general, their approach leans toward the notion of the instrumental, or goal oriented, nature of violence rather than "expressive" or uncontrolled violence. This is the notion which is followed here. However, my focus is not so much the violent criminal acts which may precede or lead to any given term of imprisonment, as the prison culture where violence is considered to be a norm. My basic argument is that the culture of violence in prisons has evolved largely through the state sanctioned and enforced containment of numbers of (often violent) people in an institutionalised setting for long periods of time. Further, the acceptance of violence in prison culture is produced and maintained by the processes of institutionalisation, which demand adherence to the values and mores of the desegregated life of the total institution whereby "all aspects of life are conducted in the same place and under the same single authority" (Goffman 1961: 37). In essence, "prisons are sites of institutionalised violence. They constitute the social space where ascendancy of one group of men over the other is explicitly and legitimately based on brute power" (Aungles 1994: 185).

## Gendered nature of violence

Chappell and Egger (1995: 274) maintain that the "empirical results from research studies, official statistics and victim surveys provide unchallengeable evidence of the relationship between masculinity and violence". Indermaur (1996: 7) makes the same point. Although the masculinity-violence nexus is mediated by factors such as class, race and degree of marginalisation, he states that "when we turn to demographic differences in violence the single most important variable is gender". He goes on to argue, "not only are males within western society much more likely to engage in violence, but the degree of patriarchy of a society has also shown to be related to the level of violence". In line with this, I found the machismo nature of violence to be clearly demonstrated within the prison environs. Although the women participants in this study were subjected to equally, if not more, punitive and austere prison regimes, their coping strategies were different from those of most of the male participants.

Whilst the hierarchical structure of Bandyup women's prison was still basically patriarchal in nature, there was a higher ratio of female prison officers than at the male prisons and, of course, the inmate population was entirely female. There was also a constant presence of mothers with babies in the prison nursery. All these factors exercised a continuing influence on the nature of life within the women's prison, in what might be called an "anti-machismo" direction. However, here too were incidents of overt physical violence. These, though, were generally short-lived and rarely resulted in serious physical injury to either perpetrator or victim (personal observation, interview: Prison Superintendent, Bandyup Prison, November 2001). Most violence within the women's prison tended to be within the range of self harm or self mutilation. At the same time, brutalisation in terms of severe deprivation and emotional violence were evident. Linda talked about this in relation to the time she spent in the environment of the punishment cells in Bandyup:

> When I was under close supervision I felt really sick for a lot of the time, you know the side effects of drugs etc and I would need to see the doctor but they more or less forgot about me down there. I would ask to see the doctor but it wouldn't happen. For a couple of

*months there I felt really sick. I couldn't eat and I would vomit but the muster is that high that they just forgot about you down there. I would put my name down to see the doctor but they (prison officers) would say my name wasn't there – stuff like that ... I've done seven years all up and I'd say I've done more than half of it in punishment. You know what I mean? I've done hard jail. I've done it rock hard compared to others in the system.* (interview: December 1998)

These conditions of hardship and humiliation affect women in the remote regional prisons in particular and additional ways. For example, female prisoners of medium and maximum security rating held in Broome Regional Prison suffered under a particularly inappropriate crossover between health care and prison security. These female prisoners, mostly traditional Aboriginal women from remote areas, were often chained and handcuffed to male prison officers during medical examinations at that prison. They were also chained around their ankles when attending family visits (Harding: Verbal Report, Prison Inspectorate Community Consultative Committee Meeting: 25 July 2001).

Neither of the women participants in this study spoke of physical violence as such within the prison. However, one of the women participants was the victim of years of severe domestic violence and only escaped such violence when either she or her husband was incarcerated. In some ways prison life offered her respite from violence. Judy explained how she experienced life on the outside:

*My adult life has been one long drinking binge since I left home and went to live with my husband. I drink to dull the pain ... my husband's very violent when he's been drinking. He'd bash me and then he'd bash the kids. I'd try to leave but he'd always find me and get violent ... It's really hard to get out of all this drinking and violence. You're in so much pain that you can't see any way out except unconsciousness, so if he didn't knock me out with his fists then I'd knock me out with the drink.* (interview: January 1999)

Indermaur's arguments suggest that women are likely to act in a less violent fashion than men when subject to shame and humiliation. He claims that "in traditionally female worlds, where the tasks are centred around support and caring, violence and aggression are non-functional and thus women develop a belief that violence is non-productive" (Indermaur 1996: 8). He also argues that the pattern of men's and women's violence is different. While for men, violence is often associated with a need to take control, for women, violence is often associated with a loss of control. In other words, for men, the use of violence is generally instrumental as it is used to achieve certain social or material aims or gains.

Accordingly, the place of violence within male prisons is central and magnified by the prevailing machismo culture. Here violence, as Genders and Morrison (1996: 29) put it, may be considered a "rational" manifestation of previous experiences, a pattern of behaviour which "conforms to the norms of the culture ... in which they must live". The prisoner consultant illustrated this when he described a very violent incident that occurred between two prisoners within a maximum security prison. During the incident, one prisoner cut another prisoner's throat and killed him. This was carried out in full view of hundreds of prisoners on the prison oval, as they were moving between work, education and their units. What struck the prisoner consultant was not so much the nature of the act itself, as its potential justification. He described the scene:

> He almost had his head cut off. It was held together by one single vertebra. I'll give you my personal reaction first. My first reaction was it's about time it happened. The guy who was killed was a child molester ... the word was that one of his victims was that bloke's (the perpetrator's) son. So my reaction was 'about time' ... the reaction that was most common was that it was about time he got it. There might have been a few (prisoners) who weren't child molesters who felt stressed enough to need medication, but not many, and nearly the entire prison population saw it ... the sight of this paedophile with his head hanging off didn't worry me at all.
> (interview: September 1999)

Another act of violence against a convicted paedophile was brought to my attention by my then partner in a letter he sent to me from Casuarina prison. He wrote, "we had a barbecue at work today. I'll tell you about it when you come to visit" (extract from personal letter: 1993). The barbecue turned out to be one prisoner setting light to another prisoner's face after dousing him in flammable liquid. My ex-partner described watching the victim's face melt. The prisoner consultant was also in Casuarina prison at that time and so I asked about his reaction to the incident. I explained that I had been horrified at my ex-partner's description of, and reaction to, the event. He outlined the general reaction of the prisoner population thus:

> Your ex-partner's reaction would have been pretty much the same as most of the prisoners around at the time. The difference in your reaction is just the amount of desensitisation to violence that happens in prison ... I agree with him completely regarding violence against child molesters ... The saying in here is that they're all

*dogs. That's the general opinion with very few exceptions.* (interview: September 1999)

There was a general consensus amongst most mainstream prisoners that those prisoners classified as "dogs" or "rock spiders" were fair targets for random acts of violence. Beau described the hierarchical structure and belief system within prison culture in this way:

> *In prison terms a dog is a giver. He's someone who will sell you out for his own benefit. Also rock spiders – well child molesters – are looked upon as dogs as well because they are the lowest form. The hierarchy within the prison, on our side of the fence ... well dogs, they're at the lowest end of the scale. Lifers and murderers are at the top and everybody else fits in between ... I wouldn't talk to a dog. It's just not a done thing.* (interview: December 1998)

## Prisoners' perceptions of their own violence

Most of the male participants told me that when they first entered the prison system they considered themselves to be either non-violent or only mildly violent people. *"I don't think I was particularly violent before I came to prison. I committed what are termed violent offences but they weren't physically violent"* (interview: prisoner consultant, September 1999). Peter reinforced this notion:

> *I wasn't a violent person when I first went to prison. I committed a crime that certainly frightened some people but I didn't (physically) hurt them. When I first went to prison I was young and small built so I was picked on by a group of predators. In my first week in jail I was raped by several prisoners. I learned to be very violent very quickly after that but it was always controlled. I mean violence doesn't come naturally to me.* (interview: June 1998)

The forms of predatory behaviour or prisoner victimisation mentioned by Peter – usually against young, vulnerable prisoners – are relatively common in the prison environment where "clues to vulnerability are not picked up or where no allowance for weakness is made" by prison staff (Toch 1977: 142).

When I asked the participants about degrees of violence, they recognised a "non-violent" category of prisoners. These were people who did not provoke a physical fight and who walked away if physical violence ensued. John, who described himself as non-violent, reflected on the fact that:

> *In prison people get so annoyed with other people that there's confrontations, arguments, fights. Once that sort of animosity starts it*

*spreads like wildfire ... I've been subject to several assaults and I built up my own self protective mechanism ... I'll spend anything up to 16 to 17 hours in my cell to avoid confrontations.* (interview: September 1998)

Mark also described himself as a non-violent person and said that he would *"avoid anyone who's a troublemaker and any situation that looked as though it might end in a fight"* (interview: August 1998). One notch up, the participants recognised a "mildly violent" group of prisoners who did not set out to provoke a physical fight, who sometimes fought when provoked themselves but never used weapons such as knives, clubs or firearms and never set out to inflict serious physical injury on another person. The prisoner consultant described the typical career of a mildly violent prisoner:

*It's like this, young bloke comes to prison, looks young, slightly built perhaps, and he becomes prey ... I've seen plenty of young blokes come in. Initially they're scared, they cop a flogging or they get raped ... so what happens is they won't go looking for fights but even when they know they're gong to take a hiding they know they're never going to take a backward step again. Even a person who hasn't got the physical ability to fight or even a violent nature will learn that it's better to put up some sort of a fight than to go along submissively.* (interview: September 1999)

In line with this, Toch (1977: 97) suggests that "[m]en who have had to fight for survival are apt to gird their loins in anticipation of the next threat or challenge". Being on the losing end in an attack is often regarded as an indicator of weakness while strength is ascribed to the aggressor. Thus the incentive to fight back is high since we can assume that "where fight is subculturally admired, we can infer that flight is subculturally despised" (Toch 1977: 170).

While several of the respondents were imprisoned because they committed crimes of violence, some of them said they used the threat of violence as a means of getting their own way rather than because they wished to harm their victims in the first place. As Indermaur (1996: 12) indicates, "[t]he instrumental use of force is often not considered by offenders to be 'violence', that is, to fall within their definition of what constitutes violent behaviour". Dick's statement echoed this type of justification as well as revealing another dimension:

*Look, you set out to do a burg (burglary) because you need money for a hit. The house is empty but someone comes back while you're still in there. What are you going to do? Of course, you threaten*

*them but you're not going to hurt them. Fuck, you're more scared
than they are. You just want to get out of there.* (interview: November 2000)

Here Dick's line of reasoning supports Indermaur's (1996: 6) argument that although violence and power are constantly interconnected
"contrary to some popular views, violence is not an expression of the
existence of power but its absence".

Along these lines, several participants said that they had used weapons to threaten their victims. Their collective view, however, was that
there was a distinct difference, in terms of degree of violence, between
*threats* of harm and *actual* physical harm. John illustrated this when he
spoke of his crimes: *"I committed three armed robberies but the actual
thing I used was an empty box. I created terror in the mind of the lady
teller but there was never any risk of physical harm"* (interview:
September 1998). Dick also described what he perceived to be the difference between threats of violence and actual violence:

> *I was convicted of several armed robberies for my first prison sen-
> tence. I used various weapons to commit these crimes but,
> although I threatened or implied by my actions that I could hurt
> people, I never physically hurt any of my victims. I only threatened
> to hurt them to achieve my aim, which was to get them to hand
> over the money.* (interview: November 2000)

As Indermaur (1996: 12) observes, "[o]nce learned as a functional response, violence can easily be seen as appropriate in meeting the
perpetrator's social (power) goals".

Only two of the participants described themselves as violent people. These were Beau and David. Beau portrayed himself as a person
both capable of and comfortable with extreme violence. He described
his propensity for violence in this way:

> *With the reputation I have of being a violent person. I mean I may
> not seem that way ... If I have a fight with somebody and I really,
> really want to hurt this person I will. I will jump all over his head
> and I will beat his head in. I will make him hurt real bad and pos-
> sibly take him to the brink of death before I stop.* (interview:
> December 1998)

Beau was not released within days of this interview as expected.
Indeed, a few days after the first interview he was charged with assaul-
ting another prisoner and spent several more months in prison before
eventually being released.

## Sexual violence in prisons

> Prisons are, above all else, a closed environment with a pecking order based on brute force, gang power and fear. They have their own economy, hierarchy, discipline and even their own language ... The power stratifications of prison populations also apply to sexual relations between prisoners ... Each system has a hierarchy with 'punk' – the term punk is used for a man who is coerced ... into a passive homosexual role – at the bottom. (Heilpern 1998: 77)

According to Heilpern (1998: 41), "[o]ne-quarter of males aged 18 to 25 incarcerated in New South Wales prisons report they have been sexually assaulted while in custody" with the perpetrators of these assaults almost always being other male prisoners. Heilpern (1998: 41) further claims that "sexual assault in prison is rarely reported". It is sometimes argued that male to male sexual assault in prisons is a simple consequence of the placement of many men of sexually active age in a male only environment. However, this fails to address the question of domination related to sexual violation, regardless of gender. Like all forms of rape, prison rape is not about sexual gratification but is about power and control – this time within an all male enclosed physical and social environment where violence is viewed as a rational act and where the penis becomes one of the weapons of choice. As Heilpern (1998: 81-82) suggests, "[t]he focus is not on who is your sex partner so much as 'who is in charge, that is who is doing the fucking, the penetrating, who is the man'".

Although none of the questions asked of the participants related to the issue, several of the participants spoke about sexual assault during interviews. Three of the male participants said that they had been anally and orally raped by other prisoners on more than one occasion. One of these men acknowledged being gang raped when he first went to prison as a teenager. Another said that he had gone on to anally and orally rape other prisoners and, throughout his long prison sentence, had engaged in consensual, coercive and overtly violent sex with other prisoners. Two of the remaining male participants and the prisoner consultant said that it was not uncommon for young male prisoners to be raped or coerced into having sex in exchange for protection or drugs. One of the women participants said that she had been propositioned and *"felt up"* by both male and female prison officers and, whilst in a regional prison, had been offered rewards for sexual favours by an assistant superintendent.

Only one of the three participants who had been sexually assaulted had reported the assault to the prison authorities. He was offered no trauma counselling. John explained his situation in this way:

*When I was subject to my last assault in 1993 I had to fight the department so that I could get a representative from SARC (sexual assault referral council) to come in and see me ... They decided to give me twice weekly (counselling) sessions with the psychologist to get down to the nitty gritty of why I was like I was. And in the meantime I've had conditions playing up where I ended up having to be hospitalised because of the panic attacks I had since then.* (interview: September 1998)

John said that he had been subjected to several sexual assaults throughout his many years in prison. From his interview it was apparent that he had been led to believe, or had otherwise assumed, that somehow he was at least in part to blame for his victimisation in this way. John is physically small and frail. He is a gay man in his late 40s who has spent almost all his adult life in prison. Heilpern (1998: 41) found that "younger, smaller gay prisoners" were at greatest risk of sexual assault in prison. Indeed, my own experiences as a prison visitor and prisoners' advocate afforded me insight into the relatively high levels of coercive, overtly violent and largely unreported sexual assault against young men held in prisons. Also, what little research has been conducted into prison sexual assault indicates that a broad range of factors can increase a prisoner's vulnerability to such attacks. Characteristics such as youth, small physical build, intellectual disability, perceived passivity and those persons in prison for the first time correlate with an increased possibility of being a victim of prison sexual assault (Human Rights Watch 2001: 5, Heilpern 2005: 286).

Peter was anally and orally raped by a group of five prisoners when he first went to prison. He said, *"I was 19 but looked 15 ... they grabbed me in the shower block, beat the crap out of me, held me down and took turns butt-fucking me. I thought they were going to kill me and I thought I was going to die from the pain ... I learned how to fight dirty after that"* (interview: May 1998). Peter never reported his sexual assault to the authorities and instead attached himself to a group of prison *"heavies"* for protection. He said that he felt a great deal of shame because of what happened and had continual emotional and behavioural problems which caused him to *"act up"* and attract prison charges which resulted in loss of parole and an extended prison term. He said that *"from time to time I'd just freak out and they'd quieten me down with largactil"* (interview: May 1998).

David said that he had been sexually assaulted when he first went to prison as a teenager, and that he had subsequently exchanged sexual favours with other prisoners for drugs. He went on to acknowledge that he had sexually assaulted other prisoners, saying, *"well, you are either*

*predator or you are prey. I started off by being beaten, raped and inti-*
*midated, then I lost all fear and thought 'what's good for the goose' ...*
*most of my sexual aggression has been played out under the influence*
*of drugs but I can get all the sex I want in prison"* (interview: September 1998). David thus played out the scenario whereby victims of
sexual assault seek to regain their power "through the same violent
means by which they think it was lost" (Heilpern 1998: 90). Also, by
becoming a sexual predator within the prison, David avoided being
assigned to the bottom of the pecking order "where life is most
unbearable" (Heilpern 1998: 90).

In contrast to these accounts, Linda said that she had *"never been*
*touched or propositioned by another prisoner but I'm obviously*
*straight and they'd respect that"* (interview: December 1998). However, she also claimed that:

> *[It was a] fairly common occurrence for young, attractive priso-*
> *ners to be propositioned by prison officers, mostly male but some-*
> *times female. They'll usually suggest it subtly when you need an*
> *extra phone call or some other favour ... some of the girls will do*
> *tricks for drugs but some of the younger ones will come across out*
> *of fear.* (interview: December 1998)

I note here that during the course of the research for this book, a female
prisoner (not one of the research participants), who had been in custody
in a women's prison for more than a year, became pregnant. The prison
authorities suggested that this prisoner had obtained semen in a
container from her imprisoned male boyfriend during a public court
appearance and impregnated herself. Using this bizarre and unlikely
explanation to publicly explain the pregnancy, the authorities ignored
the occurrence of sexual activity between male prison staff and women
prisoners. As Heilpern (1998: 87) claims:

> The (prison authority's) culture of turning a blind eye is endemic –
> and enduring. Such official acquiescence is seen as the paradox
> of institutional control. Selective blindness, the creation of 'hea-
> vies', the control of privileges, and maintaining the inmates' code
> of ostracising the sexually exploited all amount to culpability on
> the part of prison authorities in perpetuating victimisation.

## The position of violence within prison subculture: the inversion argument

Criminological and sociological research on violence has most often
focused on the heightened incidence of violence amongst the socially

and economically disadvantaged within society. For example, the Newcastle "Thousand Family Study" found that "densely populated households are more likely to produce violent criminals" and that there is "an association between multiple deprivation in childhood and subsequent violent behaviour" (Jones 2000: 105). Indermaur (1996: 7) also suggests that while "social structure may influence the value of rewards of violence it may also lead to an increased propensity to violence" when "individuals who are truly disadvantaged in social power relations are likely to experience ... 'angry' aggression ... and conclude that a violent response is needed". In short, both criminological and sociological argument suggests that within wider society it is persons of least power and the lowest socio-economic status who are more likely to perpetrate crimes of violence.

In contrast, within prison culture it is those prisoners with high status who are most likely to act in a violent manner. Within the prison hierarchy it is so called "prison heavies" who wield most power and are most likely to be violent. It is vulnerable prisoners of low status – protected prisoners such as child molesters – who have little or no power and are least likely to be violent within the overall prison context, but who may replicate similar "mini" hierarchies of violence within the closed protection units.

Within the mainstream prison context, this means that protected or low status prisoners are most likely to be the victims of violence as well as being least likely to display overt violent behaviour towards other prisoners. John, a protected prisoner, explained his situation this way, *"when you're in protection you're targeted by mainstream prisoners because they think we're all tamps (paedophiles). So we have to go to places like the library or canteen all together on a Friday to cut down the risk of assault"*. (interview: September 1998)

Mark, who was also a protected prisoner, described his position thus:

> When I was in maximum at Casuarina I was in unit six. All of unit six is protection. We were always the targets for the other prisoners, you know, yelling abuse at us, threatening us with violence and ... we had to be escorted everywhere we went in the prison. We had to go to work at different times from mainstream prisoners but every now and again the officers would let down their guard and one or more of us would get beaten up. (interview: August 1998)

Conversely, Beau who agreed that he was known within the system as a *"prison heavy"* and who described himself as *"someone who is looked up to within the system, a spokesman for my people"* explained that he

88

had to occasionally *"break a few heads when the young guns try to flex their muscle and give me grief"*. (interview: December 1998) The prisoner consultant also described this phenomenon:

> *The pecking order in jail is simple. Once again it's a survival thing and if you want to do your time in some degree of comfort, and by that I mean physical safety without worrying too much, then you have to display mental and physical toughness. In here that means you have to show that you're capable of looking after yourself physically so, when you're threatened, you react with violence. Sometimes it's even necessary to be the aggressor to keep your position of strength. You don't have to act violently all the time, just often enough to be seen by others as someone who it's best not to mess with ... sometimes this can mean you do extra time.*
> (interview: September 1999)

On this, Toch (1977: 150) suggests that in prison "the index of manliness is pugnaciousness" and, conversely, that the "criterion of unmanliness is fear ... to show fear is to invite further threatening ... the most stressful environmental pressures are invoked against those who are most helplessly susceptible to stress". In sum, within the prison community, the ability to use violence or threats of violence to generate fear in others lifts the status of the prison heavy who, in turn "feels fearless because his victims ... are terrified" (Toch 1977: 152).

## Categories of prison violence

I have identified four main categories of violence. These include acts of violence against the self such as suicide attempts and self mutilation. The other categories of violence are: prisoner to prisoner violence; prison officer to prisoner violence, and prisoner to prison officer violence.

### Self harm and suicide

Self harm and suicide are amongst the most difficult issues that prison authorities face because "they have many complex contributing factors often external to prisons, but likely to be exacerbated by the life crisis which imprisonment signifies" (Goulding 2004: 52). Between 1980 and 2005 there were 150 deaths in West Australian prisons. According to the *Deaths in Custody in Australia: National Deaths in Custody Program Annual Report* (Joudo 2005: 65) 77 of these deaths were classified as suicides. Liebling (1992: 49) found that "about 90 per cent of prison suicides are accomplished by hanging and that they are most likely to occur at night". The number of incidents of self harm in prisons is more difficult to calculate accurately as, according to the State Ombudsman (2000: 172), there is no accurate reporting mechanism for incidents of self harm within West Australian prisons and this has resulted in the Department of Corrective Services not knowing "the true extent of self harming activity in its prisons". Biles (1994: 23) suggests that self harming activity is likely to be "at least 16 times" more prevalent than completed suicides. A recent study of women in prison in Western Australia found that 46 per cent of participants had self harmed or self mutilated in the recent past (Goulding 2004: 34). Although it is generally acknowledged that "women in prison consistently report higher incidence of suicidal thoughts and more frequent suicide attempts" than their male counterparts (Salomone 2002: 2), within this study, five of the 11 participants had self mutilated and/or attempted suicide whilst in custody.

The violent and brutalising culture of prisons, together with the effects of institutionalisation, often lead to despair and self loathing in . prisoners. David spoke of his experiences of self harm:

> I've only ever harmed myself when I've been really strung out to the point of total confusion. It's been when I've been at my most powerless to get anywhere ... like, recently, when the screws kept winding me up, saying I had more prison charges and wasn't being released on my due date ... I couldn't find out anything ... one screw would tell me 'yes' and the next would tell me 'no'. It fucked with my mind so much I got hold of a razor blade and slashed up my ears. I've done that a few times, cut bits off my body. (interview: September 1998)

Judy said that she had attempted suicide when she first went to prison. She said that she "had to go cold turkey from the grog and I was seeing things and it felt real dark. It was the worst feeling: feeling nothing really. I got hold of some pills and swallowed the lot but it wasn't enough to kill me" (interview: January 1999). Linda also told me that she had wanted to die when her baby was taken from her in prison. She said that she started using heroin again and "never cared if I overdosed. Sometimes I thought it'd be better if I never woke up" (interview: December 1998). John spoke of the hopelessness some prisoners felt, "you get the constant tension in here ... there's some mornings you wake up feeling you can't face the world ... take all these deaths in custody. It's pointing out how much desperation there is here" interview: September 1998).

Liebling (1992: 67) supports the participants' accounts and reports that self harm "is a continuum along which one step may prove to be the first stage of a pathway of despair". Johnson and Toch (1982: 82) also suggest that:

> If a prisoner is placed in an unbearably stressful situation with no means at his disposal to cope with this overwhelming experience, he may divert his feelings of hopelessness towards himself. This 'self destructive breakdown' has been identified as unique to the prison setting, and it is seen as an index of the personal difficulties that face prisoners.

## Prisoner to prisoner violence

According to the participants, violence between prisoners is the most common category of prison·violence. The prisoner consultant explained the pervasive nature of prisoner to prisoner violence in these terms:

> *You've got the nature of the person who's in prison ... they may not be violent out there but they're not really upstanding members of the community either. To them, to go and bash someone sense-less is not as serious as it is to someone in the community. It's a whole set of different values in here. The most common solution to problems in here is to use violence ... It's not just the violence but you need to quickly adjust to the prison routine, how things are done and the pecking order ... this is a different world. Every-thing's magnified in here, every problem, every deprivation ... and the level of violence that's acceptable is also magnified ... so you quickly become desensitised to violence and all the little daily humiliations. They all become part of your life as a prisoner.*
> (interview: September 1999)

The participants talked about several types of violence between priso-ners. These were "payback", "predatory" and "random" or "impulsive" violence. The prisoner consultant said that payback violence was normally the most extreme form and often resulted in some degree of permanent physical incapacitation or even death:

> *Payback violence in prison probably accounts for the most extreme forms of violence because it's an emotional thing. If something has been done to you or someone close to you then you've really got to make an example of the person who did it ... you've got to, or you'll be seen as weak and therefore likely to become the victim of violence at some stage ... Payback violence is probably worse than the rapes and sexual violence. Payback is probably the worst phy-sical violence of the lot. I have seen prisoners die from payback violence.* (interview: September 1999)

Beau agreed that payback was the most serious form of violence and potentially fatal for its victims. He said, *"if some punk does something to you or your cobber or a family member then you've got to sort them out. You lose face if you don't ... and inside [prison] you're likely to have an audience egging you on so you might take it too far ... then that can lead to more payback and so on"* (interview: December 1998).

John also spoke of payback violence and claimed that the most common form of payback was *"when you're arrested with someone and he tells the police on you to get a lighter sentence then his payback will usually come in prison. It'll usually be a severe beating at the very least"* (interview: September 1998).

Predatory violence between prisoners is usually used to cement position or recruit subordinates to a group or gang. According to the prisoner consultant, *"predators prey on the young, weak prisoners, often those with a habit ... they see a young bloke come in scared and if he hasn't got some form of protection arranged then they'll target him. They'll flog them, rape them or just take their gear. It's like a jungle: survival of the fittest"* (interview: September 1999).

John acknowledged that he had been the victim of both predatory and random violence. He described his experience of what he termed predatory violence in this way:

> *I've been sexually assaulted on several occasions. I know it's because I'm physically small and weak but the animals that assaulted me wanted me to be their 'boy'. They wanted me to do stuff for them and the sexual assault was their way of forcing me to be part of their group ... I went into protection because of that but you're not safe from predators there either. There's a pecking order in protection too and that's why I spend most of my time in my cell.*
> (interview: September 1998)

David acknowledged that the authorities classified him as a predator within the system. He said that he had, on occasion, used threats of violence towards other prisoners in order to achieve certain objectives. He claimed that instrumental violence such as this might be used to *"get some gear (heroin) or avail myself of some sex or even just to make sure the other bloke knew who was in charge, especially if he was sharing my slot. Also, you've got to establish your position of strength or you're fucked"* (interview: September 1998).

Like David, Beau believed that the prison authorities saw him as a predator. He explained it this way: *"I tend to be a spokesperson for my people and that gives me position ... but by the same token, if there's a bit of family feuding in the wind or someone's poked sticks at me I'll have to front up and that means you see another side of me that not many people like ... I can be very scary"* (interview: December 1998).

Impulsive or random acts of violence between prisoners are also recognised in the prison environment, linked to sudden dislikes or expressions of hatred rather than the planned, instrumental or rational use of violence. In talking about his "predatory" forms of violence, Beau also recognised the impulsive nature of his behaviour:

> *In a fight I tend to lose my temper to a degree where I can really hurt somebody and not know because my temper takes over like I'm not thinking logically. It has to go full cycle before I wind down ... I have been like this on several occasions and hurt people real bad but then the upside is it reinforces my position and lets them know not to mess with me.* (interview: December 1998)

On the other side of the fence, John said, *"because I'm in the protection block other prisoners just assume that I'm a tamp (paedophile) and I can just be walking out of the unit and another prisoner will kick my legs out from under me or push me around ... that can happen any time"* (interview: September 1998).

The prisoner consultant described impulsive violence as *"part and parcel of being in prison ... someone looks at the wrong crim in the wrong way and can cop a belting, even if you bump into someone accidentally it can be seen as an insult and end up in a fight ... that sort of violence is usually no big deal, no one usually dies from that"* (interview: September 1999). Dick said that random acts of violence happen frequently in all areas of the prison. His reaction to such violence was, *"[i]f you see a couple of blokes at it (fighting) you usually turn away and see nothing. Violence usually flares up quickly and subsides just as quickly, especially if a screw comes along ... the only time I'd get involved is if it's a mate copping a flogging"* (interview: September 1998).

## Prison officer to prisoner violence

The participants maintained that prison officers were at times violent to prisoners. In this respect, they spoke of both officially sanctioned and hidden violence. Officially sanctioned violence includes official use of violence via various punishment and control mechanisms such as authorised use of shackles, hobbles and chains, use of chemical restraints such as mace and pepper sprays, enforced use of prescribed drugs, enforced orifice searches and in extreme cases, the use of the five point restraint bed. I asked the prisoner consultant to describe how a prisoner is shackled. He said that there were two main ways to shackle a prisoner:

*It depends how they apply the shackles which position you'll be in. If we're talking a MSU (Metropolitan Security Unit) escort shackle ... I mean this is how I'm shackled if I've got to go to hospital. You're shackled leg to leg at the ankles, arm to arm at the wrists, then there's a chain from the arm to leg shackle and you're hand-cuffed to an officer and can just about walk upright (demonstrates an upright shuffle). However, that chain from arm to leg can be shortened to any length they like. For a prisoner who's been violent or is going off then they'll drag that chain and shorten it to keep you in the foetal position ... shackles are certainly over used in this system ... there are guidelines for their use but individual officers just make that decision and sometimes it's only because they don't like the bloke and just for the fun of it they'll shackle him.* (interview: September 1999)

The inappropriate use, by the West Australian prison authorities, of restraints such as shackles has been widely noted (Goulding 2004: 18). Indeed the Inspector of Custodial Services (Report of an Announced Inspection of Bandyup Women's Prison June 2002: 77-78) reported that:

Recently a female prisoner gave birth by caesarean section in a public hospital and was restrained with either shackles or hand-cuffs for almost the entire duration of her stay in hospital. Prior to the operation, the prisoner went into theatre still wearing restraints. These were removed ... only after the anaesthetic had taken effect. The restraints were replaced when the prisoner was recovering in her room but still unconscious. The prisoner wore shackles while having a shower before giving birth, and after delivery when bathing and feeding her baby ... We would argue strongly against the routine use of restraints on women going out of prison on medical escorts ... Women should not be subjected to the use of restraints during labour or while giving birth, and restraints should not be used in circumstances where the patient's medical condition and circumstances effectively preclude her escape.

In addition to the use of physical restraints the prison authorities also rely on the use of medically administered drugs to control prisoners who present serious management problems caused by psychological and/or psychiatric conditions. In this context I asked the prisoner consultant about the enforced use of prescribed medication to subdue prisoners or modify their behaviour. He said:

*I've seen blokes get a needle, say today, and for the next 10 days they don't know who they are. It's a two-week drug ... I used to watch blokes in U Division when I was in the SHU in Fremantle. You'd think they were shackled from the way they shuffled in ...*

*they'd sit down to eat and just fall in their food. They'd go to have a shower and forget to take their clothes off. They'd be like that ten days in a row every single day. That was the drug they used as a control for people with psychotic problems. Medical staff or psychiatrists give the shots ... what was common was prescribing Largactil. Some of the prisoners used to take so much of it you could smell it coming out of the pores of their skin.* (interview: September 1999)

David said that he had been physically subdued on several occasions by the enforced administration of drugs. He described his experience in this way:

*When I've gone off on occasion and they've done a cell extraction on me – which means at least four screws or the MSU (Metropolitan Security Unit) all kitted up coming in and getting me – then they've dragged me off to an obs cell, generally giving me a going over on the way and zonked me out with a needle full of whatever ... you might not wake up for two days.* (interview: November 1998)

The use of unofficial violence by prison officers against prisoners was less common and generally conceded to be a form of payback violence. According to the prisoner consultant:

*It's very unusual for prisoners to be violent against screws, but if they are or even if they complain about a screw, then they can expect payback ... that payback usually involves ongoing and long term punishment and continuous revenge from other prison officers. This can be as simple as a continuous violation of the prisoner's rights but most often it also involves regular floggings ... most crims won't complain because it just means more floggings.* (interview: September 1999)

The prisoner consultant has spent almost 17 years in various West Australian prisons and claimed that overt physical violence by mainstream prison officers has lessened in the past decade. He described what he felt might be the worst case scenario:

*About the limit of violence against prisoners now by normal prison staff is about eight or nine officers will shackle him up, drag him to observation and he'll be shackled up, legs chained up while they wait for the medic to come along and give him some drug to subdue him. If he continues swearing then an officer will jump on him and kick him.* (interview: September 1999)

Against this, the prisoner consultant also claimed that the Metropolitan Security Unit (MSU) was trained to instil terror in prisoners in situations such as cell extractions or riots. He described MSU methods of prisoner restraint in this way:

> They'll come in with their boots and their batons, their shields and their helmets, their yelling and whatever else they use ... and they'll flog the living sense out of somebody to subdue them ... I'm not trying to be brave or macho here but they've never really frightened me because I've been on the end of so many boots and batons ... I know I can take the pain because I know it won't last. (interview: September 1999)

Commenting generally on both mainstream prison officer and specially trained MSU officer actions, the prisoner consultant went on to say:

> In prison there is a degree of acceptance of violence like this ... often it's more of a psychological thing. I mean if you see 10 people with helmets, batons and shields then 99 times out of a 100 you're going to say 'sorry, I'll stop what I'm doing' ... that's the bottom line ... In the early eighties the physical brutality was pretty high ... physical violence was their way of doing things ... now it's more of a mental brutalisation ... There's much more psychological brutalisation goes on from officers to prisoners. That is an everyday occurrence. The constant threat that if you do this you will lose this. That's played out every day all over all prisons ... You're so deprived, it's a sensory deprivation in here, you don't want to lose what little pleasures you've got. (interview: September 1999)

Although the prisoner consultant believed that overt violence is not as common as it once was within the prison system, many deep concerns remain. At the turn of the century, the Deaths in Custody Watch Committee (WA) compiled a report on violence against prisoners in West Australian prisons and took the report to the 25th Session of the Committee against Torture in Geneva. The main aim of the report was to bring to the Committee's attention "systematic and individual cases of violations of Australia's obligations under the Convention Against Torture in Western Australian (WA) prisons and other places of detention" (2001: I). It claimed that:

> No general inquiry has addressed the large task of investigating the treatment of prisoners across the range from serious allegations of torture and assault, excessive and unreasonable use of restraints and of isolation cells in injurious, cruel and degrading conditions, to less severe but more routine and systemic abuses. As a result, the institutional culture of contempt for prisoners and the related systemic problems, which are conducive to torture and cruel, inhuman and degrading punishment ... in prisons, remain unresolved. (Deaths in Custody Watch Committee, WA, 2001)

The Report of Deaths in Custody Watch Committee provides more than 20 case summaries of examples of violations of the Convention. These are based on prisoners' statements, many of which can be corroborated by evidence "in the form of witness statements, medical reports, photographs or other materials" (2001: 11). The following extracts are indicative of many cases cited in the report, being neither the worst nor the least examples of alleged violence against prisoners by prison staff.

> Case Seventeen: A female prisoner identified as QR claims that while being escorted from the prison compound to the punishment block under suspicion of using drugs, an officer used excessive force. A urine test taken later showed no use of drugs. QR claims that on the way to compound office, the officer grabbed her arm and put a handcuff on her wrist … she had been walking quietly and cooperatively with the officer. When she turned to hand a cup she had been holding to another person, the officer lifted her up from behind, pulled her legs from under her, pushed her to the ground and landed on top of her. The officer pinned her to the ground by applying his knee to her neck while another officer handcuffed her.

> There were ten witnesses to the incident who were later interviewed and provided statements. QR suffered cuts and abrasions to both of her arms, elbows and hands, both knees were bruised, her temple grazed and bruising up the left side of her body. She was then taken to the infirmary where her injuries were photographed and documented. After her injuries were dressed she was taken to a punishment block cell in severe pain. She advised an officer that she wished to make a complaint about the incident. The officer responded by laughing and telling her she could wait until the morning.

> QR made a verbal complaint. She was told she would have to make a written complaint. Although the authorities knew she was dyslexic, she was offered no assistance. The incident was investigated internally and the officer concerned was charged with using excessive force. QR was told that when the officer was served with the charge he resigned his employment and so they could not proceed with the charge. (23-24)

Other case studies include allegations about over zealous use of batons, restraints and chemical sprays. Following is the case summary of a male prisoner identified as LM who was allegedly beaten by prison officers.

> Case Twelve: LM, who says he was cleared of involvement in an incident of prison unrest by an external authority, claims that about

97

ten officers with batons confronted him in his cell. While he was trying to find out what offence he was accused of, an officer attempted to spray mace into his eyes. LM claims an officer hit him four times in his face with a closed fist. LM claims that when he fell to the floor the officers assaulted him with batons on the back of his legs, kicked him about the body while another officer stood on his back and restrained his ankles causing extreme pain. He alleges that he had mace sprayed into his eyes and mouth. LM claims he was handcuffed and the nylon rope-hobble was attached to his ankles and hands behind his back. He alleges that an officer then sprayed mace on his genitals.

LM claims that he was pulled to his feet, which caused extreme pain as the rope-hobbles stretched tight and cut into his ankles. He says that while in this position a senior officer hit him in the face causing him to fall. According to LM, he was taken down some stairs by two officers and on the way to the Isolation Unit they smashed him against walls and grills. LM was taken to wash the mace off and officers cut the nylon hobbles off. A medical officer was called and from a distance of approximately 2.4m (8 feet) said that LM's condition was medically acceptable and left.

LM claims that his ankles were bleeding, his feet were extremely painful and his face swollen. He spent the next two days in isolation. He asked to see a medical officer. Later a medical officer looked through the door cell flap and said that his medical condition was acceptable. During this period, LM claims that no photos were taken of his injuries, and he did not believe any medical notes taken. About two days later a medical officer applied Betadine to his ankles and, on the insistence of a family member, he was x-rayed. (19-20)

Case Ten: JK who claims he was not involved in prison unrest needed a Ventolin inhaler for his asthma. He approached a medical officer saying, 'excuse me Miss'. He alleges that a senior officer told him to 'shut the fuck up'. JK responded by trying to explain to the officer that he simply wanted to request a new Ventolin inhaler. JK claims that he was then forced to the ground by at least two officers, sprayed with mace in his eyes and mouth, handcuffed and had his ankles tied together with nylon ropes. The officers stood him up and ran him down to the Isolation Unit, smashing him into walls and doorframes. He was then allowed to have a shower to wash the mace away. The same medical officer who he had attempted to talk to earlier checked his ankles, which had been cut from the rope-hobbles, and gave him the new Ventolin spray that he had earlier requested. (19)

## Prisoner to prison officer violence

According to the prisoner consultant, prisoner to prison officer violence is very rare. He states that *"it happens but usually only with a prison officer who's a real bastard and then hardly ever ... I've been in jail in WA for 17 years all up and I've probably heard of half a dozen incidents where prisoners have used actual physical violence against prison officers"* (interview: September 1999).

Most of the prisoner participants agreed with the prisoner consultant's assessment. John said, *"[m]ost prisoners wouldn't think of hurting a prison officer ... well they might mouth off about it but commonsense would prevail because the repercussions would last for the entire sentence"* (interview: September 1998).

Nonetheless, there are documented cases of serious prisoner to prison officer violence. I refer in particular to violence directed against prison officers during the Fremantle Prison Riots of 1988. The prisoner consultant was heavily involved in the riot at Fremantle Prison and I asked him about the mindset of the prisoners involved and the degree of violence.

*(How violent in real terms was the riot?)*

*Initially, very violent. The initial purpose of the riot was not violent in terms of violence against persons. It was to draw attention to problems and very bad conditions within the prison. Inhuman conditions. We were intent on destroying the prison not hurting any person. Be it prison officer or whatever. The goal was to burn the prison right down ... the purpose behind that was if the firehouse and the kitchen got burned to the ground then the prison would have to close down.*

*(So this was quite calculated. It wasn't just an ad hoc spontaneous riot?)*

*It was a strategically planned operation. What went wrong initially was that a lot of the young blokes not involved in the planning ... saw an opportunity to go berserk and grabbed any weapons that were available – iron bars, lumps of wood, anything like that and just started belting any uniform in sight. That was never the plan ... there was full on violence for about five minutes ... after that there was no more violence but there was the threat of violence in the air the whole time ... there were five prison officers held hostage in the yard and there were plenty of prison officers on the top cocking firearms, pointing them at people ... so the potential for violence was always there ... it was never meant to be a violent exercise ... although with hindsight the potential for violence was always high in a prison where conditions were so bad and feelings were running high.* (interview: September 1999)

## Concluding comments

In concluding, I emphasise that the interview schedule contained no questions relating to violence. Instead, violence was raised by each of the male participants during the course of the interviews. And, while the female participants did not specifically refer to violence, their interviews clearly outlined the systemic brutality they endured and observed during their terms of imprisonment.

Furthermore, the prisoner consultant who supplied much of the background information for the study has described the violent nature of imprisonment and has, over the years, spoken to me of specific incidents of extreme violence and the general propensity for aggression within the prison system. Because of the violent and brutal nature of prisons we cannot then assume that prisons present "a just form of punishment – which at least limits the severity of punishment to what is proportionate to the seriousness of the crime" (Duff and Garland 1994: preface to Bianchi, 'Abolition, Assensus and Sanctuary': 334).

# Chapter 5

# Recapturing Freedom?

*What a difference a day makes*
*When it's the last day...... inside*
*Can't wait to get a glimpse of the city*
*What a pity, no one there for me...... outside*
*...No one waits for me*
*It's home to bed*
*A cuppa tea*
*And, of course, TV*
*What else have they had me doing...... inside*
*I've no idea about trains and buses*
*Tickets and red tape*
*All the bloody things I need right now*
*And there's no escape*
*I have to leave to go...... outside*
*What a fucking disaster this place*
*Rules of incompetence*
*Mark the jail*
*As a place to fail...... inside*
*No help, no assistance*
*Just persistence*
*To help you get back in here*
*Poverty can take the blame*
*Oh god I'm off again...... to the outside*

Brian Steels: Karnet Prison, 1994

This chapter deals with the participants' experience of release from prison and their subsequent reintegration into the community. At the time of writing only one of the 11 participants in the study (including the prisoner consultant and the ex-prisoner) has remained consistently out of prison. Mark has remained crime free and living in the community. He alone, out of all the participants, feels that his reintegration into the community has been successful. Mark found work quickly, established some new social connections and has created for himself a relatively stable lifestyle. On the other hand, Peter managed to stay out of prison for more than three years before re-offending and being imprisoned for a short custodial term but he described his life on the outside as a constant struggle. In the five years since his initial release he has been unable to find stable employment, lives an itinerant lifestyle, struggles with alcohol and prescription drug abuse and *"continually fuck(s) up relationships with everyone"* (personal telephone conversations: 2000-05). Each of the remaining participants has been returned to prison on at least one occasion and, at the time of writing, seven of those are currently serving further terms of imprisonment for additional crimes. Both of the prisoner consultant's interviews were conducted in prison after he had been sentenced for crimes committed during his two months of freedom in the community.

This section begins with participants' voicing their anxieties, expectations and hopes for the future in the days leading up to their scheduled release dates. This is then compared with how the participants actually experienced the reality of coping with life in the community. The second interviews were conducted three to six months after release: some of these took place out in the community but seven of the follow up interviews were conducted within custodial settings. Some of the participants have maintained regular contact and so I have been able to gain some understanding of how their lives have panned out in the years since their initial release dates.

## Anxieties, expectations and hopes for life in the community

Most of the participants were anxious about how they would cope with life "on the outside". In the days leading up to their release into the community, some participants had positive expectations whereas some felt that they might not make it.

### Anxieties

Mark was to be released from a country prison. He was anxious about his relocation to the Perth metropolitan area where he had no family or social supports. However, he had no choice but to relocate to the city as his release to parole was entirely dependent on participation in a post release sex offender's treatment program which was only available in Perth. He described his concerns thus: *"I've got to do my parole in Perth because of my parole conditions and I have no friends in Perth. That's the main problem. I'll be lonely ... I really don't know what to expect when I get out. I try not to think about it too much"* (interview: August 1998).

Linda, too, was fearful about her release prospects. She had accommodation arranged with a close friend but also had major concerns regarding her ability to cope with life outside of prison.

> *(Can you tell me about the things that make you most anxious about getting out?)*
>
> *Yes. My drug use. I'm not feeling like I'm going to use but it's been a problem before and I'd be a fool to think that I'm not going to be tempted. I know that if I'm in a crisis it will be an option, a pain killer ... you get into the whole sharing thing with drugs and it makes you feel close. Also I'm afraid about lots of things ... I've done this before and failed. I'm worried about seeing things through a prisoner's eyes when out there most people see things from another place. I've been a number in a maroon tracksuit for a big part of my life ... Most of all, though, I'm afraid they (Family and Children's Services) won't give me my daughter back because of where I've been. I don't want to do crime. I don't want to do drugs and I'm anxious about all of this.* (interview: December 1998)

In the days leading up to his release, Peter's anxieties manifested themselves in acute nervousness and an inability to sleep. He felt as though he was doing the last few days of his nine year prison term really hard. He said, *"I'm worried about almost everything from walking out the gate to turning up at my girlfriend's place to meeting her parents ... I've been inside since I was 19 and I'm 28 now ... It's four sleeps till I get out but I haven't really slept for nearly a week"* (interview: May 1998).

John displayed a great degree of anxiety about his imminent release but said that he was trying to feel positive. He described his main fears in this way:

> *I've been so long in prison ... I'll be virtually like a little baby and I'll be learning to walk again and I know it's going to have an emotional impact on me. I'm hoping I'll be too busy to get psyched up ... I'm feeling a bit of sadness and a bit of joy and I know if I can stay out for the first 12 months I've made it. But, by the same token, I know that if I stuff up out there then I come back to jail that I will never leave the system alive so foremost in my mind is that I've spent 27 years of my life in jail ... That is almost ALL my adult life in jail so if I stuff up and come back and die in prison then what have I got to show for my life?* (interview: September 1998)

John also said that he had no living relatives and was being released on parole to live in a designated hostel. His release was contingent on strict reporting conditions and a high degree of regulation. I asked John whether he might find the strict release conditions a problem. He said:

> *No. I know regulation well and I'm comfortable with the strict regime. The last time I was due for release I got in such a panic that I had a heart attack but I've been having counselling and I've been 'buddied' up with someone from a church group who'll meet me a few days after I get out. The place where I'm going to live has staff on 24 hours a day so if I'm feeling anxious I can easily get help.* (interview: September 1998)

David, who was released from conditions of solitary confinement in the strict security Special Handling Unit after almost nine years in prison, was also worried about his release and expressed his concerns in this way:

> *I'm very anxious because I got out on parole before and was only out an hour before I started shooting up and drinking and I ended up in hospital with an overdose. The unknown of being out there is a big issue ... Last time I wasn't really so interested in staying out. It was like, fuck, why lose something you're so used to when you enjoy it? There's lots of security in this place ... I get everything in jail I can get on the outside – drugs, sex, food ... I have identity in jail. This is how I was thinking back then ... so I came back in and everything went down the gurgler.* (interview: September 1998)

Beau was also extremely anxious in the days leading up to his release:

> *As it gets closer to the day of release, your anxiety builds to the degree that you just want to explode ... in the past I've let anxiety get to me to the degree where I've cracked and had a siege. The anxiety for me is about being released from a maximum security prison into the community. That's huge. It's a culture shock. I'm looking forward to getting out but I'm afraid.* (interview: December 1998)

Beau was involved in a fight with another prisoner several days after this interview. He was charged with assault and spent several more months in prison before finally being released.

Judy's anxieties about release centred on extended family issues and her continual battle with alcoholism. Her main worry was centred on the relationship between herself, her extended family and alcohol. She said:

> *I have to keep away from the drink. I've been sober all the years in here and I feel good ... my mum and my cousins will support me*

*but I hope my in-laws keep away and don't start no trouble ... After a while they can wear me down. My husband won't be a problem for a while because he's still inside but they'll want me to visit him ... My biggest fear is that the people who I drank with will want to drag me down again ... it's difficult in Aboriginal families to just throw people out of your house. That's my main fear. Will I have the strength to find a way around all this without giving in to the grog again.* (interview: January 1998)

## Fear of failure

Pre-release anxiety is most often intensified by the fear of failure. Several of the participants had failed before and questioned their ability to make it on the outside. In short, life out in the wider community was seen by most of the participants as something to be concerned about. Goffman (1961: 73) identifies three major factors associated with failure to reintegrate successfully into the community. These are social deskilling, stigmatisation and loss of position.

Social deskilling is an inevitable consequence of institutionalisation whereby the general values and mores of wider society are removed in favour of the subcultural values of the total institution. This form of "disculturation" may be seen as "the loss or failure to acquire some of the habits currently required in the wider society" (Goffman 1961: 73). Beau described his previous experience of release into the community in this way:

*Last time I got out I'd done a good few years. I got on a train at Perth train station but they'd changed the system while I was inside and I hadn't got a ticket when the guard came to check. I was so fucking embarrassed and said I was from over east. I couldn't even ask someone to show me how to get a train ticket from the machine.* (interview: December 1998)

Stigmatisation shadows the ex-prisoner wherever he or she goes. As Goffman (1963: 15) claims:

We believe the person with a stigma is not quite human. On this assumption we exercise varieties of discrimination, through which we effectively, if often unthinkingly, reduce his life chances. We construct a stigma theory, an ideology to explain his inferiority and account for the danger he represents.

Imprisonment then is a "life marker". It may be particularly felt when ex-prisoners apply for unemployment benefits or jobs. Goffman (1961: 72) suggests that "not only is his social position within the walls radically different from what it was on the outside but ... his social position on the outside will never again be quite what it was prior to entrance". Dick highlighted this: *"Right, I go out there and front up at social security and the employment agency. How do I account for the last seven years? Fuck, I've been in prison, mate ... don't ring us, mate, we'll ring you. End of story. That's hard to take"* (interview: September 1998).

As far as loss of position is concerned, prisoners who have been at the top end of the prison hierarchy often find themselves suddenly relegated to the bottom of the chain of command in the wider community. This humiliation may be magnified if prisoners have to adhere to strict reporting conditions on parole. The prisoner consultant spoke of this:

> *I've done a lot of years inside and I'm pretty well known in prison circles. Most prisoners would know who I am. Not everybody likes me but they know me. In here (prison) wherever I go someone will acknowledge me with a nod, g'day, fuck off, whatever. What I'm trying to point out is that I have position here and I'm known. When I was out last time I found being anonymous hard to adjust to. I'd walk through a shopping centre for a couple of hours and no one would say hullo or smile or acknowledge me in any way. That felt weird. Weird and isolated.* (interview: August 1999)

When he was previously released from prison Beau, too, found his loss of position difficult and blamed his strict reporting conditions for his inability to find suitable employment. He told me that:

> *My parole officer just refused to compromise ... I had to do weekly piss tests and what boss is going to put up with that? Also I've got a life (driving) ban so I couldn't drive and it took me hours just to get to my parole office. I had to catch two buses to get there and two to get back, twice a week. I had no time to look for work.* (interview: December 1998)

## Hopes and expectations

Despite all of these anxieties, each of the participants said that there were things they were looking forward to in the community. Albert described his feelings about getting out of prison after 10 years inside. He felt positive and confident about his imminent release and said, *"I'm not really anxious at all. I'm pretty optimistic. You see I've got it all set up out there. I've got family support, I've got a car, a licence and work to go to. I think I'll be sweet"* (interview: June 1999). John's expectations were as simple as this: *"I'm really looking forward to walking into a newsagent, buying a newspaper and being the first person to read it instead of having to wait for five or six hours and 16 other people to read it"* (interview: September 1998). Linda said that she was looking forward to *"being with my daughter. Taking her to the park. Watching her play. Seeing her free, I've only ever seen her in captivity, well, in the jail nursery. I want to see her run after seagulls on the beach ... I'd like to buy new clothes and get my hair cut properly at a hairdresser"* (interview: December 1998).

Judy wanted to *"wake in my own bed with my kids jumping all over me. Go to the kitchen and make a cup of tea. Be able to go to the fridge and choose what I want to eat ... take my kids to Cinema City and then to McDonalds for a burger"* (interview: January 1999). Beau was aiming to *"buy some clothes. I only have what I'll leave prison in and I used to have a wardrobe worth eight or nine grand ... I'm also looking forward to getting laid and sharing myself around a bit"* (interview: December 1998).

David looked forward to *"[m]y mum's cooking, tasting prawns again ... and walking on the beach"* (interview: September 1998). He also had educational and vocational ambitions which he felt might lead him to some sense of position in the community, mentioning that he might *"do a diploma. I want to do a couple actually, maybe three. Psychology, social sciences and perhaps counselling abused people and their abusers ... I've got a TAFE pamphlet and I thought these looked interesting given my background"* (interview: September 1998).

## Reality bites: coping with life in the community

At the time of writing only one of the 11 participants has remained consistently free in the community. The others did not manage to recapture freedom. Instead, they were recaptured by the system. One participant was returned to prison within days of release, most were back inside within weeks, a few stayed out for several months, one participant remained free for almost two years and another remained out in the community for three years. Each of these participants has been returned to prison on at least one occasion and seven of those are currently serving further terms of imprisonment for additional crimes. Following are the individual stories of some of the participant's experience of life, however brief, in the wider community.

### Mark

Mark has remained crime free and living in the community for more than seven years. Although he displayed the familiar patterns of pre-release anxiety and fear of failure, Mark's story is one of a successful reintegration into the community. He was released from a regional prison after completing a four year sentence, given a bus ticket to Perth and went to live in pre-arranged, supported accommodation in a hostel type situation where he had to share a room with another ex-prisoner who was not known to him. His first day in the community was problematic and stressful because he had to travel by bus from the country. He described his situation in this way: *"Outcare (a prisoner welfare agency) told me someone would meet me off the bus but no one was there and I had to find their office and do the Centrelink stuff on my own"* (interview: January 1999).

However, Mark overcame the trauma of his first day out of prison and quickly settled into a routine. He found his flatmate messy and tended to avoid all contact with him. He found a job within days of his release:

> *I went to the job agencies and registered and phoned after every-thing I thought I could do and I got offered two driving jobs. I took this one. It's driving a truck around doing deliveries ... I work quite long hours and I have to do the sex offenders treatment program on Wednesday nights so I'm kept busy.* (interview: January 1999)

Mark also actively sought out a new set of social contacts. He said that he knew he had to make the first move:

> *I had to find other people who were lonely like me so I joined Parents Without Partners and I've made lots of friends ... We go to dances on Fridays or Saturdays and we go to each other's houses for barbecues on Sundays ... I don't go to any of the functions where there are going to be children. I'm still going to the pro-gram (Sex Offenders Treatment Program) and I know what I should and shouldn't do ... My friends are really nice people and the best thing is I could choose who I wanted to be friends with.* (interview: January 1999)

Unlike any of the other participants, Mark had no informal supports in the community he was obliged to live with. His family and friends were several hundreds of miles away and he more or less had to *"get on with it"*. He coped best by keeping busy and avoiding areas of high risk. He did, however, complain that his parole officer offered no real help, mentioning that:

> *My parole officer changes every few weeks and they don't help you at all, just ask if you're complying with everything you're supposed to ... I think the parole office could be more helpful with things like*

*arranging the sex offenders program to be at better times or at least arranging for me to miss the odd session and catch up later. A couple of times I nearly lost my job cause I couldn't do overtime and if I'd missed a session they would've breached my parole and put me back inside.* (interview: January 1999)

I asked Mark how he felt about his life now and what sort of things made him feel good. He told me, *"I feel good about everything. Having a job. Having money in the bank. Paying cash for my car. My friends and being with them. I'm moving house soon. My life feels pretty good. I feel like I'm really moving forward"* (interview: January 1999).

Mark has kept regular contact and rings every few months to let me know how he is doing. He is proud of his progress, has had a promotion at work and now rents his own house. He still has his new friends and all of them, including his employer, know that he has served time in prison.

## Peter

Peter remained out of prison for more than three years before being sent back to prison. His journey has been a difficult one and he has been arrested for drunk and disorderly conduct and various other misdemeanours on several occasions since his release. He was sent back to prison for a short term sentence on an assault charge. He has since been released and has maintained some friendships from prison but acknowledges that he finds close relationships difficult to deal with. When he was released from prison after completing a nine year term he went to live with a girlfriend he met whilst he was in jail.

The follow up interview with Peter was conducted at a place of his choice, the Broken Hill pub in Victoria Park. Peter had, at that time, been out of prison (on his first prison term) for several weeks and was already experiencing serious problems with his relationship. He outlined the nature of his relationship in this way:

*I have a set of friends but I don't get to see them because of the relationship I'm in at the moment ... She's (girlfriend) very insecure. If I'm not home by 3.30 pm that's it, she goes out looking for me ... I only get to drink or smoke Fridays. God help me if I go home drunk or stinking of smoke ... I feel basically that I'm in another jail.* (interview: June 1998)

Peter found it difficult to go to designated employment agencies and follow instructions to contact potential employers from the positions vacant list. Yet he spoke about *"doing a bridging course for psychology at university next year"* (interview: June 1998). He also expected his friends to find jobs for him. At the time of the interview he said, *"I'm feeling a bit let down because I didn't get a job a friend recommended me for. I thought it was in the bag"* (interview: June 1998). When asked if he went regularly to job agencies he said, *"No, I get uncomfortable going to places like that. I have to tell them everything and it makes me feel uncomfortable"* (interview: June 1998). Going to Centrelink and opening a bank account were also traumatic for Peter. The main concerns were with identification documentation. Peter described his first visit to the bank to cash his DSS (Department of Social Security) cheque:

> *(How did you go about cashing the cheque?)*
>
> *That was hard because I didn't have a bank account or anything. It was hard to try and open a bank account because I had no ID ... but they sort of took me on my word when I said 'I've got no ID because I've just been in prison. I spent a long time in there'. They said 'all right' and got me to sign about four different things just to check signatures and that was it, but it was embarrassing telling them where I'd been.* (interview: June 1998)

When asked what situations caused him most anxiety or stress Peter reiterated that his relationship was his main problem. He said, *"It's not getting space. Not being given the leeway to see who I want, do what I want ... also, I have absolutely no idea how to handle this situation"* (interview: June 1998). In the years since the interview took place Peter has kept in touch. His relationship floundered for several months and then broke up. Peter explained, *"I had no idea how to be in a close relationship. I still don't. I'm not much good at sex and can't handle the intimacy thing. I'm better off on my own"* (telephone conversation: December 2000). Since the breakdown of his relationship Peter has been largely homeless and unemployed, moving between men's hostels and temporary accommodation with casual acquaintances. His risk of returning to prison was high and he eventually re-offended, returned to prison, was released and is currently facing more criminal charges.

## Dick

Dick was first reinterviewed after 12 weeks in the community. At that stage he had moved in with his girlfriend and was enjoying his experience of freedom. However, he found it difficult to find paid employment and explained how this made him feel:

> *I'm an artist and because I've got certain skills I figured I'd get work okay but so far that hasn't happened. It's early days yet and*

*I'm looking at doing further studies part time. Right now, though, I'm concentrating on establishing my relationship ... my missus has a couple of kids and that's new for me ... I'm trying to find where I fit in all this and sometimes her family make me feel like I don't belong ... I'd really like a job. I'd like to contribute.* (interview: November 1998)

Dick had spent more than eight years in prison and found it particularly difficult to attend job agencies. He was unfamiliar with the computer technology and said that he *"felt stupid not knowing what to do. I found it hard to impossible to fess up to where I'd been and I couldn't approach people for help"* (interview: November 1998). He said that it was easier to hand in the form to social security and that he felt more at one with the people in the dole queue. He also told me that *"I phoned the university about continuing my art studies but when I went out there I felt like a fish out of water. I just didn't fit"* (interview: November 1998).

At that stage Dick was struggling but he was still managing to keep himself out of trouble. He explained that, with no real structure to his day, he tended to drift towards his old lifestyle and habits. Several months after the follow up interview, Dick's relationship had deteriorated and he was back in prison. He explained how he felt:

*Her (girlfriend's) mum hates me because I've been inside. She won't talk to me so that caused strain in the relationship ... then there's her mates who think I'm the pits ... a couple even threatened me and I said 'bring it on, mate'. All this because I've been inside. I grew horns in there obviously ... Anyway, I stayed off the gear (heroin) for 10 months all up and though I was struggling with everything I didn't do any crime. Then, when I was on a real downer, a couple of mates from jail came over with a hit (heroin) ... it was all over red rover. I started using again. I started doing crime to pay for the gear and here I am back inside on remand waiting to be sentenced. I feel like I've fucked up everyone's lives again. This is really hard to handle.* (interview: November 2000)

Dick had remained both drug free and crime free for almost a year. However, as soon as he started using heroin again he became immersed in the whole crime scene. He regularly associated with peers he had met in prison and, after almost two years in the community, he was charged with several offences and was returned to prison. Dick was sentenced under the mandatory sentencing Act. As Schetzer (1996:6) explains:

Mandatory Sentencing Laws were introduced into the Western Australian Criminal Code in November 1996. These Laws ensured that if a person is convicted of a home burglary and is a 'repeat offender', then that person shall be sentenced to at least 12 months imprisonment.

He is now serving another long term prison sentence. He is not hopeful for his future. He illustrated his despondency in this way: *"I'll be 40 when I get out. I doubt if Mandy will wait for me ... really, what is there out there for someone like me ... I don't know how to act in front of normal people ... I take everything they say the wrong way and react like I would in jail. I feel like a real loser, no good to anyone"* (interview: November 2000).

## Beau

Beau has been in juvenile and adult custodial settings on and off since he was 10 years old. He is now 32. At the time of writing, he is back in prison for the third time since the original interview. He remained free in the community for approximately three months before he was rearrested on serious assault charges. The follow up interview took place in Hakea prison.

I asked Beau if he could identify a point when things started to go wrong after his release. He explained that he started to go off track from almost day one:

> *I had all the best intentions of doing the right thing but it was hard because I was living under my aunty's roof and having to live by her rules. I never felt comfortable because it wasn't my own space and I had to watch how I tread ... I was used to being the one in charge in prison, the one everyone came to, and here I was at my aunty's sleeping on cushions on the floor while my cousin's wadjela (white) girlfriend slept in a bed. I felt really out of place there ... I felt negative vibes from my uncle too, like he didn't want me there ... I had an argument with him and my aunty said 'I don't want you in my house' so I left.* (interview: November 1999)

While Beau was living with his aunt, he found it difficult to attend his parole and drug counselling appointments because of the distance he had to travel and the lack of access to regular public transport from her house. A trip to the parole office took Beau *"a couple of hours and then another three quarters of an hour to Perth and a 15 minute walk to the drug counsellor's office. So three hours there and the same back – six hours all up. Also my aunty didn't have a phone and it was hard trying to find a public phone that worked"* (interview: November 1999).

112

I asked Beau if he thought that counsellors and parole officers should set aside a couple of days per week where appointments could be kept anytime between 9 am and 4.30 pm for Aboriginal clients and clients who had to use public transport. He said, *"I reckon that would be great. For us (Aboriginal people) it would be more culturally cool, and for anyone who had to get on and off trains and buses. Shit, it would help heaps. That would work well and it would cut down on the number of (parole) breaches"* (interview: November 1999).

As well as dealing with the difficulties relating to accommodation and loss of status, Beau struggled with the drug issue. He blamed his continuing drug use on the problems he faced. He put it this way: *"There wasn't a day when I wasn't walking around out there feeling weighed down ... I didn't know where I belonged any more. I wanted more or less to do as I pleased without upsetting anyone or getting in anyone's way. I wanted my own lifestyle"* (interview: November 1999). Also, Beau felt a great loss of face because:

> *I had no clothes, no money and my family couldn't give me money because they're not in that position. This was a really big thing for me because when I got out of here the only clothes I had was the shirt I had on my back, basically what I stood up in.* (interview: November 1999)

> *(Could you tell me how long you'd been out of prison before you started using heroin again?)*

> *About a month and a half after I got out ... I smoked pot and had a few drinks but I stayed off the needle. For a month and a half I stuck fast ... I'd have to say that all the stress was a strong contributing factor because it (heroin) eased my worries, you know. I'd be sitting back on the blink, you know, on the nod and it was just like, yes, this is beautiful. No worries, that sort of thing.* (interview: November 1999)

Beau found it difficult to cope with the snowball effect of things going wrong. One incident, such as missing or being late for a drug counselling or parole appointment, could escalate into breach of parole and return to prison orders. At this stage he felt a basic inability to halt his mistakes there. One thing led to another and, once again, he felt as if he had lost control over his life. His problem with finding suitable accommodation appeared to underpin all his other associated problems. He spoke at length of this dilemma:

> *I had this ongoing thing with accommodation. I was practically living out of a bag ... because I went from my aunty's house to my mum's house to my uncle's house ... and then I ended up moving*

*back in with my ex-wife ... but that was the worst move I ever made. She was using smack (heroin) and speed (amphetamines) ... I was weighing it all up and thinking I'm living the way I was before I went to jail and the result of that is usually going back to jail ... and here I am back in jail.* (interview: November 1999)

At this point Beau had breached his parole conditions. He was aware that he would face a return to prison order, so he stopped attending all parole and drug counselling appointments. His itinerant lifestyle made it difficult for police to pick him up and return him to prison. However, one night when he was under the influence of drugs and alcohol, he re-offended. He described the circumstances of his arrest in this way:

*I was at a family barbecue and my ex-girlfriend was there ... some things happened, I got jealous and I hit her and broke her nose ... my cousin came out and hit me with an iron bar so I grabbed an iron bar and took a swing at him and snapped a couple of his ribs. He smacked me on the head and blood started pissing out ... he split me head open ... I really wanted to hurt him badly and he's run inside and phoned the coppers. The coppers came from every-where and I didn't jerry that there's a return to prison order out on me. I knew that there would be but the thought hadn't registered as I'd had other things on my mind just presently.* (interview: November 1999)

Not only was Beau returned to prison to serve out his parole but he had also accumulated two more serious charges. He pleaded guilty to the charges, was sentenced and served that prison term. He was once again released into the community and has since been re-arrested on armed robbery charges. He served that sentence, was released again, re-offended yet again and is currently in custody on remand.

Beau has never received treatment for his heroin addiction whilst in prison.

## Linda

Linda's fear of failure was an almost self fulfilling prophecy. She re-offended within days of her release into the community after three and a half years in prison. She was charged, released on bail, convicted and sentenced to another term of imprisonment under the mandatory sentencing Act. Within a month of her release she was back inside, finding it difficult to cope with her circumstances and doing her prison term "hard". The follow up interview with Linda was conducted in Bandyup prison.

Linda was originally released from prison a few days before Christmas and told me that things started to go wrong almost immediately. She had been sick, lost a lot of weight in prison and was released on a hot summer day in old winter clothes that were several sizes too big. She felt bad about herself and described her feelings in this way:

> When I got out the gates I felt very apprehensive. I was wearing clothes that didn't fit because they (prison authorities) wouldn't give me a liberty spend ... It was a few days before Christmas and I didn't feel confident about anything. I just wanted to see my daughter and get her some presents for Christmas. That's all I could think about – getting to see her on the outside for the first time since she was a tiny baby and just be her mum ... I was scared and I felt really low ... I went to my friend's place and then I had to do things like contact social security to sign on the dole, contact Family and Children's Services about visits with my daughter and organise to do a parenting course. Trying to do all that seemed to be beyond me. I never seemed to do anything right or get a positive result. (interview: August 1999)

Linda was dogged by feelings of failure from the outset. Because her small daughter was in foster care, she had many things to organise. She said that she had been told by Family and Children's Services that she could see her daughter over Christmas and that had been her main focus in the days leading up to her release.

> (Tell me about your visits with your daughter.)

> Well I was promised that I would have contact with my daughter over Christmas. It was to be supervised at first but I was led to believe that I would have a lot of time with her over Christmas. Someone from FACS came around and told me that the place where I was living wasn't suitable as it was near a main road ... that was the first setback. Then they told me that because it was the holiday period they couldn't provide supervision so I couldn't see my daughter over Christmas. By this time it was almost Christmas Eve and nothing could be organised and I felt awful. I had promised my daughter we could be together for some time over Christmas ... how could I face her and tell her I couldn't see her? I wanted to buy her a present and I had no money ... I felt low, depressed and couldn't face my life so I had a hit. On Christmas day I felt so depressed I wanted to die. I never got to see my daughter and I had no present for her. There was no food in the house or anything. (interview: August 1999)

At this stage, only a few days after release, Linda's life was already spiralling out of control. The formal supports that she had expected were either unavailable over the holiday period or were breaking down around her. She felt that she was unable to control any aspects of her life. The only way Linda knew how to escape from her emotional pain was to use heroin. This is what she did.

*(Okay, your supports are breaking down, it's Christmas Day and you haven't been able to see your daughter. You're feeling very low so what did you do?)*

*Everything was out of control. I was arguing with my friend and I didn't have the ability to sort anything out at all. I went out for a walk and saw a nice house with a Christmas tree and decorations and parcels and a small bike under the tree. The house was open and seemed to be empty so I went in and took the bike and a few other things for my daughter. Someone saw me and gave the police a description ... the police came around and charged me. The man whose house it was wanted to drop the charges. He sent me some things for my daughter but the police went ahead with the charges anyway. This was my third charge of this type so I sort of knew I'd come back in (to prison). It's mandatory sentencing and the judge doesn't really have a choice.*

*(Did you go back to prison immediately?)*

*No. My boyfriend went surety for me so I was out on bail until I was picked up in January.* (interview: August 1999)

Linda described the period of time between being charged and sentenced as terrible. She knew that she was going back to prison but she hid this fact from Family and Children Services because her supervised visits with her child had commenced after the holiday period and she told me, *"I was scared in case they stopped me seeing my daughter"* (interview: August 1999). Fear of being kept apart from her daughter exacerbated Linda's problem. If a scheduled visit with her daughter coincided with the reporting conditions of her bail then she would visit with her daughter and breach bail conditions. This resulted in a bench warrant being issued for Linda's arrest and she was eventually picked up by police and taken back to Bandyup Prison.

Linda spoke about her drug use on the outside. She said, *"I started using occasionally when I couldn't face not seeing my daughter over Christmas ... I hoped it would kill the pain but it didn't. I felt as though I'd let everyone down, especially my daughter ... I failed her. I failed everybody"* (interview: August 1999). Linda said that she felt like a loser. I asked her if she thought that the prison authorities could have better prepared her for life on the outside. Linda said:

*I think they should have but I don't think they could have. I think they want to justify their own existence by ensuring you come back. Several officers told me I'd be back. 'We'll see you in a couple of weeks'. More or less setting you up to fail. The system sucks. It turns you into this robotic being who can't think for themselves. Who just exists every day by being told when to eat, when to sleep, when to be punished and then lets you out into a world where you no longer fit ... I need outside help. I need counselling, not just for drug use but for life coping skills. I need help to make me feel good about myself because I feel like a total failure. Here I am 31 years old and this is my life. In and out of prison ... maybe I feel as though I don't belong out there. I don't know ... I can feel myself retreating into a black hole.* (interview: August 1999)

Although Linda had several supports organised in the community they were, in the main, with a boyfriend and friends with whom she had previously shared drugs. Her situation was all the more strained by the circumstances surrounding her small daughter in foster care and the compulsory conditions with which she had to comply in order to access supervised visits. She said that she did not have the ability to confront or even deal with bureaucracies such as Family and Children's Services and that she simply accepted their decisions without question. She put it this way: *"I could have done with some practical help like someone to support me when I needed to confront FACS to have my daughter at the unit. I had no ability to be assertive with them. I just accepted what they said and hated myself for it ... I needed someone to help me help myself"* (interview: August 1999).

Linda was sentenced to a mandatory one year prison term for stealing the toys for her daughter. She was eligible for parole after four months but, because she accumulated several prison charges, she eventually served her sentence in full. Once again, she spent much of her prison term *"down the back"* in the punishment area. She was also clinically depressed for much of her sentence. When she was not on punishment regime, Linda had regular visits with her daughter. At the completion of her sentence, Linda, a heroin addict, was once again released into the community with no help to fight her addiction. She re-offended to feed her heroin habit and was sent back to prison for four years. She lost her Ministry of Housing home and all her possessions when she went to prison. During this prison term, Linda had another baby who was taken from her at birth and made a ward of the State. At the time of writing she is nearing release, has been drug free for an extended period of time, has completed an intensive parenting program and has regained conditional custody of her two children. This time around Linda is much more optimistic about her prospects for successful reintegration into the community (personal conversation: January 2006).

## Judy

Judy spent three years in prison. When she spoke of her release from Bandyup women's prison she said, *"It felt great walking out the gate here. I was hugging the kids and we were laughing ... it felt great. It also felt strange ... I half expected a screw to step out in front of me and bring me back. That feeling stayed with me for a few weeks"* (interview: June 1999). Judy remained out of prison for several months before she breached parole conditions and was returned to Bandyup to complete her sentence.

The fears that Judy expressed immediately before her release proved to be real obstacles to her successful reintegration to the community. Initially things appeared to be going fairly smoothly. Judy moved in with her mother and her children and she said her only problem then was:

> *Sometimes the kids played up for me ... they were used to mum being in charge and they'd ignore me ... well I'd been away for three years and I felt bad that their memories of me as their mum were so bad. I was giving in to them all the time and mum would chip me for it. That'd piss me off and then I'd argue with me mum ... I spent a lot of time feeling guilty about one thing or another.*
> (interview: June 1999)

Nonetheless, the first few weeks of freedom were relatively pleasant for Judy. She remembered that *"mum took me out and bought me some new clothes and I had my hair cut and blow dried ... all of that felt good"* (interview: June 1999). Then Judy's husband's family made contact with her and some family arguments ensued. On several occasions her brother-in-law arrived at her mother's house drunk and abusive. Judy tried to find her own accommodation with the Ministry of Housing but, because of an old debt, was turned away. She said, *"They wouldn't even give me bond assistance to get a private rental ... anyway, I started to feel like a fucking failure again and I didn't know what to do or where to go. Mum was always on about being worried ... the whole thing started to crumble around me"* (interview: June 1999).

Some months after her release, Judy started sleeping at a friend's place. As she felt that her children were better off at their grandmother's, she left them there. At this point, she had remained sober and complied with her parole reporting conditions which included regular urine tests. She explained how she was returned to prison:

*All this time I'm reporting to me parole officer and doing urines. All these weeks I've not had any grog ... when things started going downhill I started thinking I'd like a drink, but I never did, not while I was at mum's ... then I felt I had to move out of her place with all the bother from his family ... so I started sleeping at me friend's and his brother came around and started abusing me, calling me a slut and he hit me ... then one night I got drunk and there was a fight out the front and I passed out ... the police came and I got arrested with some others and they breached me and I'm back in here.* (interview: June 1999)

Judy said that she still had some hope for the future because she had stayed sober all the time she lived with her mother. She recognised that she needed help to deal with issues relating to her husband's family. She explained that she has family obligations to him because he is the father of her children and that such family obligations run deep within Aboriginal culture. She put it this way:

*Grog is the problem for most of my husband's family and there's a lot of family violence. It's the normal way of life for them. My family has a past history of violence too but my mum broke away and went to the church ... Aboriginal people, we've got a whole history of being hurt by white authority and compared to that even a violent family life is the one you'd pick. It's hard to explain to a white person.* (interview: June 1999)

On balance, Judy felt that the months she had stayed out of prison had been a positive part of her life. She said that she felt bad about letting her children down again but that on good days she could still feel some direction in her life. However, she added, *"I can't take the knocks ... on bad days I just get into those black moods and feel like I'm no good to anyone and everyone would be better off if I was dead. Sometimes it's just like there's no place for me out there. I'm not sure where I belong. Maybe I belong in here"* (interview: June 1999).

## John

John's follow up interview took place in Casuarina prison. When John was released from custody after an 11 year prison term he remained free for only 10 days. The worst of his anxieties and fears about being out in the community were realised and he told me that, out there, he felt like an alien. He described his feelings on being returned to prison:

*Once I got back to Casuarina (prison) it was like someone had lifted a huge weight off my head and all the tension just went ... I was back in my security blanket. I was back in the one place I felt secure.*

*(Was it specifically Casuarina prison that made you feel secure or was it simply prison?)*

*It was simply prison, any prison.* (interview: December 1998)

To date, John has spent more than 30 years in prison; this constitutes nearly all his adult life. He has no other home.

Although John was hopeful that he might succeed in establishing himself in the community, from day one he experienced extreme difficulties. I asked him if he could give me some indication of how long he had been out before he knew he was not coping. He described his state of mind upon release in these terms:

> *My emotional stability was negative ... I think the main contributing factor to my re-offending and coming back in was that I was so tied to the system, my mind was so conditioned to regimental routine. When I got out of the system I was like a duck out of water ... that's what happens with a person who's been in jail for 10 to 15 years ... It's like putting a person in a box and sealing them up tight as you can for 10 years. The person gets quite comfortable in that box, right, and after a period of time they just shut off. They just close down like a machine that's got certain parts missing. That's what jail is, they just shut down certain parts ... Your emotions go sort of in stand by mode ... my emotions completely shut off in here. I think when I got out I was still in that mode. I had been conditioned.* (interview: December 1998)

Hampton (1993: xvii) describes "emotional shutdown" in this way:

> Emotional withdrawal and cynicism are survival tools in the prison system, used in dealing with the bureaucracy, other inmates and even family members. Being released doesn't guarantee the resurfacing of emotional vulnerability, either at the time or even years later. The revival of emotions is a longish process if it occurs at all.

John committed the offences which resulted in his return to prison in full view of bank security cameras without benefit of disguise and used a modus operandi that was specific to him and would have been readily identifiable to police. The first of these offences was committed four days after his release. I asked John if he had offended in order to return to prison. He said, *"[b]asically, yes ... there's no other reason. I duplicated everything, even to the extent that I left a trail of evidence so wide they could have followed it with a bulldozer. It was so obvious. I even used an outfit that I'd used more than 10 years ago. I used the same method that I'd used before"* (interview: December 1998).

I also asked John about the things he did and how he felt in the days before he was rearrested. He spoke of going to places such as Sci-Tech and the Omni Theatre but said, *"I felt like I was just sight seeing. I was just like a tourist ... I knew I wasn't adequately coping. I found difficulty handling money. I hadn't seen actual currency for 10 or 12 years. It was mind-boggling"* (interview: December 1998). John also said he found it impossible to communicate with people.

> *I was like a severely mentally retarded person. Mumble, mumble, mumble. I practically had to write all my communication down. That's how bad I was. The only time I could really talk clearly was when I went into the bank and the teller was standing behind one of these screens and it felt like a visit in prison ... as soon as I saw that grille I could speak okay but I went to buy cigarettes from a kiosk and because there was no grille I was like an idiot and had to point to what I wanted ... it was very embarrassing, standing there and stammering like an idiot ... I remember I felt like crawling under a paving stone at the end of the first day out.* (interview: December 1998)

John told me that the hostel where he was staying was in itself a problem as it was an alcoholic rehabilitation centre, and when he arrived there from prison:

> *[M]ost of the residents were drunk so I immediately had flashbacks of my alcoholic father. So right from the start I had the heeby jeebies and that wasn't my idea of a safe place at all ... from the start I was virtually in a tunnel ... I couldn't find up, down, sideways or anything so for the week or so that I was out I walked around in total confusion and disbelief.* (interview: December 1998)

It was evident that during John's 10 days out in the community he had no contact with anyone who could offer him formal or informal support. Although he had a pre-arranged meeting with a "mentor" from a church group this meeting never took place. He explained what happened:

> *Due to circumstances beyond my control the meeting never eventuated and the magnetic effect of the institution just took over. Because when I committed the first armed robbery I was actually on my way to meet these people ... but, as I said, once that magnetic influence of the system gets hold of you it's very hard to resist.* (interview: December 1998)

John is currently in prison.

## Simon

I was unable to locate Simon after his release. However, I was able to ascertain that he was returned to prison within a year for parole breaches.

## David

David was released at the end of a finite sentence. He was picked up outside the prison gates by a member of a prisoner's advocacy organisation with whom he was going to stay for two days until he flew home to Melbourne to go and live with his family. His mother had booked his flight and paid for his air ticket. As far as David was concerned, his sentence was finished and he owed no prison time.

Immediately upon his release he was taken to Centrelink to register, did some banking and shopping and was shown how to use the train and the bus. He then participated in some low key recreational activity with the family he was staying with. He also made phone calls to his mother and sister in Melbourne to finalise homecoming plans. Later that evening, about 12 hours after his release, a Salvation Army Chaplain who had regular contact with David in prison arrived to take him out for coffee. Within several minutes of leaving the house, David was arrested at gunpoint in the chaplain's car.

According to David's account, the arrest was particularly dramatic in nature. Two or three police cars with lights and sirens forced the Salvation Army Chaplain's car over to the side of the road, and several armed police officers then forced both David and the chaplain out of the car at gunpoint. The elderly chaplain, who was severely traumatised, was subsequently allowed to leave the scene in his car and David was taken to the police lockup (personal conversation: Salvation Army Chaplain, September 1998). The arrest occurred because of an outstanding warrant for David from a juvenile offence in Victoria some 10 years before, with the West Australian police behaving as they did because they had been informed that David was "violent, psychopathic, manipulative and dangerous" (personal conversation: arresting officer in charge, September 1998).

David spent several days in the austere conditions in the police lockup while his extradition to Victoria was arranged. He subsequently spent several more days in the lockup while the police negotiated with the airlines who were, by then, reluctant to fly David back to Victoria. He was eventually transported in handcuffs and under police escort to Melbourne where he appeared in court. The breach of the juvenile custodial parole order from ten years prior was dismissed, the court apologised to David for the inconvenience and he was released to go home with his mother (personal conversation: prisoners' advocate who was present in the court). David remained free in the Victorian community for three months before returning to Western Australia where he re-offended and was returned to prison.

David explained how he felt about life out of prison: *"It felt good at first, being home with my mum and my sister ... getting to know them again, that sort of thing ... my sister even introduced me to some of her girlfriends and my mum got me some casual work but it's not easy to adjust and my mum was always checking up on me"* (interview: January 1999). He said that the lack of structure and routine in his life on the outside was disconcerting, and mentioned that he felt a need to search for something familiar. I asked about his social life and how he handled meeting new people. He answered this way:

> *My sister introduced me to her friends and took me to parties and other social gatherings ... everyone tried to make me feel part of the group but I had difficulty feeling like I belonged there. There seemed to be no place where I felt at ease. I more or less felt like an outsider ... I even met a woman and tried to start a relationship but, truth is, I had difficulty equating sex with tenderness and it just didn't work ... so I started going to the old haunts, seeing the old familiar faces and I was pointing myself in the direction of doing crime again. My mum was worrying about me and trying to control my movements and we were arguing so I decided I needed help and came back to Perth.* (interview: January 1999)

I asked David at what stage he started using heroin again. He said:

> *Well I never really stopped. That's a marriage made in heaven ... the only thing is I didn't have to do crime to get it this time ... then I came back to Perth to try and straighten myself out, got involved in an old relationship with an old mate from prison, the drug use got out of hand, I got violent, and here I am, locked up again.* (interview: January 1999)

David also said that he *"sort of linked up with a few non (heroin) users"* through his sister but added that *"they bored me. They basically bored me ... I didn't necessarily feel as though I fitted in"* (interview: January 1999).

David maintained that, beginning with his unnecessary arrest just after his release, things just went wrong. He told me that he felt everything was against him and that there was almost an inevitability that he would end up back in prison. He said, *"[a]fter all, if you remember, the screws at Casuarina were making bets on how many days I'd be out. Well I stayed out three months or more and none of them gave me those odds"* (interview: January 1999). David was released after the subsequent conviction but re-offended yet again whilst on parole and is currently serving an indeterminate prison sentence.

## Albert

Albert was one of the few participants who expressed optimism regarding his pending release. He had served more than 10 years of an indeterminate sentence at the Governor's Pleasure and had already participated in intensive pre-release programs as part of his release conditions. He told me that he had sound employment prospects on the outside, a driving licence, had a place to live with established informal family supports, and had already purchased a car. In the days leading up to his release, he felt that he was most unlikely to re-offend or breach his parole conditions and be returned to prison. However, through no fault of his own and after only a few weeks in the community, Albert was arrested and returned to prison. His follow up interview took place in Casuarina maximum security prison during the ongoing lockdown conditions subsequent to the 1998 Christmas Day riot.

Albert had been out in the community on work release and parole conditions. This meant that he had to adhere to a strict reporting regime with his Community Based Service Officer and he also had to submit to random urine tests. Because of this, he had found casual part time employment with a friend so that he could easily comply with his parole conditions. On the day of his arrest Albert was at home. He explained what happened:

> *I was sitting at home watching TV when several detectives banged on my door with a search warrant and said they were arresting me for an armed robbery. You get to know the score and you don't resist but I had no idea what they were talking about and tried to tell them that, but they cuffed me and took me to the police station anyway ... I was a known armed robber out in the community so they came straight to me.*

> *(At the time of your arrest did you feel that this would get sorted out right away at the police station?)*

> *I suppose so. I certainly didn't think I'd be brought back to prison. I knew I hadn't done what they said ... How it happened was like this; my partner, Alice, was at a local shopping centre having a coffee with a friend at one of those cafes in the mall when the cops went by with two young blokes cuffed. They'd just been arrested and they recognised Alice from visits at Casa and one of them shouted to her 'tell ... (Albert's nickname) we've been done for ...'*

*whatever it was they'd done. Well the cops recognised my name,*
*assumed I was part of the deal and came to my house and arrested*
*me ... Six weeks down the track I'm still here (in Casuarina prison)*
*and I'm pretty well pissed off.* (interview: September 1999)

Albert spent a total of seven weeks in custody on remand in Casuarina
prison, under conditions of 23 hours per day lockdown, before he was
finally released. On his account, he was cleared of involvement in the
crime within two weeks of his arrest but it took a further five weeks to
achieve his release.

Albert was angry both at the police for arresting him and at the
prison authorities for taking several weeks to effect his release. He felt
quite clearly that he had been wrongfully arrested and spoke of the
effect of being held in custody under these circumstances. He put it
this way:

*I can't fucking win ... I was going real well when this happened*
*and it's knocked me back like you wouldn't believe ... I've lost me*
*job, it's affected my relationship ... my confidence is up to fuck*
*now. I'm never going to be sure when this might happen again ...*
*it's fucked. I've done time and now I'm marked for any armed*
*robbery that goes down.* (interview: September 1999)

In this, he echoes Bianchi's view that: "the 'criminal' stigma is always
a social life sentence" (Bianchi cited in Duff and Garland 1994: 338).
Similarly, Albert found it difficult to get employment when he was
released again and both he and his partner suffered financial and emotional trauma as a result. They spent his first Christmas out of prison
*"on the bones of our arse and we couldn't even afford Chicken Treat*
*... we ate bread and marge because that's all we had"* (interview: July
2001).

Albert's troubles continued. Over the next two years he found
several jobs but lost them when his employers found out he had served
time in prison. And, while he remained crime free and drug free, he
was once again arrested and taken into custody almost two years after
his original release from prison. On this occasion, it was two officers
from the Department of Immigration who arrested him. He described
what happened:

*Alice and I were at home in the afternoon and there was a bang on*
*the door. When Alice answered the door there were two*
*immigration officers and about eight police officers standing there*
*... they asked to speak to me and one of the immigration officers*
*said words to the effect of 'as of now you have no more legal rights*
*in Australia. We're taking you into custody and you're being*
*deported'. Well, Alice grabbed hold of me and started screaming,*

125

*the officers threw both of us to the floor, cuffed me and dragged me
off to the car with Alice still hanging off me crying. I had no bloody
idea what was going on. She was hysterical and they just took me
away without any other explanation.* (interview: July 2001)

[Albert's position with regard to the deportation order merits a brief
explanation. Albert's British born parents brought him to Australia
more than 40 years ago in 1963 when he was a small child of four
years. He claims that he cannot remember anything about Britain and
he has no family or friends there. As is the case with many British
migrants of that era, Albert's family felt no need to obtain Australian
citizenship for themselves or their children. Although the family eventually did apply for Australian citizenship, by that time, Albert was in
prison and had missed his opportunity. After spending 10 years in
prison, Albert was flagged by the Department of Immigration as "a
person of bad character" and was earmarked for deportation to Britain.]

During the interview, Albert spoke of his feeling about awaiting
deportation to a country which was foreign to him, where he had no
family supports and where he feared he would be more or less desti-
tute:

> *This situation has blown my mind ... I feel Australian ... Australia
> is the only home I remember. My entire life is here ... my wife is
> Australian, I have two Australian step-children, five Australian
> nieces and nephews, my young brother was born in Australia and
> my parents are Australian citizens ... This place is all I've ever
> known ... If I was back in prison at least I'd have some contact
> with my family ... if they deport me I'm fucked. I'll have nothing
> and no one.* (interview: July 2001)

Albert felt that he had paid the penalty for his crimes and that,
although he had fought hard to overcome his heroin addiction and
become a responsible citizen, he was given no credit for his efforts. He
believed that he had been targeted and harassed by the authorities since
his release from prison, and questioned whether he had any meaningful
future anywhere: *"I'm not sure what I've got to do to prove that I'm
doing the right thing ... it all seems pointless now, all the hard work ...
when they tell you that you don't belong in your own country. I don't
belong in England either so where do I belong?"* (interview: July
2001).

Albert was eventually released from custody and is living at home
with his partner. He spent an additional four months on remand in prison because of the immigration issue and had to fight a lengthy legal
battle against his deportation. Unsurprisingly, Albert is deeply pessi-

mistic regarding his future prospects, feeling that he is now forever defined by his term of imprisonment and persona as prisoner.

In conclusion, 10 of the 11 participants have been returned to prison at some point. This indicates the failure of the prevailing prison system to prepare prisoners for life in the wider community. The inability of the majority of the participants to "recapture freedom" is continually revealed in their reflections that they *"don't belong out there"*, *"don't fit in"*, *"feel like an alien"* or, *"don't know where I belong"* (participant interviews: 1998-2002). John's description of how he felt during his few days of freedom encapsulates these feelings of alienation in the wider community. *"When I got out, I felt like ET. I wanted to phone home"* (interview: December 1998).

The failure of the majority of the participants to "recapture freedom" is based on a combination of:

1. In some instances, a return to social networks – friends or family – in which old behaviours such as alcohol and substance abuse and the use of violence are more likely.

2. Perhaps even more important, the existence of 'prisons in the mind'. This is exemplified in a number of ways:

   (a) missing the security, routines, familiarity, being known and/or "being somebody" in prison.

   (b) taking from the prison certain codes of behaviour which are likely to count as "offences" in the community. This could be resorting to the use of violence when angry or threatened.

   (c) having a fear of "bonds" or "constraints" – and a notion of freedom that is based on "no-constraint" that means an ex-prisoner is often intolerant of the normal social "bonds" (family ties – mother/partner etc) which hold people together. This exemplifies in the desire to "break loose". It is interesting to note that this exists *together with* the previous factor (b) in a paradoxical relationship that points back to prison.

# Chapter 6

# Reflections, Recommendations, Radical Change

> Representatives and managers of the criminal law system cherish the pretension that their organisation could protect society from such a dangerous threat as criminality. In fact ... the organisation, since it was established in its present form about the end of the 18th century, has, in every respect and on all counts, failed to accomplish what it promises. Quite the reverse. For a long time the criminal law organisation has been escalating dangerously. Any enhancement of the punishing power of the organisation has so far led to more rather than less criminality. (Bianchi cited in Duff and Garland 1994: 336)

This chapter reflects on the negative impact of imprisonment on both individuals and community, revisiting the issues of harm, violence and brutality inherent in current prison systems. It looks once again at the consequences of these factors on the individual participants as they try to reintegrate as free citizens into the wider community.

This chapter needs to do more than identify what is wrong. So, drawing on the participants' suggestions and my own ideas, I use it to propose initiatives which might ease the transition from prisoner to responsible citizen. These proposals are set against the prison system as it currently stands. However, I believe that unless prisons themselves are radically reformed, these proposals will be band-aid solutions at best. My fundamental and more far-reaching argument is that prisons must undergo sweeping philosophical change if they are to function as places of rehabilitation and correction. With that in mind, the final part of the chapter explores the concept of the restorative and transformative prison as a viable and acceptable alternative to current retributive prison systems. The establishment of restorative and transformative prisons would involve a radical theoretical change, starting with a commitment to transparency and accountability within prison systems which currently, and by their very nature, negate the involvement of community and active victim participation in prisoner rehabilitation.

## Reflections: retribution, brutalisation and the reproduction of criminality

> The prison cannot fail to produce delinquents. It does so by the very type of existence that it imposes on its inmates: whether they are isolated in cells or whether they are given useless work ... The prison also produces delinquents by imposing violent constraints on its inmates; it is supposed to apply the law, and to teach respect for it; but all its functioning operates in the form of an abuse of power ... The prison makes possible, even encourages, the organization of a milieu of delinquents, loyal to one another, hierarchised, ready to aid and abet any future criminal act ... Lastly, the prison indirectly produces delinquents by throwing the inmate's family into destitution. (Foucault 1977: 266-267)

One of the recurring themes of this book is the counterproductive, harmful and brutalising nature of imprisonment. As Aungles (1994: 185) writes, "in countries that are not at war the legal-penal sphere is the only site in which rational morality can be legitimately expressed as the physical coercion of one group of men over another". Prisons, by their nature, their hierarchical organisation and their architecture, are the embodiment of secrecy, invisibility, isolation, and lack of accountability. These factors encourage, rather than discourage, coercion, brutality and violence amongst prisoners and prison staff. One of the consequences of this is that imprisonment, as it is presently constituted, does not prepare inmates for productive and pro-social living in the wider community. Mace (2000: 2) suggests that:

> There is a real risk that people will emerge from prison feeling numb, dispirited and fatalistic rather than to any degree reformed or better equipped to lead a law abiding life when they return to the community. There is also a danger that when released they will lack a network of links with the community which might be helpful in bridging the distance between institutional life and the challenge of resuming a law abiding life outside prison walls.

There are other, more mundane, reasons why the present prison system releases prisoners ill prepared to cope with everyday life in the wider community. Most long term prisoners, even those who still have some family supports in place, do not know where they fit or where they belong in their families and/or in society. Their lives have been so rigorously regimented and restricted for many years within the prison environment that their ability to cope with extended physical and social space, choices, and personal responsibility is severely diminished. In addition, their ability to solve everyday difficulties and deal with adversity in socially acceptable ways is often severely eroded. This can manifest itself in parole breaches such as missed or late appointments, dirty urine tests and/or re-offending. The result is usually return to prison orders or new criminal charges which, within the context of this book, accounted for the return to custody of almost all of the participants. As Coyle (2001c: 7) argues, "it is naïve of us to assume that by excluding large numbers of people from our society behind the high walls of a prison for a specified period of time we will somehow turn them into better citizens".

Beau's experience clearly illustrates the general inability amongst most of the participants to deal with adverse situations when they are trying to establish themselves out in the community:

> *It was pretty fucked out there from day one ... If I had a place of my own to live, even a flat, where I didn't have to feel obligated and grateful ... If I could've had some transport to get to my parole officer and drug counsellor more easily ... everything was just too hard to organise and there was no leeway given. I mean if I missed one appointment I was threatened with a breach, then if I was late for another that was something else to get me further in the shit ... In the end it just seemed pointless trying ... At first I felt useless then I got angry at the whole system ... I was fucking up and jail was beckoning.* (interview: November 1999)

John said that he could not resist the pull of the system as a familiar environment and comfort zone. He described his feelings of alienation in the few days he was out in the community:

> *I went out and about and I knew I was functioning but I didn't feel as though I was functioning. My body was working and my brain was working but nothing was connected. I was walking around in a virtual dream state. Nothing was real. It was like a bad dream ... and by the time I re-offended I was under such stress that when they (the police) were questioning me I had another heart attack.* (interview: December 1998)

John feels that he is locked into the prison system and knows no other place or way to be. He put it this way: *"I know the system so well. I'm part of the system and the system's part of me. Nothing changes in the system. Where else could I go?"* (interview: December 1998).

Mark, who has successfully reintegrated into the community, also experienced some initial difficulties with his transition from prison life. He said, *"[l]ook, it was really hard at first. Making the first move and joining Parents Without Partners was really scary but I had to find other people who were lonely like me. The job was the easy bit ... that, and I had enough money to buy a car so I could get around easily"* (interview: January 1999).

David also described the positive aspects of being out of prison but acknowledged that, even on good days, anxiety and a general inability to cope caused him to question his ability to stay free. He said:

> *Being out was very different from prison. I did some normal things. I went for a walk on the beach and I went to the shop for milk, things like that ... Having a choice made it different ... but there were issues that developed that caused me to recognise some signs that I was getting into the whole high risk situation again. That I was going to end up in prison sooner rather than later ... I was into heroin and getting into guns and I knew I had to do something drastic to keep out of prison. I was beginning to spiral out of control again.* (interview: November 1998)

Linda's ability to cope out in the community was extremely precarious when I first interviewed her. She had received no treatment for her drug use while inside during her first three prison terms and had left prison as an entrenched heroin user although she said she had been clean for several weeks. She described how she felt in the few weeks she was out of prison:

> *I just felt like one of these people who are losers. I expected to fail ... when something goes wrong I just seem to fall down and stay there.*
>
> *(Do you feel that if you had more supports you may have made it?)*
>
> *The few times I can think rationally I do. I think if I felt better about myself, if I had clothes that looked okay, if I hadn't got out so close to Christmas, if I could have had my daughter, if I could have got on the Naltrexone program – all that and some counselling then maybe I could have had a chance. But they weren't there and I didn't cope and here I am back here and doing it very hard this time ... really, I knew my situation was hopeless. There were too many things going against me. Too many things I couldn't overcome ... I just didn't cope with anything.* (interview: August 1999)

Although Linda went to live with her long term boyfriend when she left prison she said that their lifestyle had never been family oriented and added, *"[o]ur relationship has included things like us using together and that's a habit in itself ... when things started to go wrong and I was depressed, my friends offered me a hit ... that's the only way they knew how to help me. That was to try and kill the pain"* (interview: August 1999).

In addition, many long term prisoners lose touch with their families and other support networks during their sentences. Most of these priso-

131

ners face the prospect of a lonely and isolated existence when they are released into the community.

> Their lives are often defined by exclusion and ineffectiveness which, upon release, can manifest in their inability to cope with the series of demands imposed by parole and other statutory reporting requirements, and an inability to relate effectively with others. (Goulding 2004: 53)

Often, their only alternative to social isolation is to contact peers whom they associated with in prison. Associating closely with other ex-prisoners is considered to be of high risk and is likely to lead to previous offending behaviour patterns. The prisoner consultant faced this situation when he was initially released on home leaves. In theory, home leaves are designed to be part of the re-socialisation process for long term prisoners. The prisoner consultant had spent 15 years in custody and all his friends and acquaintances on the outside were ex-prisoners. He described the nature of his home leaves in this way:

> *Everyone I knew in WA were either crims or ex crims. Also, I've never known a real family life so I went out to my mates and my number one priority was sex ... I didn't want a relationship – a woman I had to talk to and take for a meal and all that stuff. I just wanted sex, so I did the round of the brothels and just got laid. That's how I spent my home leaves ... No re-socialisation, nothing that would help me on my release ... they (prison authorities) didn't check up when I said I'd be visiting restaurants and art galleries and the like ... I spent every home leave in brothels ... With hindsight and being realistic, I know I should've tried to make some attempt to re-socialise myself but after all that time inside I had neither the will nor the ability to know how to.* (interview: August 1999)

Consequently, in general terms the participants found the transition from prisoner to free citizen, at best, difficult and, at worst, impossible to deal with. The first few days out in the community are fraught with difficulties for ex-prisoners who have been stripped of the appropriate social skills for life outside of prison. In other words, the framework within which their constructed identity as prisoners was formed, has now been removed and the results, as depicted in this study, are often catastrophic. As Taylor claims:

> They would be at sea, as it were; they wouldn't know anymore, for an important range of questions, what the significance of things was for them ... and this situation does arise for some people ... an 'identity crisis', an acute form of disorientation, which people often express in terms of not knowing who they are ... they lack a

frame or horizon ... this is a painful and frightening experience. (1990: 27-28)

What we see, then, are the fundamentally perverse workings of a system which deliberately and systematically strips individuals of their social identity in order to institutionalise them into manageable prisoners and, which, just as systematically, ignores the need to re-skill and re-communalise those same individuals as they prepare to re-enter the community.

## Recommendations for practical change: the here and now

I now turn to measures which could ease the transition from prisoner to free citizen. For the moment, I place the need for fundamental reform to the prison system *per se* on hold, but will return to it shortly.

### The halfway house

The participants identified a number of measures they felt crucial in assisting them to negotiate the prison to community transition successfully. These were the *immediate* availability of reasonable, low cost accommodation for those who needed it, sufficient funds to buy food and pay for other essentials such as rent, power and clothes, and readily available information regarding informal and formal supports in the community. Over and above these measures, a top priority was support to ease the cultural transition, to reduce the difference between prison life and community life. To this end, several of the participants raised the notion of some form of halfway house.

Halfway houses may be seen as places which effectively bridge the cultural gap between the world of the prison and the wider community, where prisoners could spend the last few months of their sentences in an effort to both deinstitutionalise and re-communalise. Such dwellings would be placed throughout the community and be readily available to all prisoners due for release. It is envisaged that such halfway houses would be secure and have round the clock supervision. Intensive supervision would help in addressing community safety concerns and would also assist prisoners through constantly available counselling services.

Those participants who mentioned the concept of a halfway house were adamant that this should be incorporated into their sentence plans and should not be in addition to their sentences. Beau outlined what he felt might serve as an appropriate bridge between imprisonment and freedom:

133

*Look, I wouldn't want to be released at the end of my sentence to a supervised house, but if it were part of my sentence it would be beaut. I envisage a dwelling, secure like a women's refuge, where there is round the clock supervision, where blokes due for release might spend the last few months of their sentence. They could spend time under supervision in the community, perhaps with work commitments and strict curfews. That would have the effect of reducing the culture shock that happens when, like me, you get released from maximum security jails.* (interview: November 1999)

John also supported the idea of a halfway house and felt that, for prisoners like himself who had spent a large proportion of their lives in custodial settings, some form of supervised housing out in the community would provide a safety zone in which an effective transition to community living could be supported. He said:

*I feel as though for me to be adequately equipped for preparation for the outside world after such a long time in maximum security jails they should start my transition at least a year before they release me. Because there's no way you can put a person through a six week course after they've done most of their adult lives in an institution and think they'll be okay ... If I could've felt safe, say in a secure house with other people like myself where I could be accompanied out into the community and maybe retrained in how to act out there, how to approach different people in shops, doctors, public transport and so on. I mean to say, just handling money scared the living daylights out of me ... If there were places like that then people like me might stand a chance.* (interview: December 1998)

Dick, too, suggested, *"as part of the sentence we should spend time under supervision out in the community in a place where we can have more contact with ordinary people. Maybe a halfway house where we can have proper family visits. Okay, we'd be under curfew and possibly locked in at night, but it's like one step at a time"* (interview: November 2000).

Judy's proposal was more far-reaching. She suggested that women prisoners who presented little or no threat to the community should serve their entire custodial terms in *"secure houses in the suburbs where they can have much more access to their kids. Where they can get skills like budgeting and parenting and maybe get access to education so they can survive out there in the real world, get jobs, and feel good about themselves"* (interview: June 1999).

The idea of halfway houses is not new. Several of the older participants mentioned that there were such places in existence within the Perth metropolitan area in the 1970s. At this time there is no legislation in place which would permit the use of secure houses for prisoners out in the community, but the use of s 94 of the *Prisons Act 1981* (WA) could be extended to enable their immediate establishment and use. Indeed, the work camp initiative of 1995 was supported by an extension of the existing powers under s 94 of the *Prisons Act*. Section 94 allows prisoners to obtain permission to leave a prison to take part in an activity program approved by the Minister for Corrective Services. The activities detailed in s 94 are: community work, charitable work or voluntary work associated with the operation of the prison, sport, religious observation or any other approved activity. All programs need ministerial approval and run for a six-month period with the possibility of six monthly extensions (personal conversation: Robert Stacey, Office of the Inspector of Custodial Services, December 2001). Such initiatives could be adapted for halfway houses, which would suit long term prisoners who are to be released within the Perth metropolitan area. Alternatively, legislation specifically for the establishment of secure halfway houses out in the community could be introduced.

Success for halfway house measures have been claimed by Prison and Outreach Ministries, a Uniting Church in Australia, volunteer based organisation. This community organisation runs a mentoring scheme with halfway house type accommodation for serious sex offenders who have completed sex offender treatment program requirements in prison. Volunteers from the organisation visit relevant prisoners for at least six months before their release. These volunteers establish stable and supportive relationships with prisoners. Low cost, supervised accommodation is also provided for at least six months after release. This scheme has been successful in terms of resettlement of prisoners into the community and has continuously, over many years, maintained a very low recidivism rate (personal conversation: Prison and Outreach Ministries volunteer, December 2001).

In sum, my suggestion is that supervised accommodation such as this could be introduced as part of an end of sentence strategy to reduce the degree of institutionalisation in all long term prisoners, thus easing the transition from prison to community. Because deinstitutionalisation cannot occur within a prison, the use of halfway houses in the community would be a major step forward for long term prisoners in particular who need intensive assistance and supervision with structured program content which can be lessened gradually as appropriate social skills are reclaimed. Halfway houses could also provide a safety zone for all newly released prisoners and relapse prevention strategies for those who have minor setbacks.

## Post-release support

Prisoners who are released to home leave, work release or parole conditions are, it is true, monitored by the authorities. However this is more to ensure compliance with release conditions and program requirements, less than to make certain, as far as possible, that they have the practical necessities and necessary skills to live in a law abiding and pro-social manner in the community. In addition, the prison authorities relinquish responsibility for prisoners who are released at the end of a finite sentence (those not released to parole or work release conditions) as soon as these prisoners exit the prison.

The over-riding problem facing most newly released prisoners is poverty. Currently, most prisoners are released into the community without even the basic material necessities of life. The participants identified the absolute minimum material requirements to survive in the community as:

- Somewhere affordable and reasonable to live immediately upon release.
- Sufficient money upon release for rent, rental bond and food.
- Adequate and reasonably smart clothing of the appropriate size, which is suitable for the climatic conditions at the time of release.
- A mentor or 'buddy' to meet those prisoners released without support networks.
- A safe place such as a dedicated "drop-in" centre for ex-prisoners, which could supply information on available community supports.

All of these requirements are necessary for a reasonable quality of life, but the need for shelter dominates all. The harsh reality is that there is an acute shortage of emergency accommodation in the Perth metropolitan area and newly released prisoners do not receive priority for housing. At the time of writing, the Ministry of Housing does not have emergency accommodation available specifically for prisoners due for release and few newly released prisoners can afford rental bonds, advance rent requirements and most cannot supply references. Lack of suitable accommodation, then, is generally the most immediate problem facing prisoners upon release. There are several short term supported accommodation programs available through non-government service providers such as Outcare, Ruah Women's Support Service and Centrecare but demand for supported housing constantly outstrips supply and is subject to "tenancy time constrictions of three to six months" (Goulding 2004: 51).

The vast majority of prisoners are released from prison without secure employment arrangements in place. As unemployed persons, they are entitled to some form of unemployment payment from Centrelink. In order to obtain a Centrelink payment, prisoners must be able to produce several forms of identification. This is often difficult for long term prisoners who are most likely to lack relevant identification such as a current driver's license or Medicare card. In the past difficulties also arose in relation to prisoners receiving Centrelink payments on the day of release and many prisoners exited prison with little or no money. The participants in this study all experienced these difficulties. Consequently, many newly released prisoners had to wait up to a week even for the appointment stage of social security processing. In recognition of this problem, Centrelink has now implemented a structured process within all State prison systems to ensure that, in the vast majority of cases, prisoners receive their first payment from the prison authorities on the day of release.

However, as social security payments are paid directly into clients' bank accounts another difficulty arises because many long term prisoners have no current bank accounts and do not generally possess the necessary 100 identification points needed to open one. In addition to this, and with regard to Centrelink entitlements, Centrelink Officers have the discretion to remit emergency or hardship payments by cheque and may have an arrangement with a local bank to cash such cheques. Though, from the perspective of prisoners the process is ad hoc, problematic and frustrating, particularly as they have generally lost the skills to negotiate with official representatives of banks and/or social security offices.

Often the only identification newly released prisoners possess is the Release Form from prison which adds humiliation to all the other problems encountered. Peter spoke of this: *"It was three days before I could get in to see the social security officer and then she told me my dole would go straight into my bank account ... then I tried to open a bank account but hadn't enough ID so I had to explain where I'd been for the last nine years"* (interview: June 1998).

Beau's experience was similar:

*I went to Centrelink and had an argument with the bloke there because I couldn't get to see anyone until next day ... Then when I got to see someone I had to argue again for an emergency cheque because I had no bank account. I got that and they asked for ID at the bank to cash the cheque ... I had my Exit Prison form so they cashed it but when I went to another bank to open an account to have my unemployment payments paid into I didn't have enough*

*ID to open the account. I had no driver's license, no Medicare card, no birth certificate – nothing ... I got so angry I could've easily fucked up there and then ... they don't make it easy for you. That stuff should be sorted before you leave jail.* (interview: November 1999)

When the problem of accommodation is combined with the problem of poverty, situations of crisis proportions may arise. Even when social security payments are forthcoming, the amount of entitlements will not generally cover rent in advance, rental bond requirements, sustenance costs and power. The consequence of this is that many prisoners are released into situations that lead them immediately to high risk of re-offending through poverty. There are several possible solutions to this problem. These are first, the introduction of halfway houses which would ensure that, through the mentoring and rehabilitation process out in the community, these issues were dealt with as part of the program requirement within the progression of re-socialisation. Second, reintroduction of the enforced savings system which ensured that all prisoners within the West Australian prison system saved 10 per cent of their income or gratuities over the duration of their sentences. Previously, these savings were made available to prisoners on the day of their release as a cash payment, thus ensuring that no prisoner exited prison without some money. In the case of long term prisoners, who are more likely to be on higher rates of pay, such enforced savings would mean that they had sufficient funds to pay at least one week's rent and would effectively alleviate some degree of anxiety regarding both food and shelter.

Here it is important to note that prisoners are not paid at standard community rates. The legislative framework for prisoner wages is contained in *Prisons Regulations 1982* (WA) (see regs 44-50). In the late 1980s the Department of Corrective Services introduced a compulsory saving policy involving the deduction of 10 per cent of prisoner earned gratuity. The legislative basis for this is contained in regs 48(2) and 50. However, the rising cost of canteen purchases reduced the ability of most prisoners to save any proportion of their prison earnings. Also, the Consumer Price Index (CPI) adjustments made on such low wages did not compensate the rapidly escalating prices brought about through increased taxation on tobacco – a highly sought after product in prisons. This situation of financial hardship for prisoners was further exacerbated by the introduction of the Arunta telephone system in 1995. The new telephone system shifted the cost of calls from the Department of Corrective Services to the prisoner. It then became common practice for prisoners to seek exemption from the compulsory savings policy, which was eventually abandoned (personal conversation: Robert Stacey, Office of Custodial Services, December 2001). That notwithstanding, some adjustment to the legislative framework for prisoners' wages is called for. Such an adjustment would effectively bring payment closer to minimum community standards. This would permit the reintroduction of the compulsory savings scheme and ensure that all prisoners exited prison in receipt of enough funds for their immediate needs; a seemingly commonsense approach to attempt to reduce levels of re-offending in the first few days after release.

As indicated earlier, the availability of suitable clothing was one of the prisoner participants' main priorities. Clearly, suitable clothing is vital to an individual's feelings of self worth and confidence as he or she is about to re-enter the community. Within the West Australian prison system, prisoners who have served sentences of more than one year are entitled to a "liberty spend" to assist with the purchase of new clothing. However, four of the participants in the study mentioned that they were denied their liberty spend because they owed money to the prison. This debt was usually to pay for "dirty" urine tests.

Inadequate and inappropriate clothing was a major concern for many of the participants. At the time of the initial interviews, immediately before release, two of the participants had spent eight years in prison and three had spent more than 10 years inside. After such extended periods of time in custody, the participants' civilian clothes were ill fitting and considerably dated, thus causing feelings of concern that they would look odd or stand out. Participants wanted to blend seamlessly into the community and there was a general anxiety that, in old outdated clothes, they would stand out as "ex-crims". Linda left prison on a hot summer day in heavy winter clothes, which were out of date and several sizes too big for her, and she said that *"my skirt was held up with a piece of string and I felt like a bag of shit"* (interview: August 1999). Beau was also released from prison *"with the clothes I stood up in. I owned nothing else and wasn't entitled to a liberty spend because I owed for dirty piss tests"* (interview: November 1999). For many reasons, but most particularly to induce positive feelings of self worth in soon to be released prisoners, it is imperative that the liberty spend entitlement is not contingent on any conditions. Long term prisoners, especially, need to be able to access this prerogative without fear of denial from prison authorities because of money owed to the institution for whatever reason.

The concept of a mentor or "buddy" for long term prisoners without family or other informal support networks is also highly desirable.

Currently, some church groups and other voluntary organisations supply mentors for newly released prisoners but these arrangements are not formalised through the prison system, are ad hoc in nature and rarely meet the immediate needs of prisoners at the time of release. John's experience was a case in point. A church organisation had arranged for a volunteer to meet with him a few days after his release but his needs were more urgent. Immediately upon his release, John became panicky, and, by the time he was to attend the arranged meeting with the mentor, he had already re-offended.

The solution to this problem is that those community and church organisations which provide supportive mentoring programs to prisoners should be pre-arranged and coordinated through prison officers or community based service officers so that prisoners who need these services can rely on them immediately as they exit the prison.

## Radical change: towards the restorative and transformative prison

As indicated earlier, this chapter deals with both suggestions for improvements to the existing prison system and also with recommendations for far reaching and fundamental change to prisons *per se*. It is to this radical change that I now turn. Here, it is useful to revisit the insights of Chapter Four, which highlight the extent and nature of prison violence. There I argued that violence and brutality are endemic in prison systems. They are not isolated phenomena that flare up here and there, or now and then. During the course of the research for this book, which spans several years, all of the prisoner participants, those prisoners and ex-prisoners consulted for background information and the non-government organisations contacted, told stories which indicated that brutality and violence are everyday occurrences in most prisons in Western Australia (prisoner and ex-prisoner interviews: 1998-2001, prison chaplain interviews: 1998-2002, DICWC (WA) Report to the Committee Against Torture: November 2001). Most alarming is the claim that certain forms of brutalisation are officially sanctioned. For example, as a matter of officially sanctioned routine, it has been reported that in one regional West Australian prison all medium and maximum security prisoners must attend family visits wearing ankle chains and medical examinations handcuffed to prison staff (Harding, Inspector of Prisons: Oral report to Community Consultative Committee, September 2001).

One of the points stressed in Chapter Four was that each of the male participants spoke about the prevalence of violence in prisons even though the issue of violence was not mentioned within the research questionnaires. Further, these men spoke about extremely violent acts in a manner that suggested they were no big deal. Put simply, violence was something that had to be dealt with: something that was part and parcel of everyday life as a prisoner. This, in turn, supports Bottoms' argument "that prison culture might exhibit a perverse kind of order in which violence is the norm" (cited in Edgar, O'Donnell and Martin 2003: 6). Acceptance of violence, then, is a major feature in the makeup of the subcultural baggage that most prisoners take with them when they are released back into the community. If that factor alone does not worry those amongst us who formulate and pass relevant legislation and policy then it should. Put bluntly, as a social researcher who is also a mother, I know with certainty that if any of my children were sentenced to a term of imprisonment I would simply lose all peace of mind. I know I would be deeply concerned for their physical safety, state of mind and general wellbeing.

By and large, I have argued throughout the book that imprisonment as it is presently constituted is counterproductive and encourages, rather than discourages, the growth of criminality. Nevertheless, I do not argue here for the abolition of prisons. Nor do I argue for the elimination of punishment, because a primary aim of punishment is "to communicate to criminals a justified criticism of their crimes" (Duff and Garland 1994: preface to Bianchi, 'Abolition, Assensus and Sanctuary': 334). The concept of punishment also gives voice to social mores and principles, without which, society, as such, would be unthinkable. Integral to Durkheim's notion of social solidarity is the idea of punishment "as a straightforward embodiment of society's moral order, and an instance of how that order represents and sustains itself" (Garland 1990: 25). Put succinctly, my suggestion is that *imprisonment* as punishment should only be used as a tool of last resort for those individuals who pose a serious and immediate threat to the community.

I also contend that the process and nature of imprisonment must undergo radical change. That is, prisons:

- should not make people worse;
- should be places of safety for both prisoners and prison staff;
- must become transparent, accountable and open to government and community investigation and evaluation;
- must promote pro-social behaviour amongst those incarcerated; and this involves recognising, and working to undo, the harms to which these people, in their turn, may have been subjected;

- should be bound by human rights principles which require close attention to the health, safety and wellbeing of all people who are incarcerated;

- should include prisoner counselling and/or programs which seek to identify the underlying issues associated with the individual's offending behaviour and actively seek to challenge that behaviour; and

- should include programs and work practices which promote victim empathy, and reparation and healing for harm done to individual victims and communities.

Currently, the prison system cannot realistically claim to embody any of these principles.

## Restorative and transformative justice principles within the prison setting

> Conventionally, the criminal justice system separates the offender from the victim and the community. While this is sometimes important, if separation is all that happens, offenders can quickly distance themselves from the harm they have caused, forget it, deny it, or create elaborate justifications for why they did it, which absolves them of all responsibility ... Where the traditional justice separates the victim and the offender, restorative justice brings them together. (Newell: 2001b: 4)

The concept of restorative justice has, in recent years, attracted much attention from penal reformers, justice activists, criminologists and others within the field of criminal justice. In the first instance restorative justice presents a challenge to prevailing adversarial criminal justice systems, which are organised under the notion that crimes are perpetrated against the State rather than recognising that crimes are perpetrated, in the main, against victims and/or communities. Restorative justice is a "philosophy that moves from punishment to reconciliation, from vengeance against offenders to healing for victims, from alienation and harshness to community and wholeness, from negativity and destructiveness to healing, forgiveness and mercy" (Consedine 1995: 11). Further, restorative justice is based on the concept of re-integrative shaming which stands in stark contrast to the notion of stigmatic shaming which is prevalent within current criminal justice systems. Put simply, the re-integrative shaming process attempts to shame the action rather than the actor and encourage mutual understanding and forgiveness amongst all parties involved. Braithwaite (1989: 55) explains the concept in this way:

142

Re-integrative shaming means that expressions of community disapproval, which may range from mild rebuke to degradation ceremonies, are followed by gestures of reacceptance into the community of law-abiding citizens. These gestures of reacceptance will vary from a simple smile expressing forgiveness and love to quite formal ceremonies to decertify the offender as deviant. Disintegrative shaming (stigmatisation), in contrast, divides the community by creating a class of outcasts.

Broadly speaking, restorative justice is a process that involves active victim participation, requires offenders to take responsibility for the harm they have done and to make apology and amends to their victims. One of the basic principles of restorative justice is a willingness to restore the balance between victim, offender and community, being mindful that "in many respects the victim is badly served by our current adversarial system of criminal justice" (Coyle 2001b: 6). Restorative justice also seeks to bring all parties (victims, offenders and communities of interest) together with a view to achieving some form of reconciliation through a mutually acceptable outcome. In support of restorative justice principles, Judge McElrea claims that:

> Criminal justice has been divorced from the community for far too long. Justice has come to be seen as a contest between the state and the defendant … As a result there is little incentive for anyone to take responsibility for the offending itself or for putting right the wrong. By contrast restorative justice is essentially a community-based model that encourages the acceptance of responsibility by all concerned and draws on the strengths of community to restore peace. (cited in Bowen and Consedine 1999: 56)

My contention is that the basic principles of restorative justice could be successfully adapted for use within the prison setting; thus moving the brutalising and punitive characteristics of the current regime, as outlined in this text, towards a more reparative and healing approach. This would be to the benefit of victims and communities as well as prisoners. However, simply restoring harmony and balance for individual victims and communities and encouraging offenders to take responsibility for their offending behaviour is generally insufficient to substantially reduce recidivism rates. Newell (2001a: 3) claims that the "potential for restorative justice in prisons is considerable". He goes on to say that "it should not however be seen as a tool towards reducing recidivism but as a means towards empowering offenders to take responsibility for their actions and to make amends to their victims and their communities". The restorative justice process is specific in what

143

it sets out to achieve and we should not claim for it what it does not achieve.

Although restorative justice practices have effectively heightened victim and community satisfaction when compared with current adversarial justice systems (Goulding and Steels 2006, Maxwell and Morris 1993: 120), there is still a need to address the problem of high re-offending rates and the consequent production of more victims. This is where the principles of transformative justice come into play. Unlike the restorative justice process which sets out to heal the effects of crime, repair damage done and restore harmony and balance to fractured relationships, the transformative justice component is designed specifically to challenge offending behaviour. It is modelled on a process of mutually agreed plans, which involves the active participation of offenders together with their support networks of family and friends who seek to explore the underpinning factors which culminated in any criminal behaviour. Some transformative justice processes, in terms of meaningful rehabilitation programs, are already an important component in those few prisons that work within a restorative framework. However, I feel it is important to *name* the inclusion of transformative processes within the prison setting and not just assume their existence as part of the restorative process.

Because the transformative justice element takes place in the presence of family and/or friends, it diminishes the likelihood of offenders hiding underlying problems and/or addictions. In line with restorative practice, the transformative justice process also makes use of the re-integrative shaming process before any restorative course of action. My argument here is that restorative justice practices are most likely to achieve successful outcomes for all participants if utilised in conjunction with other supportive measures, such as the transformative justice process, which not only effectively investigate the underlying issues of individual criminal behaviour but also apply challenges to such behaviour patterns on an individual basis. In this way the combined restorative and transformative model has more chance of reducing re-offending rates as well as achieving increased victim and community satisfaction (Goulding and Steels 2006).

The term "restorative prison" seems, at first sight, oxymoronic in nature. The question here is "how can restorative and transformative processes work within traditional retributive custodial settings"? It has, therefore, to be acknowledged that "at one level there can be no such thing as a restorative prison" but, according to Coyle (2001b: 7-8), "that is too negative a message and, in the interests of prisoners, of prison staff and of civil society one has to set one's ambitions higher than that". It has already been accepted that the prison systems that we already have in the developed world fail to compel offenders to take responsibility for the harm they have caused in the perpetration of their crimes, fail to recognise the importance of victims in the equation and fail to demonstrate the values inherent in civil society.

In order to work effectively within the prison setting, restorative and transformative justice processes should address some fundamental areas of concern. These are:

- Providing reparation to victims and communities through meaningful prisoner work activities which effectively assist individual victims and/or communities.

- Restructuring of all grievance procedures within prisons to include and promote alternative dispute resolution processes. This would include prisoner to prisoner disputes, prisoner to prison staff disputes and all prisoner and prison staff grievances.

- Encouraging prisoners to recognise that their criminal actions have caused harm to victims and their families, their own families and communities.

- Encouraging prisoners to engage in counselling and/or programs within the prison with supportive networks of family or friends in order to address the underlying issues which resulted in their offending behaviour patterns.

- Encouraging prisoners to engage in interaction with victims (not necessarily their own victims) where appropriate within the prison setting.

- Building positive relationships between prisoners and prison staff.

- Fostering new relationships between prisoners, the prison and local communities as a first step towards reconciliation and successful prisoner reintegration.

- Counteracting the negative stereotypical images of prisoners within local communities, increasing the opportunities for successful reintegration.

According to Coyle (2001c: 10), the truly restorative and transformative prison setting would:

> present prisoners with a series of duties, challenges and learning opportunities. It would invest trust in the prisoners' capacity to take responsibility for performing tasks, for meeting challenges

and for using learning opportunities. The task for prison staff at every level and in all departments would be to work with prisoners to identify the skills, guidance and support they need to restore their lives, equipping themselves for renewed citizenship and a life away from crime.

A key factor in a restorative and transformative prison is an environment of safety for both prisoners and prison staff. This stands in marked contrast to the violent and brutalising nature of our current prisons. As Newell (2001b: 3) argues:

> Unless prisoners can avoid experiences of being victimised in prison they are unlikely to be able to focus their attention upon those they have damaged by their offending behaviour. Thus the need to create and sustain safe healthy prisons is vital for restorative justice to flourish.

## The restorative prison at work in other jurisdictions

This section on the functioning of restorative prisons is heavily reliant on Newell's (2001a; 2001b) and Coyle's (2001a; 2001b; 2001c) work. Basically, the concept of restorative prisons is relatively recent and more or less limited to the Belgian prison system and the current research in this area by the International Centre for Prison Studies. Thus there is a paucity of other published sources.

As previously pointed out, restorative prisons are a relatively new concept. In Belgium an action research project involving the introduction of restorative justice practices into six prisons was introduced in 1998. Newell (2001b: 1) reports that this was in response to "the horrors of the Dutroix affair of child abuse and child murder in the summer of 1996" and subsequent community concerns regarding the "malfunctioning of the criminal justice system". The fundamental concern within the Belgian community was that victims of crime and concerned communities were effectively ignored within the criminal justice process. The dreadfulness of the Dutroix crimes gave victim groups and communities the necessary impetus to lobby parliamentarians and to push for radical change. Newell (2001b: 1) goes on to say:

> The decision was made to involve victims within the criminal justice system using the principles of restorative justice ... This focus was partly in response to the repeatedly formulated requirements of an active self help group of parents of murdered children and several groups of battered women and because there were trends within criminology that gave some direction towards the possibility of reform ... From surveys of victims Belgian research

showed there was great dissatisfaction with the way that public agencies like the police, public prosecutors and judges dealt with the aftermath of crime. Victims expected there to be a public reaction to delinquent behaviour, which includes listening to the needs of victims ... repairing the harm done to individual victims and of the need to restore the confidence of the victim, his neighbourhood and the public belief in the functioning of the criminal justice system.

The catalyst for change within the Belgian criminal justice system was widespread community concern that what existed did not achieve the basic aims of crime deterrence, rehabilitation of criminals and general community safety. It was this awareness of the failure of prisons to challenge offending behaviour, the victim's need to be heard, together with insistence on more effective actions to implement greater community safety, that provoked the Belgian authorities to seek alternative options within the criminal justice system. It was also the courage and vision of prevailing politicians that directed such public outcry towards a restorative rather than a more retributive criminal justice system.

Newell (2001b: 2) states that the Belgian experience "focused on the restoration of damage caused by crime and towards the resolution of conflict between people and communities". He goes on to comment that there have been some very good examples of restorative projects with juvenile offenders. He spoke of "a project about material damage at the police station ... and the experiments of victim-offender mediation in cases of serious violent crime". Each of these projects has undergone evaluation and the outcomes suggest that most victims, judicial decision makers and offenders support the restorative process. Newell sums up by saying "it became clear to be really effective, the victim's perspective must be integrated in all stages of the criminal justice procedure, including any period of custody" (Newell 2001b: 2).

The positive evaluation of the restorative initiative in the six Belgian prisons concerned resulted in the Minister for Justice introducing restorative justice practices to all Belgian prisons. According to Newell (2001b: 2), "each of the thirty (Belgian) prisons now has a restorative justice counsellor appointed to work with the governor in order to introduce concepts and practices in line with those developed within the community".

In January 2000 in Britain, the International Centre for Prison Studies at King's College, London, also embarked on a restorative prison project. This was the result of one of the recommendations from "A New Agenda for Penal Reform", an international conference on prison reform organised by the International Centre for Prison Studies. One of the main themes to emerge from the conference was the recognition that "formal criminal justice systems have marginalised victims of crime and have failed to oblige offenders to face up to the damage and harm which their actions have caused" (Coyle 2001c: 6). The ensuing argument was that prisons could become more effective as places of rehabilitation if they were run within a restorative framework which actively encouraged "prisoners to take responsibility for the consequences of their behaviour by providing greater opportunities to make amends, and by establishing formal channels of mediation between prisoners to resolve conflict" (Coyle 2001c: 7).

The British restorative prison project has been implemented in collaboration with the Prison Service in England and Wales and includes the active involvement of three prisons in the north east of England. One of the main aims of the project is to generate debate "about the purpose of imprisonment and prisons by examining the relationship between the prison, the prisoner and the wider community". There is also an effort to discover whether "the development of a restorative regime inside a prison can contribute to altering human relationships and to changing the perceptions that prisoners, prison staff, victims and the wider community have of each other" (International Centre for Prison Studies Web Page: November 2001).

Indeed the restorative prison project has effectively enhanced relationships and perceptions amongst the aforementioned social groups. For example, the Albert Park Project in the north east of England involved prisoners from two local prisons in a total renovation of the badly run down public facility. A boat had been "rebuilt by prisoners in the workshops of one of the local prisons. Men in nearby prisons had also produced mosaics for the ... visitors' centre, had built tables for its café and had constructed the ornamental railings surrounding the lake" (Stern 2005: 8).

At a press conference held to launch an information booklet on the Albert Park renovation, the Director General of Prisons (cited in Stern 2005: 8) said:

> It gives me enormous pleasure to launch this publication. I was brought up just round the corner from Albert Park. I saw it gradually fall into disrepair. Now it is being refurbished with a major contribution from prisons in the area ... The prisoners are putting something back into the community. They are learning useful skills. And, hopefully, when they leave prison they will feel that they have more of a stake in the community and be able to make a new start in life.

Another restorative justice park project in Reading was completed by young prisoners. A public park area which had also fallen into disrepair, become a dumping ground for rubbish and was frequented by drug abusers was cleaned up and is now used again as a local park and children's playground. During the clean-up there were reports of local community members taking refreshments to the teams of young offenders. According to Leathlean (2004: 3) the parks projects gave:

> offenders a chance to undertake active, meaningful work, and make direct amends to the community. Offenders have clearly valued this opportunity, and have been moved to see how much it has meant to the residents. In the words of one offender: 'You can feel good that you are doing something for the community, not just sitting back and doing your time. And it was nice to see that they had faith in us, that they believed that we could be rehabilitated. In that sense, they were giving something back to us'.

Within a restorative prison setting, prisoners have the opportunity to make some form of reparation to local communities through meaningful work. This could be by way of supplying goods manufactured in the prison to charitable organisations or through the sale of such goods with profits donated to the relevant organisation. According to Coyle (2001c: 9):

> The prisons are working with a non-government organisation called 'Inside-Out' refurbishing goods, such as motorcycles, spectacles and books, for use by disadvantaged people in the United Kingdom and in other countries ... Non-governmental organisations and other voluntary groups report that, when offered the chance, prisoners will work with enthusiasm on projects they know will help people who are more disadvantaged than they are: the old, the ill, the poor ... The high motivation, active commitment and ongoing enthusiasm that people in prison can bring to work of this kind and what they can achieve should not be underestimated.

Various restorative and reparative processes are currently in place in prisons in several other jurisdictions around the world. However, these have been described as "piecemeal, uncoordinated and largely dependent on the initiative or chance involvement of enthusiastic individuals" (Liebmann and Braithwaite cited in Mace 2000: 2). Liebmann goes on to say that such initiatives "can often be short lived or become marginalised under the pressure of other priorities if they have not been integrated as part of the prison's regime". Currently, Belgium is the only country which has its entire prison system based on restorative justice practice which includes, but is not limited to, prisoner reparation to victims and community, victim and community involvement in the process and prison staff who are trained in the principles of restorative justice.

Within the West Australian prison system a few reparative projects are currently in place. For example, in Casuarina a few prisoners re-classify used spectacles as part of an international eye care project to enhance sight within the populations of third world countries such as Nepal. In support of Coyle's previous argument, these prisoners have a sense that they are contributing to society in a positive manner by helping those they perceive to be worse off than themselves (personal observation and conversations with the prisoners and prison officers concerned, November 2001). Similarly, prisoners at Karnet prison farm have, for many years, built specially designed bicycles and tricycles for children and adults with disabilities. These reparative activities do not, however, occur within a restorative prison setting. In line with this, Liebmann and Braithwaite (cited in Mace 2000: 2) found that there were few prisons worldwide which had adopted restorative justice as a "total philosophy informing all their activities".

## The implementation of a restorative and transformative prison system

The Belgian experience began "with the cultivation of a prison culture which allows and stimulates restoration processes between victims and offenders" (Newell 2001a: 3). In order to implement restorative prac-tices and establish the underpinning philosophy, all prison staff in the initially selected Belgian prisons had to undergo extensive training and education in the principles and practice of restorative justice. Many obstacles had to be overcome, not the least of which was the attempt to combine restorative practices with traditional prison modes of admini-stration. Newell (2001a: 4) suggests that the tension between the two is still apparent. He maintains that:

> Restorative justice requires respect, the assuming of responsibility and the freedom to solve problems by those involved in the con-flict. These attitudes are opposed to the deprivation of freedom and limited personal responsibility that form the basis of current prison practice.

In the Belgian reforms prison staff needed to develop generic thera-peutic skills to facilitate restorative and transformative processes in diverse situations. The restorative and transformative procedures require a fundamental lack of prejudice on the part of staff, who have to deal with offenders and their support networks (and victims and their support networks) regardless of the criminal act which led to the prisoner's incarceration. These skills are also displayed in managing (restoratively) situations of conflict between prisoners and between prisoners and prison staff. In order to better accommodate the transition from retributive to restorative systems, consultants are employed in each prison to raise awareness of restorative processes and to establish meaningful dialogue between prisons and community.

In their turn, prisoners have to learn to accept responsibility for the harm their criminal activities have caused to individual victims, family and neighbourhood. This largely transformative component is implemented at the beginning of any given prison sentence and is maintained throughout the term of custody. Newell (2001b: 3) outlines the process in this way:

> Staff organised support to help them (prisoners) take up responsibility for the crime and the consequences for the victims ... Prisoners are given awareness training so they are conscious of the psychological and emotional consequences for the victims. This program is called 'Victim in Focus' and is a confronting approach aimed at changing attitudes.

Prisoners are also made responsible for any financial compensation owed to victims. To this end, a restoration fund has been established and prisoners are now able to earn money in order to pay victim compensation. This has the effect of instilling some degree of responsibility in prisoners whilst providing reparation for victims.

In the early stages, both victims and community were given preparation for the radical change towards a restorative criminal justice system. This was initially through provision of information about restorative justice practices and "the situation of imprisoned offenders and what is likely at the end of their sentences" (Newell 2001b: 3). Victim aid groups were also consulted throughout the introduction of restorative practices, which came into play from initial arrest of offenders, through the investigation process, the court process to incarceration in restorative prisons. In Belgium then "at all stages of the process victim orientation and the possibilities for mediation, reparation, community service or other alternative ways to react to lawbreaking are becoming the norm" (Newell 2001b: 3).

## Restorative and transformative prisons in the West Australian context

For principles of restorative and transformative justice to work in the West Australian prison system there would need to be profound cultural change. This would need to occur among the prisoners, prison staff and community members. Rather than attempt to achieve this across the board – an unlikely proposition as it would probably meet with strong resistance and do little to initiate real cultural and philosophical change – the suggestion here is that an action research project involving two wholly restorative and transformative prisons be considered. These are; the privately run Acacia Prison and the new low security women's prison, Boronia Pre-release Centre for Women. Acacia Prison and Boronia Pre-release Centre have, arguably, stood alone in resisting the entrenched punitive culture of the State run prison system. Although Boronia is a State run facility, it was planned and built on assumptions more in line with restorative concepts.

## Acacia Prison

Acacia is a 750 bed relatively new prison largely staffed by personnel with little or no experience in the State prison system and, consequently, the prison is not yet steeped in the punitive and divisive cultural practices which have haunted most State prisons. Further, because it is a privately run prison, Acacia is somewhat distanced from its State counterparts. As a result, prison management and staff may be more prepared to adopt restorative and transformative practices than those who are entrenched in the traditional State system. In addition to these factors Prison Fellowship (Australia) has already introduced their faith based restorative "Sycamore Tree" program within Acacia where surrogate victims meet with prisoners, explain restorative justice philosophy and engage in symbolic actions of responsibility taking, apology and reparation

At the time of writing, Prison Fellowship (Australia) has completed two "Sycamore Tree" programs at Acacia Prison. Conversely, senior management at State run prisons has been reluctant to introduce the restorative program, offering little or no support to the concept. Certainly, for those implementing restorative programs in custodial settings, it is important to acknowledge that prisons prioritise security concerns and run to rigid schedules which, if interrupted, can cause logistic problems for staff.

Within a West Australian context, the already established "Sycamore Tree" program in Acacia Prison addresses one of the four main elements required in a restorative and transformative prison environment; that of promoting an awareness of the impact of crime on victims through direct mediation between victims and offenders. The remaining three elements are considered to be:

- The implementation of meaningful workplace activities for prisoners so that a proportion of their time is spent working for the benefit of others within a spirit of reparation.

- Incorporating restorative justice principles into dispute, grievance and disciplinary procedures.

- Initiating positive relationships with local communities in order to illustrate the need for prisoners to be "reconciled with the wider society and received back into it" (Francis 2001: 2).

In the case of the new women's prison, the current Attorney General and then Minister for Justice, Jim McGinty, had indicated his desire to change the direction and mode of imprisonment for women in Western Australia. His vision ensured that the architectural design of the new women's prison is closer to community living standards with accommodation made up of small clusters of house-type dwellings. Since changes to architecture and environment alone do not transform traditional practices and assumptions, it is timely to embark on a project of fundamental change for a wholly restorative and transformative prison. This would necessitate selecting staff open to cultural change and willing to undergo training in restorative and transformative practices. It would also mean that the new prison would need to be administered separately from Bandyup Women's Prison.

There is no set formula or plan for the establishment of a restorative and transformative prison. Such prisons are few and far between. Even so, valuable lessons can be learned from the Belgian experience and from the current research being conducted by the International Centre for Prison Studies in Britain. What is clear from the outset is the need for intensive training and education of prison staff at all levels in the theories, practice and generic applications of restorative and transformative justice. This would require, as in the Belgian system, the employment of restorative and transformative justice consultants (reporting directly to the prison superintendent at each prison) to initiate, maintain and oversee ongoing development and implementation of positive practices. Running parallel with prison staff education and training, there ought to be an intensive program of community information similar to that carried out by the Belgian authorities. This would require the close involvement of victims of crime, victim aid groups, church and community organisations and the general public.

I acknowledge that the concept of a restorative and transformative prison in Western Australia involves sweeping change from within the criminal justice system. The introduction of such radical transformation would require clear vision and political fortitude from relevant

West Australian Government Ministers. However, the prison system we have does not serve the community well. It is economically unaffordable, reproduces criminality and comes with a tremendous social cost. The restorative and transformative model has provided the Belgian community with a more effective and pro-social system, which satisfies most community concerns with regard to the workings of the complete criminal justice system. As Newell (2001a: 1) points out:

> Whilst we continue to regard restorative justice and prisons as opposite points of the spectrum the public will not recognise its validity as a realistic approach to resolving the conflicts involved in the decisions central to criminal justice. The debate about prisons must become more central in seeking to establish restorative justice as more than an interesting alternative for the less serious offenders and offences. The victims of serious crimes are being let down by the current exclusion of prisons as places of restoration for offenders, victims and their communities.

In conclusion, all of us who constitute "community" – including victims of crime and offenders, as well as ordinary community members – are being let down by retributive prison and criminal justice systems which do little to heal the effects of crime and nothing to create safer communities. The concept of a restorative and transformative prison system in Western Australia may seem a remote possibility at present. But it must be acknowledged that the vast majority of our prisoners have come from local communities and, in time, all but a handful will return to these communities; most of these men and women will have been harmed and made worse by their experience of imprisonment. It is my contention that prisoners who have served their time in restorative and transformative custodial settings would be returned to the wider community with a vastly better chance of successful reintegration as law abiding, valued citizens than those long term prisoners who participated in this study.

Finally, it is appropriate to conclude with some words from a prisoner. Linda put the case for reforms more succinctly than any academic. She had this to say:

> *Several officers told me I'd be back. They said, 'We'll see you in a couple of weeks'. The system sucks ... it lets you out into a world where you no longer fit. I don't think they (prison officers) were capable of helping me to adjust to the outside because the inside is where they have all the power ... If your life revolves around ordering people around how can you help those same people adjust to a normal life? They (prisons) need more people who care. Perhaps social workers but not prison officers who put you down*

*the back and punish you further ... how can you relate to them?*
*You know, at the end of the day, I'm just an ordinary person who*
*wants to make a nice home for my daughter and be her mother.*
(interview: August 1999)

# Appendix A: Research Design

## Doing qualitative research: understanding the everyday world of the long term prisoner

Qualitative research methodology was used throughout this study. Indeed, the underpinning ethos of the book is that the prisoner participants, not the researcher, are the experts of the prison experience. Consequently, the prisoners' own accounts of their experiences of imprisonment are central. In this sense, it is largely an ethnographic or "micro-sociological" study. At the same time, however, I am mindful that the prisoners' experiences are formed largely by the wider institutional context of the prison which, in its turn, is formed by the wider politico-economic context.

Because it is the prisoners' experiences of imprisonment and release that are the focal points of the study, I found symbolic interactionist, phenomenological and ethnomethodological frameworks useful analytical tools for the research process. These micro-sociological approaches support the notion that human actors engage in social interaction not simply as a response to prevailing social structures and mores, but primarily as participants who must constantly interpret situations and make active decisions to deal with what is there.

Symbolic interactionism, phenomenology and ethnomethodology together present a challenge to positivistic social theory. Positivism, which grants centrality to social structures and diminishes the importance of the individual actor, also assumes not only the "objective" or "outside" position of the researcher, but also the "superior" [more informed, more knowing, more expert] view of the researcher. Against this, Psathas argues that "methodologically, the implication of the symbolic interactionist perspective is that the *actor's* view of actions, objects and society has to be studied seriously" (1973: 6-7, my emphasis). That is, the actor's world view must be fully understood, even, at some level, "entered into". In order to achieve this, the researcher must become part of the social world she is studying. Among other things, this means that, no previously held assumptions or theoretical positions should be allowed to structure the researcher's judgment

(Psathas 1973: 7). "In this sense, symbolic interactionists seek to faithfully represent and describe the social world as it is known to those who live in it. This approach is indeed phenomenological in spirit" (Psathas 1973: 7). While the phenomenological and symbolic interactionist claim to a researcher's presumed "veil of innocence" is widely recognised to be unrealistic, the intent is clear. In practical terms, and as far as this research is concerned, this meant that I attempted, as far as possible, to comprehend the subjective world of the prisoner while acknowledging I could neither share it nor rid myself of the mental baggage associated with doing social research. With that proviso, symbolic interactionism, phenomenology and ethnomethodology provided me with a workable framework with which to approach this study. Following is a brief outline of these sociological perspectives and an explanation of their relevance to this study.

## The subjective experience

### Symbolic interactionism

Symbolic interactionist theory is based on the principle that humans act towards objects on the basis of the meanings that these objects have for them. Symbolic interactionists argue that such meanings are a consequence of the social circumstances and social interaction that human actors have with each other. Further, that "these meanings are handled in, and modified through, an interpretive process used by the person in dealing with the things he encounters" (Blumer 1969: 2). In his analysis of symbolic interactionism, George Herbert Mead argued that the self materialises out of a form of social interactionism whereby human actors internalise the role of the other. In line with this, he attributed to humans the ability to see themselves as they perceive others see them (Jary and Jary 1991: 386). He also viewed human interaction as distinguishable from that of animals "above all by language and by the huge importance of symbolic communication of various kinds" (Jary and Jary 1991: 645).

For symbolic interactionists the process of social interaction is what actually shapes human behaviour rather than simply being a medium through which such conduct is expressed. Moreover, within a symbolic interactionist framework, it is recognised that humans not only react to others but that they must possess a notion of self in order to do so. Thus, humans can recognise themselves in various social roles and can direct their actions according to how they perceive themselves at any given time. The individual actor's view of "self" is constructed and emerges from her social interaction with others and the effects of how she perceives others to define her.

As far as this study is concerned, symbolic interactionism assists in our understanding of the construction of "self as prisoner" as being largely reliant on the ways in which prisoners comprehend how others see them. This construction of self as prisoner in terms of the "other" depends on the position of the other in question. For example, within the prison environs, a different view of "prisoner" will be reflected in the eyes of prison staff and prisoners themselves. Similarly, within the wider community, members of a prisoner's family will mediate his or her identity as "prisoner" with memories and notions of the person's previous identity, in a way which members of the general community will, in all probability, not.

A key factor within the symbolic interactionist approach to social research is the notion that "[o]ne of the most powerful ways of learning is through the rich and detailed example – methodologies that attempt to do justice to detailed understandings of real social situations and actual communities" (Fine, Johnson and Farberman 1992: viii). In this research these principles underpinned a detailed study of specific prison routines and patterns of social interaction.

## Phenomenology

A significant point about phenomenology is that it claims to accurately represent subjective experience. Cicourel (1968: 331) suggests that social researchers often talk about "the actor's world view" without explaining *how* they understand the actor's perspective. He argues that "[s]ociologists have been slow to recognise the basic empirical issues that problems involving language and meaning pose for all research" (Cicourel 1968: 331). For that reason it is fundamental to studies of this nature that researchers become familiar with the world that they intend to investigate.

Within a phenomenological framework there is clear recognition that varied groups can come together to form socially diverse worlds. I have already argued that the researcher who starts from a phenomenological perspective must learn about the world she intends to study in order to understand the meanings that specific things hold for its members. This is fundamental to phenomenological research because it is recognised that "group life is built up out of social interaction, out of the constructed meanings in action in which individuals jointly engage. Institutions, roles, status positions, organisations, norms and values develop and reciprocally influence those engaged in their construction and maintenance" (Psathas 1973: 6).

158

In the case of this study the social world under observation and investigation is the prison. The phenomenological approach requires the observer or researcher to understand the nature of the social structure of the prison, the norms and values inherent within the prison and how these affect the social world of the prisoner. Arguably, though, all such insights are limited to the extent that the researcher does not actually experience being a prisoner under the prevailing prison conditions inherent in the study. Along with this it is questionable how far researchers can "bracket" or "suspend" their everyday, commonsense assumptions. Psathas' (1973: 15) argument that "I set aside preconceptions and presuppositions, what I already 'know' about the social world, in order to discover it with clarity of vision" may fail to adequately acknowledge the entrenched social, cultural and academic baggage that we, as social researchers and human actors, carry with us in *our* everyday worlds.

In his phenomenological text, *Seductions of Crime*, Katz makes copious use of interviews to describe the participants' criminal activities and their feelings when they perpetrated such criminal acts. (Throughout this book, I have also made extensive use of participants' conversations and their own interpretations of the effects of long term imprisonment on their lives.) Katz (1988: 3) suggests that most sociological studies of crime focus on the background and rarely "take up the challenge of explaining the qualities of deviant experience". He goes on to propose that "empirical research turn the direction of inquiry around to focus initially on the foreground" in order to "make it our first priority to understand the qualities of experience that distinguish different forms of criminality" (Katz 1988: 3). Katz conducts his research into criminality from the inside, making use of participant observation, ethnographic material and personal conversations.

## Ethnomethodology

Ethnomethodology recognises that social reality is "always to be seen as the 'rational accomplishment' of individuals" (Jary and Jary 1991: 205). Harold Garfinkel, the founder of the ethnomethodological approach, claimed that conventional sociology ignored the methods used by ordinary human actors in their interpretations of their everyday lives, portraying them as "cultural dopes" (Garfinkel cited in Haralambos 1995: 812). Ethnomethodologists attempt to analyse the stories of members of particular socio-cultural groups within the context of their specific group culture. Further, and because of its concerns with how individuals experience and make sense of their everyday commonsense social interaction, ethnomethodology departs from macro-socio-logical theories which focus on the larger questions of social structure. The stated task of the ethnomethodologist is to describe, interpret and understand subjective reality. Therefore, within the framework of an ethnomethodological approach, the researcher should try to under-stand people within the context of their own social environment in order to appreciate how those individuals come to comprehend that environment. Against this, it needs to be pointed out that, when a researcher enters an intersubjective relationship with a person being researched the dynamics of the situation immediately change, "conta-minating" and changing the social world in question. There is, then, no fixed or enduring social world that can be entered and left, rather, there is a fluid set of circumstances of which the researcher becomes a part. The prison world which I observed, and which – using the voices of the prisoners – I have recounted in this book, is an approximation rather than actual account of social "reality".

Like symbolic interactionism and phenomenology, ethno-methodology requires that the researcher adopt the position of "learner" as she is always inferior to those researched in terms of cultural knowledge and her grasp of patterns of communication, habits and cultural imperatives. As well as adopting the position of learner in relation to participants, it is also critical that the ethnomethodological researcher should ensure a high degree of familiarity with the subject matter and some degree of closeness or relatedness to her participants.

Adopting an ethnomethodological viewpoint meant that I acknow-ledged that prisoners already possess the ability to interpret their everyday experiences. In addition, this approach permitted me to use my own analytical and interpretative tools in the research process. Here I worked from a specifically feminist position, being deeply indebted to Dorothy Smith's (1987) feminist ethnomethodological text *The Everyday World as Problematic*. Smith's concern with the notion of "bifurcation", which she sees as "manifesting itself in the separation between social scientific description and people's lived experience" (Ritzer 1988: 308), is crucial to this study.

## Implications of micro-sociology for this study

Prisons are distinct and largely isolated communities with their own cultural norms and mores. In order to gain some perception of social interaction within the prison system it was necessary for me to engage relatively closely with prison culture. I drew selectively from the approaches described above to obtain background information and ethnographic detail. This occurred both during the study and over the years while I was working within prisons. That is, through listening, observing and interacting with prisoners I learned the specific meanings of language and symbols within the everyday world of the prison. Some frequently quoted terms within this study are:

- *Screws* – prison officers
- *Slot* – cell
- *Ramp* – search
- *Dog* or *rat* – a prisoner who informs on another prisoner
- *Rock spider* or *tamp* – a prisoner convicted of paedophile offences
- *Chogy* or *down the back* – punishment cells
- *Muster* – prisoner count

A reasonable knowledge of the language and symbols of the world of the prisoner enabled me to gain insight into the cultural practices of the prison system. More generally, Goffman's text *Asylums* was particularly useful. Goffman did extensive fieldwork in a psychiatric hospital, working as an assistant to the athletic director and, when pressed, "avowing to be a student of recreation and community life" (1961: ix). His "immediate object in doing fieldwork was to try to learn about the social world of the hospital inmate, as this world is subjectively experienced by him (Goffman 1961: ix). Although he did not present as an inmate himself, Goffman was able to gain a reasonable understanding of the language, symbols and social mores of the inmate's world. Within the context of this study, a Goffmanesque approach to symbolic interactionist method was arguably one of the most potent instruments and explains my heavy reliance on *Asylums* in Chapter Two. In addition, throughout the text, I have consistently kept true to the participants' stories and related them verbatim. However, and bearing in mind Taylor's point about the problems of the often descriptive nature of phenomenological accounts, I also depart from a purely phenomenological approach. In particular, I have also analysed and interpreted those experiences within a context of the participants' position within the institution and the institution's position within society. In other words, I have diverted to a more conventional sociological method by including my own analysis of empirical data within a broader socio-political context.

Although the micro-sociological approaches of symbolic interactionist, phenomenological and ethnomethodological thought were valuable analytical tools for this study of the world of prisoners, I make no claim to subscribe exclusively to any of these theories. I have simply utilised parts of these theoretical frameworks as tools to formulate, construct and articulate this study. And, while I have drawn on these approaches, I have also continued to maintain that the micro and macro sociological aspects are constantly interdependent.

Finally, within this study I have worked steadfastly from a feminist standpoint, which seeks primarily to establish a relatively equal power relationship between researcher and participant. In essence, I have listened to the everyday experiences of some long term prisoners as they prepare to leave and, in many cases, return to the institution. I have attempted to "remain true" to their accounts but acknowledge my own limitations as a social researcher: a person who has spent time within the physical boundaries of several prisons but who, unlike the prisoner participants in this study, could leave these prisons at will.

## Ethical considerations and feminist methodology

A central fact of feminist research is that research with disempowered and marginalised groups should be used for the empowerment of participants. In this study, I collaborated with the prisoner participants concerning what would be done with the research as far as publicity and social outcomes were concerned. It was, then, a collective decision that the results of this study should be used to raise both government and public awareness of the problems associated with long term imprisonment. To this end, and with participants' consent, I have used some of the knowledge gleaned from participants to lobby relevant parliamentarians and senior bureaucrats for positive change within the West Australian criminal justice system.

Conversely, feminist research methodology, whilst reducing the power differential between researcher and researched and allowing silent voices to be heard, has the potential to be exploitative. That is, the social isolation which is often characteristic of marginalisation and which, in terms of this research, is also part of the experiences related by the prisoner participants, can mean that they give too much information in the relief of finding a space within which to speak. Thus the irony is that although feminist methodology claims to establish a relatively equal power relationship between the researcher and researched, at the same time it may increase the vulnerability of marginalised and powerless participant groups, particularly if expectations are raised which cannot be met.

In general terms, the safeguards used in mainstream social research to ensure confidentiality and anonymity are inadequate in research with disempowered groups at the margins. This is particularly the case with in-depth interviews which actively encourage an intimate and trusting relationship between interviewer and participant. Undoubtedly, during interviews, I found that the prisoners' narratives were open and frank, demonstrating a real desire to tell their stories. In this way the potential for betrayal of trust exists for "the very intimacy of qualitative research undermines the possibility for absolute anonymity" (Aungles 1994: 252).

During the interviews I became aware that the question of trust is constantly problematic in research *on, from* and *about* the margins. Although I acknowledge that the prisoners could choose whether or not to participate in this research, in reality, they had little control over their information once they had given it to me. To minimise this loss of control I returned transcripts to participants for their scrutiny so that they could determine whether I had "written up" their interviews accurately, retaining the true spirit of their stories.

Since most of the participants returned to prison during the time span of the research, I had to obtain special security clearance to take the transcripts into the relevant prisons. I also had to stand my ground on several occasions when prison officers insisted on scrutinising the transcripts before they were given back to the prisoners. On the first occasion, I was extremely concerned that the transcript might be forcibly removed from me. I put the transcript, which had been in my hand, back into a folder. The prison officer insisted that he should take it to his superiors whilst I, in turn, insisted that it could not leave my person unless it was handed to the participant. The officer called on a senior security officer and I explained the situation to him, showed him my letters of approval to conduct the research in conditions of confidentiality and told him that I felt it was particularly important that prison staff did not have access to prisoner transcripts. I then negotiated a compromise with the prison security officer on the basis of which, I remained with the prisoners while they read their transcripts. I then retrieved the transcripts and took them from the prison with me. Had I not complied with this rule and let the prisoners retain the transcripts after I left, I could have been charged with trafficking within the prison. Whenever instances of this nature occurred I was reminded of my own marginalised position within the maximum security prison. Wherever I was in the prison, either interviewing participants or discussing transcripts, I was locked in, albeit temporarily. I had to make a concerted effort to remain calm, reclaim some control and negotiate my position.

To summarise the issues so far: first, I felt that the research had to be used in some way to better the lives of the marginalised prisoner participant group and the wider social population of prisoners. Secondly, I had to constantly consider my position as researcher in terms of the "trust/betrayal" factor and ensure that I did not exploit the participants who talked so freely of their experiences of imprisonment. Thirdly, I had to clearly position myself as a researcher from the margins who "was on their side" and engaged in research designed to achieve social and political results. Finally, I needed to make clear to the participants that there was no guarantee that this research would make any positive contribution to their lives or the lives of prisoners in general.

## The participants

Ten long term prisoners and one ex-prisoner were involved in the research. One of the long term prisoners provided background information about prison life in general and is referred to as the "prisoner consultant". The other 10 formally participated in the study and were interviewed in the week leading up to their release and then again three to six months after their release. The recently released ex-prisoner was approached at a later stage of the research because I felt that additional information regarding an individual's original introduction to prison and the initial process of institutionalisation was needed as a base or context for the prison experiences described by the other participants. I chose this individual – I call him "Brad" – because I had known him for some time and he was willing to talk to me. Brad has served more than one custodial term.

Because of the logistics involved in gaining access to long term prisoners due for release, I did not use normal sampling methods. The participants were simply selected as they became available. That is, when I found out or was advised by the Department of Corrective Services, that a prisoner who fitted the criteria of "long term" was about to be released, I approached prison authorities at the relevant prison, made an appointment to visit the prisoner, explained the purpose of the research and requested his or her participation. Of the prisoners approached to participate one refused. The only adjustment made to the process of sequential selection was the inclusion of two female long term prisoners. Within the West Australian prison system, there are very few women prisoners who fit the criteria of "long term" as it is defined for the purposes of this study, and I bypassed two possible male participants in order to include the women in the study.

## Selecting and approaching participants

For the purpose of this study, I used the term "long term prisoner" to mean any prisoner who had served, during his or her current sentence, a minimum of three years in custody. I had initially defined "long term prisoner" as any prisoner who had served a minimum of five years in custody but as there was only one female prisoner due to be released who fell within this category I widened the group to include those who had served three years in custody.

I was able to locate long term prisoners due for release because my involvement as a prisoners' advocate gave me access to the relevant information. In addition, a senior Department of Corrective Services staff member was given the task of informing me which prisoners were due for release. This enabled me to achieve a reasonably efficient timetable for interviews. There were, however, several problems involved in identifying prisoners through this process. In the main, these related to prisoners who were to be released on licence to work release or parole conditions.

In Western Australia prisoners may be released into the community when their sentences are finite or they may be released on licence to parole or work release. A finite sentence is one that is served in full and the prisoner who is released on a finite sentence is discharged into the community as a free citizen. In contrast, a prisoner released to parole or work release conditions is still classified as a prisoner, released into the community on licence. McCleary (1978: 17) defines parole in this way:

> The status of being released from a penal or reformatory institution in which one has served part of his maximum sentence, on condition of maintaining good behaviour and remaining in the custody and under the guidance of the institution or some other agency approved by the parole board until a final discharge is granted.

If parole or work release conditions are breached, then the prisoner may be returned to prison to serve out his or her sentence. Prisoners who are eligible for parole or work release are given an earliest date of release and their release is contingent on a positive decision by the Parole Board. At the time the interviews took place it was prevailing practice that the Parole Board in Western Australia met to consider prisoners for parole or work release on three Fridays of every month. In terms of this research, problems occurred when the Parole Board made a decision on a Friday to grant parole to a long term prisoner whose earliest date of release was the following Monday or Tuesday.

Consequently, on several occasions I spent time in prisons trying to locate prisoners who had already been released.

In the event, I enlisted the assistance of seven of the 10 prisoner participants through using information obtained in my role as prisoners' advocate. This group included both women participants. The remaining participants were found with the assistance of the Department of Corrective Services. Those participants that I found through my own resources were approached by me, initially, through official visits. That is, I telephoned the prison, booked an official visit, met with and spoke to each prisoner about my research and asked if he or she would like to participate. In these cases I had obtained prior security clearance to pass on letters of information and to have informed consent forms signed by relevant prisoners.

The procedure for accessing potential participants found via the Department of Corrective Services was somewhat different. Subsequent to Parole Board meetings on relevant Fridays, the Department's representative would call me if there were any prisoners due for release. The vast majority of these were short or medium term prisoners and did not fit the research criteria. It is pertinent to note that most prisoners within the West Australian prison system are categorised as either short term or medium term, as a result, it was often difficult to locate potential participants. When I established that prisoners did fall within the guidelines of the research I then had to adhere to official protocol, contact the relevant prison and approach the superintendents and then the prisoners for permission to conduct the research interviews. Two of the participants were held in a regional prison and were contacted by letter. This was problematic because I also had to contact their unit officers to explain the nature of the research and to ensure that the prisoners were made aware that participation was purely voluntary.

The protocol for interviews was similar for both groups of participants. There was a minimum of 24 hours notice to individual prisons to access prisoners, explain the research and seek informed consent. There was a further 24 hours notice to make appointments to conduct interviews. I also had to contact the senior security officer at the appropriate prison to ensure that I could take a recording device into the prison to record interviews. I also attempted to make sure that this clearance was in place at the front gate of the relevant prison. There were several obstacles that hampered the smooth running of these procedures. These obstacles included messages not being received at the front gate regarding security clearance for the recording device. On several occasions prison officers refused me permission to enter prisons with the recording device and I had to wait for lengthy periods until senior security staff could confirm my security clearance. Also, on several occasions prisoners were unavailable for interviews for various official reasons and, on one occasion, the authorities were unable to locate a specific prisoner.

My initial intention was to interview 20 long term prisoners in the days immediately before their release. I would then conduct follow up interviews with the participants approximately six to 12 weeks after their release. Given that all of the prisoner participants were due for release into the community I had anticipated that most of my interviews would take place on a fairly casual basis in minimum security prisons. However, seven of the nine participants were released into the community from maximum security prisons. One of the participants was released from the Special Handling Unit at Casuarina prison. This is a secure wing that is used "for prisoners who pose a significant management problem" (Executive Director, Prison Services: 19 December 2000) and is classified as a "maximum security prison within a maximum security prison". There were a number of difficulties involved in conducting research within maximum security prisons but, by and large, it was the lengthy process involved in doing the interviews that caused me to reconsider the number of participants in the research. Each interview generally took somewhere in the vicinity of two hours to complete. This meant that the time spent within the prisons was usually around three hours. On average, it took approximately 30 minutes to get from the front gate to actually meeting face to face with each participant and a further 15 to 20 minutes to exit the prison. Also, transcribing interviews verbatim took me anywhere from three days to a week. For ethical reasons I could not allow anyone else access to interview material. Consequently, I felt that it would be more beneficial for the study to conduct 20 in-depth interviews with 10 prisoners plus the ex-prisoner rather than a larger number of more straightforward interviews.

## Characteristics of participants

Of the 11 people interviewed, nine were male and two were female. Their ages ranged from 24 to 47 years. Their served terms in custody on their current sentences ranged from three and a half years to 16 years. Two of the participants were serving their first prison term as adults. All of the others had served two or more prison terms in adult prison systems. One of the male participants had served a total of 27 years in various prisons. One of the women participants had three school-age children and the other had a child of pre-school age. Three of the men were fathers but only one of those had any contact with his children.

Several of the participants had lived some part of their childhood as wards of the State in institutions and/or foster care. Both of the female participants had spent part of their childhood in foster care and institutions and both had suffered physical and sexual abuse. The prisoner consultant had spent most of his childhood in institutions, much of his adolescence in juvenile detention centres and almost all his adult life in prison. Nine of the participants acknowledged a past or present problem with substance abuse (illicit drugs and/or alcohol) and five of those used, or still use, heroin on a regular basis. None of those participants who use or used heroin had been offered recognised forms of drug rehabilitation whilst in prison. Although one of the women was, at the time of the second interview, receiving methadone treatment within the prison, this was only because she was in receipt of such treatment in the community before her second term of imprisonment.

Only one of the prisoners I approached to participate in the research project refused. He was fighting a heroin addiction and was extremely anxious regarding both a pending Parole Board decision and his potential release. He has contacted me since his release and spoken to me about the problems he faced when first released into the community. I have not used his information within this study except as general background information.

## Interview schedule

I used in-depth interviews as the main method of gathering information from participants. For this purpose I designed interview schedules built around open-ended questions. The questions were used more as prompts than scripted questions, mainly to ensure that I covered all of the relevant issues. What I have defined as interviews could best be described as long conversations or dialogues with each participant. There were two research schedules (see appendices B and C respectively). The preliminary schedule was used for initial interviews in the week before release from prison. The post release schedule was used for follow-up interviews three to six months after release. However, seven of the follow up interviews, although conducted after the initial release, were in fact conducted within the prisons as the participants in question had been returned to prison for one reason or another.

The questions in the initial schedule related to life within the prison environment. The questions in the post release schedule were reflective of the preliminary questionnaire but related to life out in the community. I explored the following issues:

- daily routine within/outside the prison
- social relations and social life within/outside the prison
- anticipated changes either positive or negative
- formal and informal supports
- prison pre-release programs
- practical and emotional preparation for change
- the experience of change, positive and negative.

I selected these issues as I wished to explore how the strict prison regime impacted on the social and personal lives of the prisoners both before and after release. The questions relating to the participants' daily routine were designed to illuminate the degree of routine and diversity available to individual participants. These issues were mirrored in the questions related to prisoners' social relations and social life. Here I wanted to gauge the degree of choice available to participants within the confines of the prison, particularly regarding people or situations they might wish to avoid or attract. I also asked questions about the anxieties and expectations concerning release in order to compare how these anxieties and expectations measured up to everyday experiences once participants were out in the community. In the same way, the questions on anticipated community supports were of a comparative nature and sought to establish whether prior expectations were realised for the participants upon release. The questions about pre-release programs were included to gain participants' views about the relevance of these programs to their transition from prisoner to free citizen. In the same vein, I asked participants about their own practical and emotional preparation for release to explore the availability of informal supports within the prison and to ascertain participants' knowledge and use of these supports. The final series of questions were designed to gauge participants' general feelings in the days leading up to their release.

As indicated earlier, seven of the follow-up interviews were conducted in prison because participants had been returned to prison either for breach of parole conditions or for committing further offences. This meant that the follow up question schedule needed to be modified. In these instances I simply let participants tell their stories and, once again, used prompts (see Appendix C) to ensure that all relevant issues were covered.

Although there were no questions specifically about violence in the interview schedule, all of the male participants told stories of extreme physical violence directly related to their experiences of prison life. While the female participants did not articulate their experiences of prison in this way, several events which they talked about during interviews were certainly brutal or violent in nature. So, whether male or female, the participants talked in different ways about their experiences of violence within the prison. Some prisoners were victims of violence, some were perpetrators of violence and several had experiences of violence as both victims and perpetrators.

As the participants related their experiences, the interviews began to take on a life of their own. This, in turn, made me realise that the study would be less concerned with an individual prisoner's experience of the transition to freedom but would become more of an account of the nature of prison life. Further, the centrality of violence as a topic within the participant interviews was a decisive factor in my decision to include the prisoner consultant in the study. He had served many years in most of the prisons in Western Australia and was able to provide insights on violence as well as a number of other issues directly relevant to the study.

In the case of the prisoner consultant, I elected not to follow the format from the original research schedules. Instead, I spoke to him about the purpose of the research and the "prevalence of violence" issue in my interviews with the other prisoner participants. I asked him if he would be willing to talk to me about his prison experience in general, explaining that I would be guided by his expertise with regard to what he considered to be the main issues of imprisonment. From this discussion, we decided to have two interviews. Each interview lasted more than two hours. The first interview covered issues such as institutionalisation, control and surveillance, the role of prison officers, re-socialisation and the prisoner consultant's brief experience of life in the wider community. The second interview dealt only with violence in prisons. During both interviews I was guided by the prisoner consultant's imperatives and simply listened, questioning him only to clarify some meaning or when prompted by a lengthy pause or silence.

## The journey to the interviews in maximum security facilities

I found each of the interviews conducted within the maximum security prisons stress inducing and upsetting. The main contributing factor to my feelings of anxiety was the impact of my journey from the front gate to the visit area. I have described this as an "officially sanctioned ritual of depersonalisation that must be followed by visitors before each visit. This ritual becomes part of the transition of status involved for each visitor, for the duration of each visit" (Goulding 1997: 34). The journey, through a series of locked doors and surveillance checks, involved a symbolic warning that I was entering an area generally bereft of conventional community social mores and interactions, and intended to induce in me what Goffman (1961: 149) describes as an institutionalised frame of mind.

The trek from the front gate to the official visit area involved ritualised surveillance checks by prison officers. In broad terms, the principles underpinning these procedures are uniform within all West Australian prisons. All visitors, social and official, must proceed through a series of locked doors and surveillance checks in order to reach the visit area. Surveillance checks vary subtly between individual prisons, usually dependent on the availability of hi-tech equipment. For example, at some prisons a "walk through" metal detector was used, while at others I was frisked by an officer using a hand held detector. Any paperwork or equipment that I carried with me into the prison was checked. Paperwork, apart from interview transcripts, was either scanned or scrutinised and equipment, such as my recording device, was opened and checked for contraband. I was given verbal warnings not to give paperwork to prisoners and not to obtain their signatures without prior permission from security personnel.

Although I entered the prisons on these occasions as an official visitor and social researcher, my reception at the front gates was often influenced by my prior position as a family visitor and, in particular, by my more recent and sometimes adversarial roles as official prison visitor, prisoners' advocate and justice activist. Several members of the prison staff whom I encountered at the front gates knew me in these roles. As a family visitor, I assumed that I might be viewed by some staff as a security threat because it is common practice within prisons to target family visitors as the most likely source of illicit substances within prisons. As a prisoner advocate and high profile justice activist I could be seen as a threat to the system and, sometimes, as a personal threat to a few officers I had complained about within the system.

## The interviews

Eight of the preliminary interviews and six of the follow up interviews were conducted in maximum security prisons. Only two preliminary interviews took place in minimum security facilities. The remaining follow up interviews occurred out in the community but two of those participants subsequently returned to prison. Both interviews with the prisoner consultant were conducted in a maximum security prison. The interview with the ex-prisoner was carried out in my home. I found it stressful and difficult conducting interviews in the maximum security prisons because I could never be entirely sure whether the interviews were being monitored or recorded by prison authorities, and the atmosphere in these prisons was generally unfriendly and often intimidating.

The interviews took place in the following prisons; Casuarina Prison, Canning Vale (now renamed Hakea Prison), Bunbury Prison and Bandyup Women's Prison – all classified as maximum security facilities. I conducted one interview at Karnet Prison Farm and one interview at Bunbury Minimum Security Prison. Both are classified as minimum security facilities. I had originally anticipated that most initial interviews would take place within minimum security prisons because prisoners who have served a substantial period of time in custody are expected to undergo some form of re-socialisation process. Such re-socialisation generally includes time served in a minimum security prison immediately before release. This is because minimum security facilities are deemed to be more culturally compatible with life in the wider community and it is anticipated that this should ease the transition from prisoner to free citizen.

The interview which took place at Karnet minimum security prison farm was, in relative terms, relaxed and casual in nature. Prison officers were friendly, did not object to the recording device and let the participant choose where he wanted the interview to take place. We conducted the interview under a tree in a garden area. The participant was relaxed, jovial and positive about his future. He had already had several home leaves which meant that he had experienced several hours out in the community as a day release prisoner. The atmosphere in minimum security prison farms is relatively stress-free in terms of regular prison regimes. Most prisoners in minimum security facilities are close to their release dates and, during the time span of the interviews, there were no high walls or razor wire around the perimeter.

In terms of collating rich and meaningful information, the interviews themselves went well. The participants all displayed a willingness to speak at length of their prison experiences. I believe that this is clearly illustrated in their narratives and the open, honest and casual nature of the general conversations.

## Data analysis and interpretation

Because of the sensitive and confidential nature of the interview material, I chose to transcribe all interview tapes myself. This was an enormous task in terms of the actual physical transcription from tape to paper. However, the most disturbing factor was "reliving" some of the more emotional and traumatic parts of several interviews as I read the transcripts through. As I immersed myself in the data I began to pull out the main themes of the study. I identified the main themes as institutionalisation, patterns of surveillance and control, the "us and them" culture, prison violence and brutality, and a general inability to re-integrate successfully into the wider community.

# Appendix B
# Interview Schedule – Preliminary

## Inside Prison

## 1. Daily routine

*I'd like to start by asking how your life is right now. Could you tell me your daily routine? I'm interested in things like –*

*Prompts*

- going through your day – from awake to sleep
- diet
- sleep
- work/study
- leisure – reading; TV; clubs; conversations with friends; other relaxation
- other

## 2. Social relations/social life

*I'd like to know a bit more about your social relations – in particular, who you talk to, the time you spend alone, and the situations you may try to avoid –*

*Prompts*

- close friends and general acquaintances
- people turned to for support
- people or situations that are avoided
- time spent alone
- visitors
- other

# Transition Issues

## 3. Anticipated changes (positive and negative)

*There are obviously going to be many changes when you get out of prison. Could you say something about the kind of changes you expect and whether you think they will be good or bad?*

*Prompts*
- social relations
  - family
  - sex
  - friends
- housing
- work
- money
- leisure
- food
- transport
- other

## 4. Anticipated support

i. *Could you comment on where you think you may get support from when you are released from prison?*

*Prompts*
- informal
  - partners
  - other family members; immediate or extended
  - friends
  - other
- formal
  - financial support – Department of Social Security (DSS)
  - employment services
  - non-government agencies
  - other

ii.  *How adequate do you think this assistance is likely to be? Are there any areas in which you feel you may be pretty much on your own?*

iii.  *Finally, are there any people/groups who you feel may have a negative effect on you?*

## 5.  Prison pre-release programs

i.  *I'd like to ask you about the prison's pre-release programs. Have you:*

- attended any pre-release program?
- sought counselling?
- been contacted by Community Based Corrections (if negative confirm if parolee or end of sentence)
- sought help from any other outside agency

ii.  *How useful did you find them?. Why?*

iii.  *If you decided not to approach any of these programs, can you say why?*

## 6.  Own practical and emotional preparations for change

*In addition to the prison's programs there are all your own prepar-ations for change. I'm thinking about the planning you may do; the conversations you may have with people you trust, and the way you may try and prepare yourself emotionally. Can you say something about this?*

### Prompts

- seeking informal help – other prisoners, prison staff, visitors
- doing mental planning
- emotional preparation
- other

## 7.  Current feeling about the change

i.  *Are there things that you are feeling anxious about as far as get-ting out of prison is concerned? What are they?*

ii.  *Are there things that you are really looking forward to as far as getting out of prison is concerned? What are they?*

iii.  *Overall, how are you feeling about getting out of prison?*

# Appendix C
# Interview Schedule: Follow up

## Post Release

### 1. Daily routine

*How is your life now? Could you tell me about your daily routine now? I'm interested in things like –*

*Prompts*

- going through your day – from awake to sleep
- what do you eat and when
- sleep
- paid employment/organised study
- leisure/entertainment
- other

### 2. Social relations/social life

*I'd like you to tell me about your social life now. I'd like to know who you talk to, the time you spend alone, situations you are attracted to and situations you might try and avoid.*

*Prompts*

- close friends and general acquaintances
- people turned to for support
- people or situations that are avoided
- time spent alone
- what do you do/where do you go for entertainment
- other

## 3. Changes in your life

*You have obviously experienced many changes since you were relea-sed from prison. I'd like you to tell me about the kinds of changes, how they made you feel and whether you see these changes as good or bad.*

### *Prompts*

- social relations
  - family
  - friends
  - sex
- housing
- work
- money
- leisure
- food
- transport
- technology
- cultural/social change within the community
- other

## 4. Support systems

*i.   Could you comment on where you get most support from.*

### *Prompts*

- informal
  - partner
  - other members of immediate or extended family
  - friends
  - other
- formal
  - financial support – Department of Social Security (DSS)
  - employment services
  - Community Based Corrections
  - non-government agencies
  - other

ii. *How adequate do you feel this support has been? Are there any areas where you feel you've been left pretty much on your own?*

iii. *Finally, are there any people or groups, formal or informal, who you feel have had a negative effect on you?*

## 5. Prison pre-release programs

i. *If you attended any of the prison pre-release programs can you tell me if you feel they prepared you adequately for the 'real life' situations you now face?*

ii. *Can you explain why you feel this and can you perhaps give me some idea of things that would be helpful in such programs?*

iii. *If you did not attend any pre-release programs do you think this left you at a disadvantage?*

## 6. Own practical and emotional preparation

i. *When you were in prison you indicated that you had tried to prepare yourself for release in various ways. Can you tell me if these preparations assisted you in the changeover from prisoner to free citizen.*

ii. *Which strategies/preparations helped you the most?*

## 7. Current feelings about your changed circumstances and status

i. *What sorts of things now cause you most anxiety as a free person?*

ii. *What sorts of things give you the best feelings and make you feel good about yourself now?*

iii. *In general terms, how do you feel about being out of prison?*

## 8. Other

*Is there anything else that you would like to add that you feel is relevant to this research?*

# Bibliography

Aboriginal Affairs Planning Authority, 1992 "Brief Chronology of Aboriginal Affairs in WA", Unpublished Paper.

Aboriginal Justice Council Annual Report, 1998.

Aboriginal and Torres Strait Islander Social Justice Commissioner, 2004 *Social Justice Report, Chapter Two*, "Walking with Women – Addressing the needs of Indigenous women exiting prison": <www.hr eoc.gov.au/social_justice/sjreport04/2WalkingWithTheWomen.html>.

Adler, P, and Adler, P, 1997 *Constructions of Deviance*, Wadsworth Publishing Company, California.

Athens, L, 1980 *Violent Criminal Acts and Actors: A symbolic interactionist study*, Routledge, London.

Aungles, A, 1994 *The Prison and the Home*, Institute of Criminology, University of Sydney Law School, Sydney.

Australian Bureau of Statistics, Incarceration Rates, March 2006.

Ayris, C, 1991 "Changing the Guard", *The Big Weekend, West Australian Newspaper, 7 September 1991*.

Barnacle, H, 2000 *Don't Let Her See Me Cry*, Bantam Publishing, Australia.

Becker, H, 1966 "Labelling Theory Reconsidered" in *Outsiders: Studies in the Sociology of Deviance*, Free Press, New York.

Berger, P, and Luckmann, T, 1967 *The Social Construction of Reality*, Penguin Books, UK.

Bianchi, H, 1994 "Abolition: Assensus and Sanctuary" in *A Reader on Punishment*, Duff, A, and Garland, D, (eds), Oxford University Press, Oxford.

Biles, D, 1994 "Deaths in Custody: The Nature and Scope of the Problem" in *Deaths in Custody: International Perspectives*, Liebling, A, and Ward, T, (eds), Whiting and Birch Ltd, London.

Blumer, H, 1969 *Symbolic Interactionism: Perspective and Method*, University of California Press, Berkeley, USA.

Bowen, H, and Boyack, J, 1999 "Community versus State in New Zealand", Unpublished Conference Paper, ANU February 1999.

Bowen, H, and Consedine, J, (eds) 1999 *Restorative Justice Contemporary Themes and Practice*, Ploughshares Publications, New Zealand.

Boyle, J, 1977 *A Sense of Freedom*, Canongate Publishing, Edinburgh.

Bozovic, M, (ed) 1995 *The Panopticon Writings*, Verso, London.

Braithwaite, J, 1989 *Crime, Shame and Reintegration*, Cambridge University Press, Cambridge.

Broadhurst, R, 1988 "Aboriginal and Nonaboriginal Recidivism in Western Australia: A Failure Rate Analysis" in *Journal of Research in Crime and Delinquency,* Vol 25, No 1, February 1988.

Bullock, A, Stallybrass, O, Trombley, S, 1988 *The Fontana Dictionary of Modern Thought*, Harper Collins Publishers, London.

Burns, T, 1992 *Erving Goffman*, Routledge, London.

Butler, T, and Allnutt, S, 2003 *Mental Illness Among New South Wales Prisoners,* New South Wales Department of Corrections Report.

Cain, M, 1986 *Realism, Feminism, Methodology and Law*, Academic Press Inc, London.

Carlen, P, 1994 "Crime, Inequality and Sentencing" in *A Reader on Punishment*, Duff, A, and Garland, D, (eds), Oxford University Press, Oxford.

Chappell, D, and Egger, S, (eds) 1995 *Australian Violence: Contemporary Perspectives II*, Australian Institute of Criminology, Canberra.

Choo, C, 1989 "Black Must Go White", unpublished thesis, University of Western Australia, Perth.

Christie, N, 1993 *Crime Control as Industry*, Routledge, London.

Church Agencies, 1988 *Prison the Last Resort: A Christian Response to Australian Prisons*, Collins Dove, Blackburn, Victoria.

Cicourel, A, 1968 *The Social Organization of Juvenile Justice*, Wiley Publishing, New York.

Cohen, S, and Taylor, L, 1972 *Psychological Survival: The experience of long-term imprisonment*, Penguin Books, London.

Consedine, J, 1995 *Restorative Justice Healing the Effects of Crime*, Ploughshares Publications, New Zealand.

Coyle, A, 1994 *The Prisons We Deserve*, Harper Collins Publishers, London.

Coyle, A, 2001a *The Restorative Prison Project,* "The Myth of Prison Work", International Centre for Prison Studies, King's College, London.

Coyle, A, 2001b "Prisons and the Democratic Process", Unpublished Conference Paper, New Initiatives in Penal reform and Access to Justice, Hyderabad, India, 20 October 2001.

Coyle, A, 2001c "Restorative Justice in the Prison Setting", Unpublished Conference Paper, International Prison Chaplain's Association, 13 May 2001, Driebergen, The Netherlands.

Cromwell, P, 1996 *In Their Own Words: Criminals on Crime*, Roxbury Publishing Company, California.

Daly, K, 1999 "Reassessing the Relationship between Restorative and Retributive Justice", Unpublished Conference Paper, ANU, February 1999.

Dandeker, C, 1990 *Surveillance, Power and Modernity*, Polity press, Cambridge.

Deaths in Custody Watch Committee (WA), 2001 *Report to the 25th Session of the Committee Against Torture.*

Department of Environment and Heritage, 2005 "Fremantle Prison: A Brief History": <www.environment.gov.au/heritage/national/sites/fremantle-factsheet.html>.

Duff, R, 1999 "Penal Communities" in *Punishment and Society,* The International Journal of Penology, Vol 1, No 1, July 1999.

Duff, R, and Garland, D, 1994 *A Reader on Punishment,* Oxford University Press, Oxford.

Edgar, K, O'Donnell, I, and Martin, C, 2003 *Prison Violence: The dynamics of conflict, fear and power,* Willan Publishing, Devon.

Electoral and Referendum Amendment (Enrolment Integrity and Other Measures) Bill 2004.

Emery, F, et al, 1973 *Hope within Walls,* Centre for Continuing Education, ANU, Canberra.

Fatic, A, 1995 *Punishment and Restorative Crime Handling,* Ashgate Publishing Ltd, Aldershot.

Felson, R, and Tedeschi, T, 1993 *Aggression and Violence: Social Interactionist Perspectives,* American Psychological Association, Washington, DC.

Fine, G, Johnson, J, and Farberman, H, 1992 *Sociological Slices,* JAI Press Inc, Connecticut, USA.

Finnane, M, 1997 *Punishment in Australian Society,* Oxford University Press, Melbourne.

Foucault, M, 1977 *Discipline and Punish,* Penguin Books, London.

Francis, V, 2001 *The Restorative Prison Project: Discussion Paper Two,* "Restorative Practices in Prison – A Review of the Literature, Paper one: Work with Victims", International Centre for Prison Studies, King's College, London.

Garland, D, 1990 *Punishment in Modern Society,* Clarendon Press, Oxford.

Garland, D, 1997 "Governmentality and the Problem of Crime", *Theoretical Criminology,* Sage Publications, London.

Genders, E, and Morrison, S, 1996 "When violence is the norm" in *Dangerous People,* Walker, N, (ed), Blackstone Press Ltd, London.

Gilligan, C, 1988 *Mapping the Moral Domain: A contribution of women's thinking to psychological theory and education,* Harvard University Press, Massachusetts, USA.

Glazer, B, and Strauss, A, 1967 *The Discovery of Grounded Theory: strategies for qualitative research,* Walter De Gruyter Inc, New York.

Goffman, E, 1961 *Asylums,* Doubleday, New York.

Goffman, E, 1963 *Stigma,* Penguin Books, London.

Goulding, D, 1995 "The Punishment of Innocents: A report on the social and emotional impact of imprisonment on prisoners" families", Unpublished Independent Study Contract, Murdoch University.

Goulding, D, 1997 "Issues of Identity Relating to Prison Inmates and Their Support Networks of Family and Friends: an analysis of institutional identity", Unpublished Honours Thesis, Murdoch University.

Goulding, D, 2004 *Severed Connections: An exploration of the impact of imprisonment on women's familial and social connectedness,* Murdoch University Print, Perth.

Goulding, D, and Steels, B, 2006 "Restorative and Transformative Justice", Unpublished Seminar Paper, Murdoch University.

Grant, D, 1992 *Prisons The Continuing Crisis in NSW,* Federation Press, Sydney.

Green, R, 1998 *Justice in Aboriginal Communities – Sentencing Alternatives,* Pierich Publishing, Saskatoon, Canada.

Haebich, A, 1988 *For Their Own Good,* UWA Press, Perth.

Hairston, C, and Lockett, P, 1987 "Parents in Prison: New Directions for Social Services" in *Social Work,* March/April 1987, National Association of Social Workers, Indiana University.

Hammond, M, Howarth, J, and Keat, R, 1991 *Understanding Phenomenology,* Basil Blackwell Ltd, Oxford.

Hampton, B, 1993 *Prisons and Women,* New South Wales University Press, Sydney.

Haralambos, M, et al, 1995 *Sociology: Themes and perspectives,* Collins Educational, London.

Harding, R, 2001 *Report of an Unannounced Inspection of the Induction and Orientation Unit and the Special Handling Unit at Casuarina Prison,* Report No 1, Office of the Inspector of Custodial Services, Western Australia.

Harding, R, 2002a *Report of an Announced Inspection of Nyandi Prison,* Report No 10, February 2002, Office of the Inspector of Custodial Services, Western Australia.

Harding, R, 2002b *Report of an Announced Inspection of Bandyup Women's Prison,* Report No 13, June 2002, Office of the Inspector of Custodial Services, Western Australia.

Harding, R, 2004 *The Diminishing Quality of Prison Life: Deaths at Hakea Prison 2001-2003,* Report No 22, March 2004, Directed Review into Deaths at Hakea Prison, Office of the Inspector of Custodial Services, Western Australia.

Harding, R, 2005 *Directed Review of the Management of Offenders in Custody,* Report No 30, November 2005, Office of the Inspector of Custodial Services, Western Australia.

Harding, R, 2006 *Thematic Review of Offender Health Services,* Report No 35, September 2006, Office of the Inspector of Custodial Services, Western Australia.

Harding, S, (ed), 1987 *Feminism and Methodology: Social Science Issues,* Indiana University Press, Bloomington, USA.

Hearn, J, and Parkin, W, 1987 *"Sex" at Work: The Power and Paradox of Organisation Sexuality,* Wheatsheaf Books Ltd, Brighton, Sussex.

Heilpern, D, 1998 *Fear or Favour: Sexual Assault of Young Prisoners,* Southern Cross University Press, Lismore.

Heilpern, D, 2005 "Sexual Assault of Prisoners: Reflections" in *UNSW Law Journal,* Vol 11, No 1, August 2005, pp 25-28.

Heritage, J, 1984 *Garfinkel and Ethnomethodology,* Polity Press, Cambridge.

Heywood, A, 1992 *Political Ideologies,* MacMillan Education Ltd, London.

Hodge, B, 2000 *One of Many: Poems from Prison*, Fremantle Arts Press, Western Australia.

Hope, T, and Shaw, M, 1988 *Communities and Crime Reduction*, Home Office Research and Planning Unit, Her Majesty's Stationery Office.

Howe, A, 1994 *Punish and Critique: Towards a Feminist Analysis of Penality*, Routledge, London.

Human Rights Watch, 2001 *No Escape: Male Rape in US Prisons*, Human Rights Watch Publication.

Hunt, G, et al, 1996 "Changes in Prison Culture: Prison gangs and the Case of the "Pepsi Generation'" in *In Their Own Words: Criminals On Crime*, Cromwell, P, (ed), Roxbury Publishing Company, California.

Indermaur, D, 1996 "Perceptions of Violence" in *Psychiatry, Psychology and Law*, Vol 3, No 2, November 1996.

International Centre for Prison Studies, King's College, London: <www.prisonstudies.org>.

Jary, D, and Jary, J, 1991 *Dictionary of Sociology*, Harper Collins Publishers, Glasgow.

Johnson, A, 1995 "Prison Culture, Violence and Sexuality" in *Cultures of Crime and Violence: The Australian Experience*, La Trobe University Press, Melbourne.

Johnson, R, and Toch, H, 1982 *The Pains of Imprisonment,* Sage Publications, California, USA.

Jones, S, 2000 *Understanding Violent Crime*, Open University Press, Buckingham.

Joudo, J, 2005 *Deaths in Custody in Australia: National deaths in Custody Report 2005,* Australian Institute of Criminology, Australian Government, Canberra.

Katz, J, 1988 *Seductions of Crime*, Basic Books, Harper Collins Publishers, New York.

Kirby, S, and McKenna, K, 1989 *Experience, Research, Social Change*, Garamond Press, Toronto, Canada.

Leathlean, R, 2004 "The Role of Restorative Parks: Projects in Community Safety", Thames Valley Partnership, UK.

Liebling, A, 1992 *Suicides in Prison*, Routledge, London.

Liebling, A, Price, D, and Elliott, C, 1999 "Appreciative inquiry and relationships in prison" in *Punishment and Society,* The International Journal of Penology, Vol 1, No 1, 1999.

Liebmann, M, and Braithwaite, S, 1999 *Restorative Justice in Custodial Settings*, Report for the Restorative Justice Working Group in Northern Ireland.

Lowman, J, and MacLean, B, 1992 *Realist Criminology, Crime Control and Policing in the 1990s*, University of Toronto Press, Toronto, Canada.

Luckmann, T, (ed) 1978 *Phenomenology and Sociology*, Penguin Books, Melbourne.

Mace, A, 2000 *The Restorative Prison Project*, "Restorative principles in the prison setting: A vision for the future", International Centre for Prison Studies, King's College, London.

Mahoney, D, 2005 *Inquiry into the Management of Offenders in Custody and in the Community*, November 2005.

Mauer, M, 2003 *Comparative International Rates of Incarceration: an examination of causes and trends*, Report presented to the US Commission on Civil Rights.

Maxwell, G, and Morris, A, 1993 *Family, Victims and Culture: Youth Justice in New Zealand*, Social Policy Agency, Institute of Criminology, Victoria University of Wellington.

Maxwell, G, and Morris, A, 1999 "Researching Reoffending", Unpublished Conference Paper, ANU, February 1999.

Maxwell, G, and Morris, A, 2001 "Putting Restorative Justice into Practice for Adult Offenders" in *The Howard Journal of Criminal Justice*, Vol 40, No 1, February 2001.

McCleary, R, 1978 *Dangerous Men*, Sage Publications, London.

McDonald, J, and Moore, D, 1999 "Community Conferencing as a Special Case of Conflict Transformation", Unpublished Conference Paper, ANU, February 1999.

McGivern, J, 1988 *Report of the Inquiry into the Fire and Riot at Fremantle Prison on the 4th January 1988.*

McHoul, A, and Grace, W, 1993 *A Foucault Primer: Discourse, power and the subject*, Melbourne University Press, Melbourne.

MacKinnon, C, 1987 "Feminism, Marxism, Method and the State" in Harding, S, (ed), *Feminism and Methodology: Social Science Issues*, Indiana University Press, Bloomington, USA.

Megahey, N, 2000 *A Community Apart: A History of Fremantle Prison, 1898-1991*, PhD Thesis, Murdoch University.

Menninger, K, 1968 *The Crime of Punishment*, The Viking Press, New York.

Ministry of Justice, *Report of an Inspection: Woorooloo Prison Farm*, 12-17 August and 14-17 November 1999.

Morgan, R, 1999 "New Labour "law and order" politics and the House of Commons Home Affairs Committee Report on *Alternatives to Prison Sentences*" in *Punishment and Society*, International Journal of Penology, Vol 1, No 1, July 1999.

Morrison, S, 1994 "The Decision Making of Armed Robbers", *UK Home Office Paper*, Oxford Centre for Criminological Research.

Moyle, P, 2000 *Profiting From Punishment, Private Prisons in Australia: Reform or Regression*, Pluto Press, Sydney.

Nevill, M, 2000 *Report of the Standing Committee on Estimates and Financial Operations in Relation to the Financial Management of Prisons*, Western Australian Legislative Council.

Newburn, T, and Stanko, B, (eds) 1994 *Just Boys Doing Business: Men, Masculinities and Crime*, Routledge, London.

Newell, T, 2001a "Responding to the Crisis – Belgium establishes restorative prisons", Unpublished Paper in response to author's visit to the Belgian Prison Service, March 2001.

Newell, T, 2001b, "Restorative Justice in Prisons", Unpublished Paper, Restorative Justice Consortium Conference, London, October 2001.

Nieuhaus, J, 2000 Unpublished Conference Paper, SACRO Annual Conference, Heriot Watt University, Edinburgh, December 2000.

Oakley, A, 1981 "Interviewing Women: A contradiction in Terms" in Roberts, H, (ed), *Doing Feminist Research*, Routledge, London.

O'Malley, P, and Palmer, D, 1996 "Post Keynesian Policing" in *Economy and Society*, Vol 25, No 2, pp 137-155.

O'Malley, P, and Sutton, A, (eds) 1997 *Crime Prevention in Australia*, Federation Press, Sydney.

O'Malley, P, 1999 "Genealogy, Systemisation and Resistance in Advanced Liberalism", Unpublished Paper, School of Law and Legal Studies, La Trobe University, Melbourne.

Ombudsman, Western Australia, 2000 *Report on an Inquiry into Deaths in Prisons in Western Australia,* December 2000, Parliamentary Commissioner for Administrative Investigations.

Pratt, J, 1997 *Governing the Dangerous*, Federation Press, Sydney.

Pratt, J, 1999 "Emotive and Ostentatious Punishment: Its decline and Resurgence in Modern Society", Unpublished Conference Paper, UWA September 1999.

Psathas, G, (ed), 1973 *Phenomenological Sociology*, John Wiley and Sons Inc, New York.

Prison Fellowship (Australia) "Sycamore Tree" restorative justice program website: <www.users.bigpond.com/pfansw/projects/pf_sycamoretree.html>.

Rabinow, P, 1984 *The Foucault Reader,* Penguin Books, London.

Ramsland, J, 1996 *With Just but Relentless Discipline*, Kangaroo Press, Kenthurst, NSW.

Reynolds, H, 1999 *Why Weren't We Told*, Penguin Books, Melbourne.

Ritzer, G, 1988 *Contemporary Sociological Theory*, McGraw-Hill, Inc, New York.

Ritzer, G, 1992 *Sociological Theory*, McGraw-Hill, Inc, New York.

Rogers, R, 1993 "Solitary Confinement" in *International Journal of Offender Therapy and Comparative Criminology*, Vol 37, No 4.

Rose, N, 1988 "Calculable Minds and the Management of Individuals" in *History of Human Sciences*, Vol 1, No 2, pp 179-200.

Rose, N, 1992 "Governing the Enterprising Self" in *The Values of the Enterprise Culture: The Moral Debate*, Heelas, D, and Morris, M, (eds), Unwin Hyman, London.

Rose, N, and Miller, P, 1992 "Political Power beyond the State: Problematics of Government" in *British Journal of Sociology*, Vol 43, No 2, pp 173-205.

Ross, J, and Richards, S, 2003 *Convict Criminology*, Thomson Wadsworth, USA.

Rutherford, J, 1990 *Identity, Community, Culture, Difference*, Lawrence and Wishart Ltd, London.

Salomone, J, 2002 "Issues Paper 2: Mothers and Children/Babies", Department of Corrective Services (WA) Report, Low Security Women's Prison Project Paper.

SBS Documentary 2000 *Business Behind Bars: Part 1*, Screened SBS Television Network, October 2000.

Schafer, N, 1994 "Exploring the Link Between Visits and Parole Success: A Survey of Prison Visitors" in *International Journal of Offender Therapy and Comparative Criminology*, Vol 38, No 1.

Schetzer, L, 1999 Submission to the Senate Legal and Constitutional References Committee: Inquiry into Mandatory Sentencing, October 1999.

Schlosser, E, 1998 "The Prison Industrial Complex" in *The Atlantic Monthly*, December 1998.

Shearing, C, 1995 "Reinventing Policing: Policing as Governance", *Interdisziplinare Studien zu Recht und Statt*, S296 Australian Society and Politics, Course Reader, Murdoch University, Perth.

Shoham, S, 1995 *Violence: An Integrated Multivariate Study of Human Aggression*, Dartmouth Publishing Company, Aldershot.

Smith, D, 1987 *The Everyday World As Problematic: A feminist sociology*, Northeastern University Press, Boston.

Smith, D, 1988 "Feminism and the Malepractice of Sociology" in *Popular Feminism Papers*, No 003, Centre for Women's Studies in Education, Ontario.

Smith, D, 1999 in Leinert, C, (ed) *Social Theory: The Multicultural and Classic Readings*, Westview Press, Boulder, Colorado, USA.

Smith, L, et al, 1999 *Report of the Inquiry into the Incident at Casuarina Prison on 25th December 1998*.

Stanko, E, 1994 "Dancing with Denial: Researching Women and Questioning Men" in Maynard, M, and Purvis, J, (eds) *Researching Women's Lives from a Feminist Perspective*, Taylor and Francis Ltd, London.

Stern, V, 1998 *A Sin Against the Future*, Penguin Books, London.

Stern, V, (ed), 1999 *Sentenced to Die*, International Centre for Prison Studies, King's College, London.

Stern, V, 2001 "Prisons, Drugs and Society", unpublished speech, European Conference on "Prisons, Drugs and Society", Bern, Switzerland, 20-22 September 2001.

Stern, V, 2005 "'Prisons and Their Communities: Testing a new approach", An account of the Restorative Prison Project 2000-2004, International Centre for Prison Studies, King's College, London.

Strang, H, and Braithwaite, J, 2000 *Restorative Justice: Philosophy to Practice*, Dartmouth Publishing Company Ltd, Aldershot.

Sycamore Tree Program, Prison Fellowship Australia website: <www. users.bigpond.co/pfansw/projects/pf_sycamoretree.html>.

Sykes, G, 1958 *The Society of Captives: A Study of a Maximum Security Prison*, Princeton University Press, New Jersey, USA.

Taylor, C, 1990 "The Self in Moral Space" in *Sources of the Self: The Making of the Modern Identity*, Cambridge, Mass, USA.

Taylor, I, Walton, P, and Young, J, 1973 *The New Criminology*, Routledge, London.

Taylor, L, and Graham, H, 1972 "Grammars and Vocabularies: alternative approaches to a sociology of motivation", seminar paper, Department of Sociology, University of York, UK.

The Aboriginal Justice Council, 1998 *Our Mob, Our Justice: Keeping the Vision Alive*, Aboriginal Justice Council Secretariat, Perth, Western Australia.

The Association of Heads of Churches of Western Australia 2000 *Prison the Last Option: New Directions for the Millenium*, UWA Conference Report, 18-19 March, 2000.

Thomas, J, and Stewart, A, 1978 *Imprisonment in Western Australia*, University of Western Australia Press, Perth.

Toch, H, 1977 *Living in Prison: The Ecology of Survival*, The Free Press, Macmillan Publishing, New York.

Tomasic, R, and Dobinson, I, 1979 *The Failure of Imprisonment*, Allen and Unwin Australia, Sydney.

Victorian Political News (VPN): <http://robertclark.net/news/0715mcgr. htm September 2000>.

Vinson, T, 1982 *Wilful Obstruction*, Methuen Australia Pty Ltd, Sydney.

Walker, N, 1980 *Punishment, Danger and Stigma*, Barnes and Noble Books, New Jersey.

Walmsley, R, 2005 World Population List: 6th Edition, International Centre for Prison Studies, Kings College, London.

Weeks, J, 1990 "The Value of Difference" in *Identity, Community, Culture, Difference*, Rutherford, J, (ed), Lawrence and Wishart Ltd, London.

Zamble, E, and Quinsey, V, 1997 *The Criminal Recidivism Process*, Cambridge University Press, Cambridge.

Zedner, L, 1997 "Victims" in *Oxford Handbook of Criminology*, Maguire, M, Morgan, R, and Reiner, R, (eds), Clarendon Press, Oxford.

Zehr, H, 1990 *Changing Lenses*, Herald Press, Scottdale, Pennsylvania.

Zimring, F, and Hawkins, G, 1997 *Crime is Not the Problem: lethal violence in America*, Oxford University Press, New York.

# Index

restorative and transformative prisons (*cont*)
  other jurisdictions, in, 146-50
  principles, 142-6
  recommendation for change, 128, 140-2
  re-integrative shaming, 142-3
  West Australian context, 151-5
retribution, 65, 129-33
right alliance, new, 32-3
riots, 19, 20-2, 25, 74, 99
Rottnest Island, 14, 16
Round House, 14
Royal Commission into Aboriginal Deaths in Custody 1991, 15-16
Royal Commission into the Prison System in Western Australia 1989-99, 15
Ruah Women's Support Service, 136
Russia, incarceration rate, 31
savings, enforced, 138-9
self harm, 77, 89-91
sentences, indeterminate, 17
sexual relationships, loss of right to, 56-7
sexual violence in prisons, 85-7
shackling, 93-4
social de-skilling, 105
social injustice, 29
social isolation, 132
solitary confinement, 15
*Standard Minimum Rules for the Treatment of Prisoners*, 25
Standing Committee on Estimates and Financial Operations in Relation to the Financial Management of Prisons, 11
Steels, Brian, 11
stigmatisation of ex-prisoners, 105
stolen generations, 7
strip-searches, 44-5, 59-60
suicide, 89-91
surveillance, 58-9
  covert, 60-1
  impact of, 61-2
  overt, 59-60

'Sycamore Tree' program, 152
telephone calls, 138
threats of harm, 84
truth in sentencing, 28
unemployment benefit, 137
unit management regime, 66-7
United Nations
  Human Rights instruments, 25
United States
  number of persons incarcerated, 30
urine tests, 44-6, 59
violence
  categories of, 89-100
  gendered nature of, 79-82
  inversion argument, 87-9
  payback violence, 91-2, 95
  predatory violence, 92
  prison officer to prisoner, 93-8
  prisoner to prison officer, 99
  prisoner to prisoner, 91-3
  prisoners' perceptions of, 82-4
  prisons, in, 76-8, 140-1
  random acts of, 93
  self harm, 89-91
  sexual, in prisons, 85-7
  suicide, 89-91
  theories of, 78-9
visits
  contact, 70
  control over, 69-72
  non-contact, 70
  surveillance, impact of, 62
  types of, 70
Vosper, Frederick, 15
voting by prisoners, 57
'war on crime' measures, 10, 28
weapons, threats using, 84
Western Australia
  rates of imprisonment, 25-8
women prisoners, 19-20
  gendered nature of violence, 79-82
  mode of imprisonment, 153
  parenthood, 53-4
  rates of imprisonment, 25-8
Wooroloo Prison Farm, 17
work camp initiative, 135
work options, restriction of, 51-3